Essential Guide to
Dance

Essential Guide to
Dance

Third Edition

Linda Ashley

HODDER
EDUCATION
A PART OF HACHETTE LIVRE UK

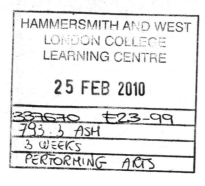
Orders: please contact Bookpoint Ltd, 130 Milton Park, Abingdon, Oxon OX14 4SB.
Telephone: (44) 01235 827720. Fax: (44) 01235 400454. Lines are open from 9.00 – 5.00,
Monday to Saturday, with a 24-hour message answering service. You can also order through our website
www.hoddereducation.co.uk.

British Library Cataloguing in Publication Data
A catalogue record for this title is available from the British Library

ISBN: 978 0 340 96 838 3

First Published 2008
Impression number   10 9 8 7 6 5 4 3 2 1
Year   2014 2013 2012 2011 2010 2009 2008

Cover photo © Nick White/Getty Images
Typeset by Servis Filmsetting Ltd, Stockport, Cheshire
Printed in Italy for Hodder Education, part of Hachette Livre UK, 338 Euston Road, London NW1 3BH

CONTENTS

337670

FOREWORD

If you are a student or teacher of dance, this book will give you an insight into the world of the professional dancer. If you are taking practical and written examinations in dance at GCSE, AS, A2 level, or at diploma or degree level, this book should be part of your studies. Teachers of dance at any level will benefit from reading this guide as it covers the essential aspects of dance and is a great source of information. Students of performing arts and drama will also find this guide very informative as it will help to broaden their knowledge and understanding of an art form that they will at some time certainly need to use.

The section on safe dance practice is very detailed and offers the reader clear definitions of the key terms associated with the main areas of body fitness. The diagrams, illustrations and photographs help the reader to visualise the key information concerning anatomy and how to look after the body to keep it fit, healthy and ready for dance. The guide gives advice on safe training and injury prevention, providing information useful for all dancers of all levels.

There is a wide range of practical tasks designed to last between ten and twenty minutes. These are ideal for members of a class to try out with teacher supervision. They are an effective way of making the theoretical side of the subject come to life and should be enjoyable as well as instructive. There are choreographic tasks, which will help the dancer to learn new ways of choreographing pieces.

The guide covers the dancer as performer, choreographer and critic. It refers to a very large selection of dance works readily available for viewing and discusses relatively new areas of dance, such as dance for camera. The works cited will appeal to a wide audience from young to old and they cover many genres and styles of dance.

The quotations from dance practitioners, which appear throughout the book, are inspiring and provide a good starting point for further research and extension tasks.

There are extensive lists of references and resources at the end of each chapter, including books, articles, videos and DVDs. The lists of websites and organisations provide a wealth of contacts for readers to investigate and make links with.

I have been using *The Essential Guide to Dance* since it was first published and I am always keen to buy the latest edition. It has served me well in the classroom where I have a class set of the guides so each student has access to one. Students find the layout of the pages and the register of the language easily accessible and consider the book somewhat of a bible. It is the first publication they turn to when working towards theory examinations and they are full of praise for the knowledge it imparts and the variety of ways it chooses to convey the large amount of theoretical and practical understanding of dance required by the young dance student.

If you are about to start teaching dance in a school at any level, you should have a copy of this book and keep it by your side. It is a fantastic teaching tool and a handy reference book.

Gail Deal, Cert.Ed., MA, FCIEA
Head of Performing Arts and Music, Esher College
June 2008

ACKNOWLEDGEMENTS

The author and publisher wish to thank the following for permission to reproduce their images:

Within Task Four,
page 14   REVELATIONS. Alvin Ailey American Dance Theater, SADLER'S WELLS, LONDON (09/07) © Linda Rich/ArenaPAL

1.09	Chris Nash
1.12	Oxford Designers & Illustrators
1.15	Linda Ashley
1.16	Private Collection/Roger-Viollet, Paris/The Bridgeman Art Library
1.20	Chris Nash
1.21	Front cover of *Strength – Broadsides from Disability on the Arts* reproduced with kind permission of Trentham Books Ltd. Photograph © Hugo Glendinning
1.27	© Houston Rogers/V&A Images/Victoria and Albert Museum
1.28	Chris Nash
2.1	© Bettmann/CORBIS
2.2	Chris Nash
2.3	© Houston Rogers/V&A Images/Victoria and Albert Museum
2.4	© Hugo Glendinning
3.3	Chris Nash
3.4	Chris Nash
3.5	© Asya Verzhbinsky
3.6	Chris Nash
3.7	© Hugo Glendinning
3.8 (a) & (b)	© Anthony Crickmay/V&A Images/Victoria and Albert Museum
3.10	Linda Ashley
3.12	Linda Ashley
3.14	© Asya Verzhbinsky
3.15	© Anthony Crickmay/V&A Images/Victoria and Albert Museum
3.16	Francis Loney/ArenaPAL/TopFoto
3.17 (a)–(d)	Linda Ashley
3.18 (a)	© michael-stifter.de - Fotolia.com
3.18 (b)	© Connie Huffa - Fotolia.com

1 SAFE DANCE PRACTICE

Prevention is better than cure

Safe dance practice has become a hot topic during the last few years. You can learn how to dance safely, in practice and performance, by understanding how to apply preventative practice. This chapter will help you to understand how to prevent injury and stay healthy. Everyone's body has limitations and strengths. Learning the names of bones, joints, muscles and about the basic physiology of how the body works will help you to dance more safely and to recognise your strengths and weaknesses. An applied working knowledge of the body, based on anatomical and physiological principles, is most useful in preventing injury. This chapter names individual parts of the body in the context of how they may arise in class or in performance. For a dancer or a choreographer, an active awareness of safe practice can serve to explain both how to execute a certain movement and why a particular phrase is giving difficulty. Unsafe practice and how to deal with injury are also examined.

Don't say, 'Oh well, we did that, and I kicked my leg five inches higher than she did.' Who cares? Did you understand the movement? That is what matters.

(Hanya Holm in The Vision of Modern Dance, *1980)*

The body of a dancer is like the piano of a musician: it is a working tool, and so must be finely tuned. This needs an intelligent, aware, sensitive and disciplined approach to dance training. Dance training pursues the improvement of capabilities which the body already has naturally. As with an athlete, these capabilities need to be developed in order for their potential to be maximised. Safety and efficiency of movement need to be ensured. You can monitor your own safety by learning more about how your body works and what it needs to train, perform and stay healthy. Practise the theory as you dance. Safe dance principles are based on improving the following main areas of basic body fitness:

- alignment;
- flexibility;

- strength and stamina;
- co-ordination and technical skill;
- general body maintenance.

Different technique classes vary in how much emphasis is placed on these areas. Often, because of the stop–go nature of these classes, there is not enough time for effective all-round conditioning of the body. This is a problem because these basic areas of fitness are all vital in ensuring safe practice and injury prevention, so extra body conditioning can help you to stay dance fit. In this chapter there are some exercises and ideas to assist you with extra body conditioning.

Let us now consider each of these five main areas in turn.

Alignment – a balancing act

During movement, the body should remain aligned, whether in a fall or jump or turn. In the well-aligned body, there is a feeling of freedom, easy movement, effortless carriage of the head and awareness of all parts of the body. It is a more expressive body that 'looks good' whatever it is doing, at any given moment. Good alignment is not static, it is a dynamic position of readiness to move and during movement. When you are dancing your teacher will be correcting and encouraging you to be aware of important alignment and other kinesthetic information. Discovering your muscular imbalances is an important part of your dancing and these can be felt when you work on correct postural awareness.

Postural awareness

Good posture is vital for control, safety and expression; poor posture or alignment of one part ricochets throughout the rest of the body.

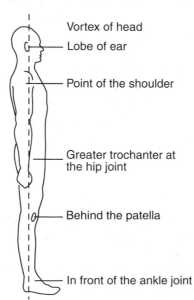

Vortex of head

Lobe of ear

Point of the shoulder

Greater trochanter at the hip joint

Behind the patella

In front of the ankle joint

Figure 1.1 To show points that the line of gravity will pass through in correct alignment

The correct postural line runs through the ear lobe, through the centre of the shoulder and hip, in front of the ankle and down through the foot (see Figure 1.1). The shoulders, hips and knees should be level.

Of course, this plumb line is imaginary. Similarly, your centre of gravity is an imagined point lying slightly below your navel (around the middle of the sacral vertebrae), depending on the shape and weight distribution of the dancer. If you shift your centre of gravity slightly you will feel your body move to keep up – like falling into travelling, running and skipping. When moving, a dancer with a deeper *plié* can lower the centre of gravity and have a greater range of control.

Now try Task One. You can use the human skeleton in Figure 1.6 to find the bones if you do not know all the names.

TASK ONE – *Finding Alignment*

KEY SKILLS Improving own learning and performance
Communication

🕐 10 to 20 minutes

In pairs, let one read instructions and the other adjust posture. Checklist for standing in parallel first position:

■ Weight evenly spread over the metatarsal arch. Check: long toes; lift inner medial arch, position of navicular for pronation.
■ The tibia and fibula (lower leg) balance on top of the talus (ankle).
■ The pelvis balances on the femur (thigh bone), so that the muscles of the lower back, abdomen and thighs are in equal contraction. Check: the thighs lift to support the hips; to check for level hips; place forefingers on the iliac crest. At the back place thumbs on the sacroiliac joint (where the two dimples are); drop the tailbone (sacrum)/flatten the abdomen so that the pelvis is in reciprocal relationship with the lumbar spine.
■ Knees relaxed; soft patella; facing straight ahead.
■ Upper back supported by thoracic vertebrae. Check: proper amount of anterior–posterior curvature; shoulder girdle rests easily on thorax. Shoulders relaxed/scapulae dropped and level.
■ Weight of head even on top of cervical spine. Check: jaw at right angle to the floor; long neck lifted lightly from ears.
■ Chest lifted, and sternum above balls of feet. Do not: lift shoulders/tighten neck/hold breath/lift chin/tuck seat under.

Now read this to your partner:

■ Now hold this position and try to rise easily. (Check your partner does not: shift their weight forward or back when rising; flex at the hip or knee.)
■ Move your arms and head easily without loss of balance.
■ Use your bones for support – think X-ray!
■ Feel control coming from the centre outwards.
■ Let your arms connect to the centre of your back.

For effective movement, each segment of the body must be in proper relationship to its adjacent sections. The anti-gravity postural muscles (see Figure 1.2) are responsible for maintaining upright posture, so that the weight-bearing points on the skeleton will be balanced and the muscles will be able to release energy for action safely and economically. Look at Figure 1.2: can you see that the abdominal muscles are on the *anterior* (front) of the torso and the back muscles on the *posterior* surface of the trunk? The *anterior* and *posterior* muscles work in balance with each other.

Figure 1.2
The main muscles controlling alignment

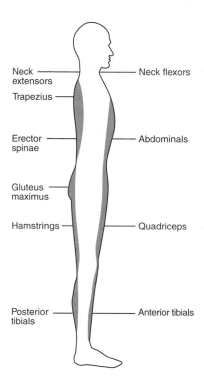

Alignment thus relies on there being balanced relationships between different muscles in each part of the body. This means that different segments of the body give and take (extended and contracted muscles) in order to maintain skeletal balance. Without this balance movement will be inefficient and possibly unsafe, as energy is wasted pulling certain segments of the body into line. A good example of this is the position of the arms in second. The arms are abducted to the sides and often dancers put strain into the lower back by positioning the arms too far back. This position squeezes together the shoulder blades (*scapulae*) and places excess weight and force into the lower back. TRY this – stand in second position, arms by your sides. Close your eyes. Raise the arms to the side (abduct) into what you think is second position (DO NOT PEEP!). Then look straight ahead when you open your eyes. Wriggle your fingers and using *only* your peripheral vision (looking straight ahead), you should be able to see your fingers. If you cannot see them, reposition your arms. Lower your arms and repeat the exercise until you can see the hands first time. If you practise this enough times your movement memory should recall this when you need the arms in a safe second position. This simple exercise is a great way to make your dancing safer and to hold a better line too.

Look at Figure 1.3 and write down the names of the four muscles, or muscle groups, that you can see on the anterior surface of the torso. In addition to these muscles, the *quadratus lumborum* connects the last rib to the pelvis and the spine. The muscle fibres of the *quadratus lumborum* are in a criss-cross weave and help to stabilise the ribcage and the *lumbar* spine (lower back). Now try Task Two.

Figure 1.3
Core stabiliser muscles of the anterior abdomen

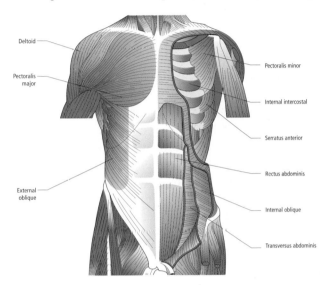

TASK TWO – *Finding Your Muscular Power House for Alignment*

KEY SKILLS Improving own learning and performance
Problem solving

🕐 10 to 20 minutes

You can do this exercise alone or with a partner to help each other with instructions or corrections. This exercise will help you connect with your abdominal muscles on the anterior surface of your torso. Don't forget to breathe properly.

1 From standing in a parallel with a well-aligned posture that you found in Task One, breathe out fully and contract the FIVE muscles of the *anterior surface* of your torso. As you do this, bend your knees and relax your shoulders and allow your arms to softly float up in front to a comfortable level. What shape is your torso now?
2 How do your back muscles feel now?
3 Breathe in and return to standing.

4 Repeat (1) – as you contract the muscles, name as many of your anterior abdominals as you can. Breathe in and return to standing.

5 Look closely at Figures 1.3 and 1.4 and notice which way the muscle fibres lie on your body for ONE of the abdominal muscles. Close your eyes and repeat (1). See if you can make an image in your mind to see the muscle fibres contract. Breathe in and return to standing.

6 Repeat for one other muscle.

Answers are on page 333.

Look at Figure 1.4 and find the large band of muscle, the *transverse abdominis*. This helps alignment by supporting your lower spine. When all of these core stabilising muscles are toned they will assist you to maintain expressive and safe alignment during dancing. These *anterior* core stabilisers are large, flat muscles, some lying deeper than others. If the *anterior muscles* are weak then the torso will lack stability and excess pulling by the lower back (*lumbar*) muscles can result in pain in the lumbar spine, or in the knees, hips or even feet. Even though the core muscles may be the problem, the pain can occur in other places, because the dancer may start to compensate for the torso muscle weaknesses by shifting the weight onto joints that are *inferior* (lower down the body). Muscles work together in sequence; therefore poor alignment in one body area can cause pain in others.

Figure 1.4 Anterior muscular system of the body

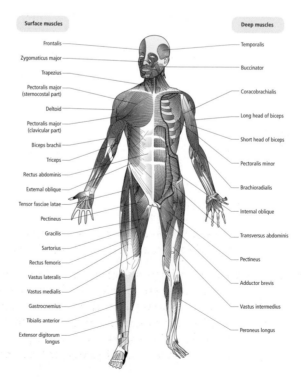

Surface muscles

Frontalis
Zygomaticus major
Trapezius
Pectoralis major (sternocostal part)
Deltoid
Pectoralis major (clavicular part)
Biceps brachii
Triceps
Rectus abdominis
External oblique
Tensor fasciae latae
Pectineus
Gracilis
Sartorius
Rectus femoris
Vastus lateralis
Vastus medialis
Gastrocnemius
Tibialis anterior
Extensor digitorum longus

Deep muscles

Temporalis
Buccinator
Coracobrachialis
Long head of biceps
Short head of biceps
Pectoralis minor
Brachioradialis
Internal oblique
Transversus abdominis
Pectineus
Adductor brevis
Vastus intermedius
Peroneus longus

The *plié* is a basic exercise for safe dance practice, because it offers the ideal opportunity to be aware of your alignment. When executed with correct alignment, the *plié* improves your feeling of being centred, strengthens the legs and increases your turn-out. All of these benefits lead to improvement in safety and quality of jumping, travelling and lifting. Obviously, you can see how important the *plié* is as part of your regular training. Now try Task Three – this will strengthen your pelvic floor and other abdominal muscles to improve alignment and ease of the *plié*.

Figure 1.5 Posterior muscular system of the body

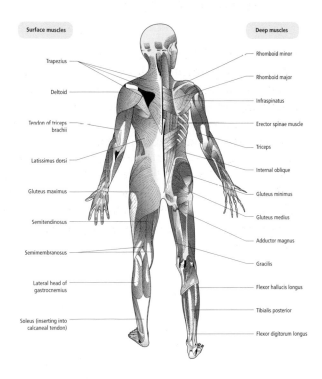

Surface muscles — Trapezius, Deltoid, Tendon of triceps brachii, Latissimus dorsi, Gluteus maximus, Semitendinosus, Semimembranosus, Lateral head of gastrocnemius, Soleus (inserting into calcaneal tendon)

Deep muscles — Rhomboid minor, Rhomboid major, Infraspinatus, Erector spinae muscle, Triceps, Internal oblique, Gluteus minimus, Gluteus medius, Adductor magnus, Gracilis, Flexor hallucis longus, Tibialis posterior, Flexor digitorum longus

TASK THREE – *The Magic of the Plié*

KEY SKILLS Improving own learning and performance

🕐 10 to 20 minutes

For this exercise to strengthen abdominal muscles and alignment, be prepared to concentrate on 'seeing' your muscles move.

■ **Part one** – Firstly, sit cross-legged or comfortably on the floor and imagine your pelvic girdle filled with water. Breathe in and allow arms to float up to second position and breathe out as arms lower slowly. Repeat this slowly and concentrate on feeling the water move outwards to fill the bowl as your pelvic bones move apart as you breathe in. As you breathe out, the bones move closer and the water

is pushed gently back. Repeat a few more times and concentrate on the pelvic floor muscle that lies in layers on the bottom of the bowl. As you breathe out, feel the pelvic bones move apart and the pelvic floor muscles lengthen (*eccentric contraction)* and the bones come closer and the muscle fibres shorten (*concentric contraction*).

■ **Part two** – Now repeat this exercise three more times standing, turned-out in second position. Stand *comfortably*, in second position turned-out, arms by your side. Leave the arms there throughout and breathe easily the whole time. Be sure not to force your turn-out. As you *plié*, use the correct co-ordination of the pelvic floor muscles – 'see' them lengthen and shorten.

■ **Part three** – Still standing in second, you are now going to concentrate on visualising the other abdominal muscles too. Check Figure 1.4 for the origin and insertion of the *transversus abdominis*. Now use your thumbs to locate the bony top of the pelvic crest at the front of your hip girdle. This is the *anterior superior iliac spine* (ASIS), which is the iliac crest that marks the origin of the *transversus abdominis*. This muscle is the pair of the pelvic floor and they work in balance as OPPOSITES – it shortens as you *plié*. To feel the *transversus abdominis* shorten, place your hands on the front of the ASIS and as you *plié* slide them in towards the centre. Can you feel the shortening of the *transversus abdominis*?

■ As you straighten your legs, slide the hands back to where they started and concentrate on feeling a lengthening of the *transversus abdominis*.

■ Finally, repeat more *pliés*, trying to feel both the pelvic floor and the *transversus abdominis*, as they lengthen and shorten to balance your alignment. Adding an image of a string from the top of your head pulling you up as you *plié* down will help the action to be smooth and fluent and elongate your neck and spine.

At this point it would be helpful to examine three specific areas of the body which are crucial for good alignment:

■ the skeleton   ■ the spine   ■ the foot.

The skeleton – the bones of the matter

The main functions of the skeleton are:

■ support;
■ protection of organs, e.g. brain, heart, lungs, spinal chord;
■ to allow accurate movement when muscles contract by giving rigidity;
■ to provide red marrow – some bones contain red marrow which is a part of the blood-forming tissue;
■ storage of minerals, such as calcium and some fats for energy.

The skeleton is divided into two parts:

1 The axial (head, chest, pelvis): the skull, vertebrae, clavicle, scapulae, sternum, ribs, ischium, ilium.
2 The appendicular (legs and arms): the humerus, radius, ulna, carpal bones, metacarpals, tarsals, metatarsals, phalanges, femur, tibia, fibula.

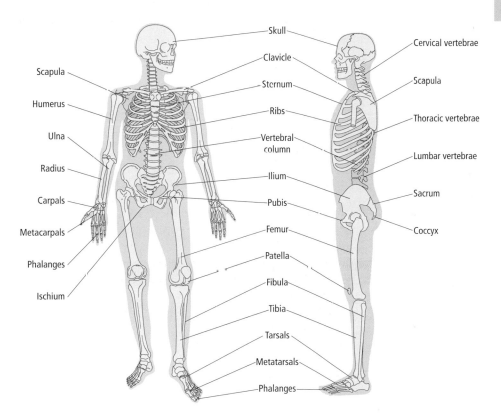

Figure 1.6 The human skeleton

The bones

Bones make up the skeleton. There are four types: long, short, flat and irregular. The size of these depends on their function: bones bearing larger body weights are bigger and denser, whereas those bearing lesser body weights are smaller and lighter. Bones provide attachment surfaces for muscles, ligaments and tendons so that joints can move.

■ **Long bones** – tibia, fibula, humerus, radius, ulna, metacarpals, phalanges.
■ **Short bones** – carpal and tarsal.
■ **Flat bones** – skull, scapulae, sternum, ribs.
■ **Irregular bones** – sacrum, innominate bone, vertebrae.

Here are some examples of bones and their function:

- The femur of the thigh (long bone) supports more weight than the humerus of the upper arm, and so it is larger and heavier.
- The vertebrae (irregular bone) of the spine are larger near the bottom to support the increased mass from above.

Similarly, the shape of a bone depends on its function. For example:

- The vertebrae are like rounded building blocks stacked to form the spinal column which surrounds and protects the spinal chord.
- The ribs are slender and curved to protect the lungs and heart, and also offer a broad surface for muscle attachments.
- Bones like those in the lower arm – i.e. the radius and ulna – are long and slender to allow the system of levers to operate efficiently.

Bone is very hard connective, living tissue and exercise helps to build stronger bone by imposing stress. As the condition of bone improves, calcium salts, in the matrix of the bone, are deposited. Bone density reaches a peak by the age of 20, so the younger you start to look after your bones, the longer into your future they will last.

Table 1.1 Injuries to bones

Injury	Symptoms/causes	Treatment
Stress fracture (including 'shin splints')	Localised cracks in bones due to repeated stress on one area of bone. Causes: Use of unsuitable (unsprung) floors. Poor alignment in any of following: fibula – sickle foot/inversion; tibia bow – weight back; lumbar vertebrae – weak abdominal muscles	Rest Remedial correction of weaknesses, including specific exercise for weak musculature. Heat. Stretch front of lower leg for shin splints (see Task Three).
Fractures	Uncommon as a dance injury. Most common is of fifth metatarsal and of ankle, when twisted – i.e. if inverted and rotated in the fall.	Plaster cast. Immobilise for six weeks or many months. May be treated with strapping if a minor fracture. Dancer may not dance, but should exercise areas not in plaster to stay strong/mobile. Once out of cast: ice and ultrasound, plus exercise of inactive muscle.

DANCE TIPS

**QUICK GUIDE TO HEALTHY BONES
– preventative practice**
- Diet: calcium intake found in dairy products, some tinned fish, e.g. sardines and salmon. Daily recommended intake: 12–15 years, 1000mgs; 16–54 years, 1200mgs.
- Regular weight-bearing exercise.

DANCE TIPS

**PUTTING YOUR BONES AT RISK –
unsafe practice**
- Smoking and high caffeine or alcohol intake affect your bones' ability to absorb calcium.
- Osteoporosis is loss of bone density, usually found in women over the age of sixty, when levels of the female sex hormone oestrogen drop. Bones can become 'brittle' and breaks are more likely to occur. However, young women who are under a healthy weight and whose menstrual cycle is disrupted may also lack oestrogen, and this may result in stress fractures in the feet or legs. Lack of oestrogen reduces the absorption of calcium. Consult your doctor if you are having problems with your menstrual cycle.

The spine – the vertebral column

The spine is a long limb . . . allow the rest of the body to balance around the curving river of the spine.

(Miranda Tufnell in Body Space Image, *1990)*

In the well-aligned dancer, the healthy spine is another power centre for moving. The way you sit, lie, stand, travel or fall is affected by the spine. Its elasticity absorbs shock waves created as you dance.

The main functions of the spine are to:

- protect the spinal nerve chord;
- support the head, ribs and hips;
- maintain upright posture;
- absorb shock of movement.

The spine has four curves (see Figure 1.6), which correspond to groups of vertebrae:

1 the cervical curve: seven cervical vertebrae (neck);
2 the thoracic curve: twelve thoracic vertebrae (chest/rib area);
3 the lumbar curve: five lumbar vertebrae (lower back);
4 the sacral curve: sacrum and coccyx (fused at bottom).

The curves of the spine help to spread the stress involved in weight-bearing, as do the cartilage discs in between the vertebrae which act as shock absorbers. The cartilagenous spongy discs are essential, for example, when landing from jumps and in allowing the spine to flex, extend and rotate. The vertebrae have transverse processes that stick out on each side, which provide attachment points for muscles.

The sacroiliac joint (where the lumbar curve meets the sacrum) is vulnerable. This is the point where the mobile spine meets the immobile pelvis. If the lower abdominal muscles are weak and combined with tight lower back muscles, there will be weakness in this joint. The erector spinae muscle runs down the back as part of a group with other muscles such as the splenius, suboccipitalis and the semispinalis. These long, thin muscles attach along various vertebrae or to the skull. Underneath them are the deeper short, thin muscles that attach from one vertebrae to another. Together these back muscles balance with the abdominal group to provide core stability for dancers.

Postural problems/injuries of the spine

Generally speaking, if a particular form of dance training encourages bad habits and unsafe practice – for example, if a dancer attempts movements beyond their ability – alignment and muscular balance will break down. Serious postural problems or injury, or both, may then result. There are also various anatomical defects – e.g. curvature of the spine – which require medical diagnosis and cannot be changed by exercise. In training, dancers with these defects need expert advice on how to accommodate the problem whilst maintaining correct posture. Some postural problems are listed in Table 1.2

The neck (the cervical curve) is also vulnerable to strain because it is so mobile and bears the weight of the head. The neck muscles must therefore be in good condition. In the event that the neck extensor muscles are weak and the flexors are too tight, the dancer's chin may jut up and the ear will be in front of the plumb line. This is known as cervical lordosis/forward head.

■ Extensor muscles are those which stretch the body.
■ Flexor muscles are those which curl or bend the body.

Many surveys report that the lower back is the most common site of injury for dancers.

A general word about injury would be helpful here. The *Fit to Dance?* (1996) survey found a link between poor fitness and numbers of injuries to dancers. It also gave examples of dance companies which planned swimming and fitness training into the dancers' contracts, to provide appropriate body conditioning.

Table 1.2 Postural problems of the spine

Problem	Symptom(s)	Causes	Treatment
Scoliosis – lateral deviation of the spine	From the back, appears as 'S' or 'C' curve.	Numerous misalignments.	If diagnosed from childhood, dance training can help ease the condition by emphasis on symmetry of movement.
Lumbar lordosis – swayback	From side view, the normal lumbar curve is exaggerated.	Weak abdominal muscle/tight lumbar spine and hamstrings.	Stretch lower back, hamstrings and hip flexors/ strengthen abdominals.
Flat back	Flat lower back (opposite of lordosis), posterior tilt of pelvis/ elongated thoracic.	Weak lower back muscles/ tight hamstrings.	Strengthen lower back and hip flexors/stretch hamstrings.
Kyphosis – round back	Abdominal round upper back (thoracic curve) as seen from side.	Tight chest muscles and weak upper back.	Stretch chest muscles of upper trunk and strengthen upper back.

The use of the spine in different dance genres

There are interesting contrasting uses of the spine in the various genres of dance. The classical ballet genre has maintained the vertical spine as one of its characteristics from the fifteenth century. This relates back to its noble beginnings when correct deportment – how to walk, sit, stand and bow – was taught and denoted status and power. The nobility would perform dances in this manner, and later this tradition was taken on by professionals to become ballet as we know it today. The style of the vertical torso gives ballet its distinctive ethereal lightness, and facilitates the execution of characteristic multiple pirouettes and soaring jumps with greater ease.

The characteristic deep back bends and high arabesques require strong abdominal muscles to resist gravity, making a stable platform for the thoracic spine to arch away from. A safety tip is to stretch the lumbar spine upwards before bending. The *épaulement* of the shoulders starts in the thoracic vertebrae. This is where the 'wind-up' preparation for pirouettes begins.

Even this defiance of natural forces was not enough, however, for the pioneers of modern dance, and at the start of the twentieth century individuals like Isadora Duncan emerged in rebellion. For her, the solar plexus was the creator of all movement, and the name of the game was freedom. Along with this went

a mobile, tilting, twisting, curving *spine*. This allowed a wider range of expressivity for the choreographer, and dance has never looked the same since. The spiral twists of the torso typical of many modern styles start in the thoracic vertebrae. The so-called 'contraction' of the Martha Graham Technique is in fact an extension of the spine, not a bend, similar to the exercise that you did in Task Two. The corset of abdominal muscles contracts as the erector spinae extends, resulting in the characteristic curving torso.

In jazz dance, too, the erector spinae is stretched and strengthened during the characteristic pelvic forward and backward thrusts. Also in the jazz body roll exercise the erector spinae is strengthened as it contracts to arch the back, on the downward, forward phase of the roll.

Ballroom dancers keep the head aligned with the spine at all times. The head may be turned, inclined, lowered or raised, but always aligned to float freely and safely on top of the spine. In the Latin hip or Cuban motion, the dancer's hips rotate independently of and around the spine by alternating bends and stretches of the knees, giving the characteristic slinky look.

TASK FOUR – *Name Those Muscles*

KEY SKILLS Problem solving

🕐 10 to 20 minutes

REVELATIONS Alvin Ailey American Dance Theater, SADLER'S WELLS, LONDON 09/07

Fill in the missing words. In the photograph a male dancer is:

1 Using a c __ __ __ __ __ __ __ __ __ of the abdominal muscles.
2 This movement of the torso is a characteristic of the M __ __ __ __ __ G __ __ __ __ __ Technique in modern dance.

> **3** As the dancer executes this move, name two anterior muscles in the torso that contract.
> **4** When the abdominal muscles contract, what does the erector spinae muscle do?
>
> *Answers are on page 333.*

The foot – a true feat of engineering

Another crucial part of the body for dancers' correct alignment is the foot. Isadora Duncan, with her defiant, rebellious barefooted look, named dance 'the religion of the foot'. It is surprising, really, that such a small device is strong enough to support the whole of the rest of the body.

There are 26 bones and many small intrinsic muscles in the foot. These intrinsic muscles, which are layered, are vital because they allow the foot to point strongly with straight toes. Weak intrinsics will cause the toes to claw because the flexor muscles will be over-powerful.

Good practice in dance training aims to increase strength and suppleness of feet. In ballet, exercises such as *battement tendu, dégagé, frappé* and *relevé* strengthen the intrinsic muscles of the feet.

The other muscles which move the foot start below the knee and connect to the bones of the foot. The movements produced by these muscles are:

- plantar flexion – pointing downward, ankle extends;
- dorsi flexion – top of the foot points upward, ankle flexes;
- inversion – inner border of foot lifts;
- eversion – outer border of foot lifts;
- adduction – turns foot inward;
- abduction – turns foot outward;
- supination – combines adduction and inversion (sickle);
- pronation – combines abduction and eversion (looks like a flat, duck-footed walk).

The foot is divided into three sections – tarsus, metatarsus and phalanges (toes). We notice these sections as we walk, run or jump. When doing exercises like foot pushes and prances, the 'going through the foot' is felt particularly clearly as springy and strong. Strong, flexible feet are one of a dancer's most valuable assets.

The tarsus section of the foot is made up of seven bones: talus (ankle), calcaneum (heel bone), cuboid, navicular and three small cuneiform bones (see Figure 1.7). In correct alignment the lower leg (tibia/fibula) rests on the tarsus on the same medial line as the ball of the foot (metatarsus) (see Figure 1.6). This means that when you plié, the knee should align over an imaginary line extending out from the middle toes. Look down as you plié in turn-out and you should be able to see your big toe and the one next to it. This is crucial for safe landing from

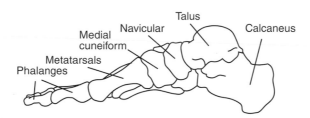

Figure 1.7 The bones of the foot

jumps. The metatarsus consists of five long metatarsals and leads to the toes (phalanges) (see Figure 1.7).

The foot has four arches for normal function in supporting the body weight, stepping and protection:

- the inside medial arch: from heel to heads of metatarsals (longitudinal);
- the outside lateral arch: from heel to head of the fifth metatarsal (longitudinal);
- two transverse arches – one across the foot at its most forward becomes the metatarsal arch (dome-shaped) and the other running across the front heads of the metatarsal bones.

The metatarsal arch is supported by ligaments and lumbrical muscles. The two most important ligaments of the foot are:

- the spring ligament (between calcaneum and navicular);
- the plantar ligament (between calcaneum to cuboid and the three middle metatarsals).

The arches give the foot its strength and flexibility and allow it to withstand the shocks involved during weight transference (stepping and jumping). Rolling in on the arches of the feet or out to the border should be avoided. Generally, a triangular distribution of weight on each foot is best (see Figure 1.8): the weight is spread evenly here between points 1, 2 and 3, under the first and fifth metatarsals and under the heel bone (calcaneus). If poor alignment is diagnosed, corrective inserts in shoes can help with treatment. The sole of the foot also provides the brain with information. It receives sensations from nerves which directly relate to a dancer's knowledge of orientation, alignment and support. For example, when jumping, the feet would tell you that there was no ground support.

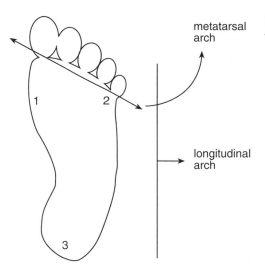

metatarsal
arch

longitudinal
arch

1

2

3

Figure 1.8 Correct distribution of weight on the sole of the foot

If arches collapse, serious misalignments occur not only in the foot but also in the rest of the body. If the body weight is placed on the outside of the foot ('sickling' or inversion), it not only looks bad but can lead to sprained ankles from incorrect landings by damage to the lateral ligament.

A collapsed medial arch leaves a pronated foot and the foot rolls in on the inner border (eversion). When this happens, you can see the navicular is misaligned nearer to the floor. Check your feet when standing to find the position of the navicular – it is the little knobbly bone sticking out on the inside of the foot just under and forward of the ankle.

Figure 1.9 Strong flexible feet are one of a dancer's most valuable assets.
Photography: Chris Nash
Photograph from cover of 'A Glance at the Toes'

Postural problems/injuries of the foot

- **Stress fracture of metatarsals.** Appearance: 'march fracture' appears as a pain under the foot when pushing through the foot in jumps, on a rise or when stepping. Soldiers marching on hard surfaces are prone, hence the name. Causes: poorly aligned body weight/barefoot work where extra pressure has been put on the metatarsal arch/increase in work. Treatment: rest recovery over approximately 6–8 weeks; physiotherapy, which encourages the intrinsic muscles of the foot to support properly.

- **Morton's Foot.** Appearance: abnormally short and hypermobile first metatarsal which can destabilise the foot and cause pain in the metatarsal area. Treatment: a foot pad to correct faulty weight placement.

- **Hallux Valgus and Tailor's Bunion.** Appearance: an enlargement on metatarso-phalangeal joint of either the first or fifth toe. Inflammation appears on the bursa where extra mineral deposits accumulate. Pain occurs when the ankle is rolling inwards. The big toe distorts away from the midline and the little toe goes towards the midline. Causes: Hallux Valgus from foot pronation combined with walking with outwardly rotated hips. Tailor's Bunion foot supination combined with inwardly rotated hips. Incorrect weight placement results. Treatment: by chiropodist placing a pad. Physiotherapy may use ice/ultrasound/corrective exercise. Check weight distribution on feet. Avoid tight shoes and barefoot work.

- **Hammer toes.** Appearance: crooked toes, big toe points upward, phalanges 2 and 3 are flexed downward, and the ends are often callused. This can lead to corns. Causes: too narrow or short shoes. Treatment: keep toes in extended position in jumping and travelling. If pain becomes too great, special footwear/surgery may be necessary.

- **Plantar fascial strain.** Appearance: aching on the sole of the foot. Causes: incorrect landing from jumps. Treatment: ice/strapping/reduce workload/ ultrasound/support pads in shoe. Can be stubborn and recurring.

- **Flat feet** (*pes planus*). Appearance: lowering of the medial arch. Aching under big toe and along to heel. Causes: unsuitable footwear/rolling in on ankles. Often related to poor turn-out and knee problems/bunion. Treatment: ultrasound/arch support/corrective exercises for the intrinsic muscles of the foot.

- **Rolling and sickling.** Appearance: if there is a bow in the tibia bone, a misalignment in the angle of the ankle joint will result. The knee will be out of line with the ankle and foot. Rolling and sickling will occur.

TASK FIVE – *Feet*

KEY SKILLS Improving own learning and performance

🕐 10 to 20 minutes

A corrective exercise for feet to strengthen the dorsi flexors and to help the prevention of, or to heal, shin splints of the lower leg:

- Sit on a mat on the floor, legs straight out in front.
- Extend one foot. Place the other foot on top.
- The top foot puts downward pressure on the bottom foot. Flex the bottom foot against the pressure for 10 seconds, then pull back the foot through the whole range of flexion.
- Repeat two or three times.

Dancers should do as many exercises for their feet as for other parts of the body, since it is so important that the feet should be strong enough for the work demanded.

Remember, healthy feet are happy feet and research has shown that people who wear sensible shoes live longer!

(Dr P. Brinson and F. Dick in Fit to Dance?, 1996)

The use of the foot in different dance genres

In classical ballet the foot is normally plantar flexed (pointed), whereas in the modern genre it is often dorsi flexed – this is particularly noticeable in the Martha Graham Technique. Some post-modern styles prefer a more neutral, relaxed position of the non-weight-bearing foot. Obviously, these all have very different expressive qualities – the light, endless line of the ballet in contrast to the harsher, broken look and more natural throw-away feel of the post-modern dancer. An even length in the metatarsals and toes will assist support in demi-pointe (weight distributed evenly on heads of metatarsals and phalanges) and full-pointe (weight on phalanges only) work. The feet on the ground gives a further contrast between the genres – the floating ethereal look of the ballerina on pointe as contrasted with the earthy, gravity-bound, flat look of the modern dancer.

Needless to say, the rigours of pointe work may cause alignment problems. Ballet dancers who work regularly in plantar flexion on pointe may be prone to tendinitis in the Achilles (the tendon of the calf muscles) at the back of the heel. Shoes must fit correctly, with, if necessary, high vamps (support pads) to protect high arches (*pes cavus*). Pointe work should never begin before the age of 12, when the bones have ossified sufficiently to cope with the weight. Continual pointe work may result in a thickening of the metatarsals, and this is why the feet may seem to widen. When pointe work is stopped completely, however, the feet will return to their original size.

Sometimes the wearing of shoes, as in high heels for female ballroom dancers, can cause problems because when the calcaneum bone (heel) is raised for prolonged periods of time it may shorten the gastrocnemius and soleus muscles in the lower leg.

No account about feet would be complete without some thoughts on tap dance. The blend of Northern English clog dance, Irish step dancing, American soft-shoe and African–American steps and rhythms is an energised and lively combination. In the eighteenth century, African slaves brought their rhythms to America but were forbidden to use drums, so they made taps and slaps to accompany their dancing instead. From Harlem, New York in the 1920s to Hollywood films in the 1940s and musical theatre, styles were varied but always tapping out captivating rhythms. Tap dance gained widespread popularity during the twentieth century and in the present day it is enjoying a revival.

Footwork requires articulate and supple ankles, toes, metatarsals and heels to make single, double and triple taps that counterpoint the music. A toe tap exercise, when the toes and metatarsal touch the floor and quickly rebound, increases ankle flexibility. While the feet are busy, the torso is counterpulling away from the feet and maintaining a dynamic alignment so that there is plenty of room for the toes to twinkle!

TASK SIX – *Toe power!*

KEY SKILLS Improving own learning and performance

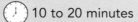 10 to 20 minutes

This exercise is useful for dancers from all different dance genres. You are going to articulate the three sections of the feet. Repetitions of this exercise can be used for warming up and the feet will be strengthened. Your co-ordination for jumping and foot alignment can also benefit.

Start by standing in parallel. If you prefer, you can use a barre for support at first. Check that your weight is evenly distributed on the triangle of the sole of your foot, as in Figure 1.8. As you work, hold your torso steady in alignment to free the feet and legs.

- Slowly peel one heel (*calcaneum*) off the floor, leaving the ball (*metatarsal*) on the floor.
- Push the toes (*phalanges*) down forcefully into the floor so that they spring off the floor quickly as they extend. Your knee will be at 90 degrees now. During this motion it is important to use only the toes and not the upper leg muscles to lift the leg. You can ask a partner to check for any misalignment of the foot at this point, such as sickling, or for any shifting of weight out of alignment.
- Once on one leg you should be balanced and aligned and able to hold the position.
- Slowly return the foot to the floor, reversing the order of the sections of the foot – toes/ball/heel.
- Repeat this a few times slowly on one foot, then the other. Try to feel the 'going through the foot' and holding your alignment that are both important for safe practice in jumping and travelling.
- Repeat on each foot, increasing the speed, ensuring that the heel cushions onto the floor each time before the next spring from

the toes. This protects the Achilles tendon from shortening in actual jumps and is important to protect it from snapping on landing. The movement should be sharp and controlled but easy and light.

■ Now you can add some music – anything you like with a moderate to fast beat. Stay aligned throughout, avoiding the wobbles or shifting weight from one foot to another. As you do this it should feel like you are able to stand on one leg for ever! Try this combination in parallel or turned out:
  – 8 foot pushes on the right and repeat on the left.
  – 4 foot pushes on the right and repeat on the left.
  – 2 foot pushes on the right and repeat on the left (twice).
  – 1 foot push on the right and repeat on the left (8 in total).
  – *Plié*, straighten, rise to demi-pointe, lower (4 times).
■ Repeat the whole set three times in total.

As well as the spine and feet, other parts and functions of the body are crucial in maintaining correct alignment:

■ The lateral flexor muscles of the trunk help to hold the trunk in place, for example during multiple pirouettes.
■ Visual cues: the eyes send information to the brain on the body's position in space.
■ Semi-circular canals in the inner ear send information on the body's orientation in space.
■ Receptors in joints, tendons and muscles provide continual information to the brain on the body's relative position in space.

Alignment – summary

It is clear that this fundamental skill of alignment is crucial to the prevention of injury for any dancer. Becoming aware of and correcting poor posture can improve alignment. The dancer requires the stretching and strengthening of appropriate muscle groups when they encounter misalignments/injuries.

Other examples of faulty alignment in training are:

■ weight too far back;
■ failing to turn out from the hips;
■ twisted hips;
■ feet overturning/rolling;
■ misuse of muscle groups during *plié* (knees flex) and *relevé* (rise on toes either demi-pointe or full pointe).

Many dance programmes nowadays stress the importance of core stability and body awareness, as taught in the Alexander Technique and Pilates, for example, which emphasise the balancing of the muscles. Regular attendance to good

technique classes in the presence of an observant teacher will help to maintain alignment and keep the chance of injury to a minimum.

Learning to dance is an extremely vulnerable activity . . . Dancers must learn to treat themselves with respect.

(Julia Buckroyd in 'Dying Swans', New Scientist,
25 December 1993/1 January 1994)

Now try Task Seven, a final quiz.

TASK SEVEN – *Quiz: Check It Out!*

KEY SKILLS Problem solving
Improving own learning and performance

 10 to 20 minutes

Test your knowledge about alignment and the skeleton, spine and feet.

1 Is your foot inferior or superior to your shoulders?
2 Is the position of your *rectus abdominis* anterior or posterior on your torso?
3 How are the fibres of your *quadratus lumborum* arranged and why?
4 Identify two ways that regular and correctly performed *pliés* improve safe practice.
5 How many arches are there in the foot and what is their function?
6 How many bones make up the tarsus and where are they found?
7 What is the purpose of the curves in the spine?
8 How many types of bones are there? Why are they different sizes?
9 Why is it important to have enough calcium in your diet?
10 In ballet, which position of the foot is often used and what is this position commonly known as?

Answers are on page 333.

Flexibility – freedom to move!

Increasing flexibility involves increasing muscular elasticity so that the range of motion (ROM) of joints will increase. Flexibility should not involve stretching the ligaments that provide the joints with stability: the elongation of the ligaments increases the possibility of injury. The limit to flexibility is either the ligaments, tendons (such as the Achilles) or bony restriction. Individual differences in the fascial sheath that surrounds the muscle will affect the range of motion/flexibility. Tight ligaments will reduce mobility, as will tight musculature.

Myth: a dancer can never be too flexible

Natural flexibility is not necessarily a bonus for a dancer. Flexible joints which are not protected by adequate muscle strength are more susceptible to injury.

(Rachel Harris in 'Dance Dates', Birmingham
National Dance Agency, 1994)

The assumption that all dancers should be able to achieve the same range of motion is thus false. Other factors which will influence flexibility are gender, age, body and room temperature, and training. When flexibility is increased through warm-up, the range of motion in the joints increases. A more flexible body helps to avoid malalignment, muscle tears and injury generally.

Recent somatic approaches, such as Feldenkrais® and the Alexander Technique, concentrate on releasing the body's full potential to move. By relaxing and using imagery, rather than forcing muscles, your ROM can improve not only during static stretches but also as you dance. As with alignment, flexibility is at its most important when dancers are moving and this is determined by being able to let go of tension and channel movement to flow freely through the body. This control involves co-ordination of movement and will be dealt with in more detail later in the chapter.

The main concerns surrounding flexibility are:

- the joints – particularly the hip, knee and ankle;
- stretching.

The joints – meeting points

Where two bones meet, there will be a joint which allows movement to occur. There are several types of joint which allow different degrees of mobility – from fully mobile to very restricted. In dance, we clearly need a wider range of movement in the hip/leg joint (the 'break' of the leg) than in, say, the knee, which needs greater stability for its protection in actions like landing from a jump.

There are three types of joint:

- cartilaginous
- fibrous
- synovial.

Cartilaginous joints

These allow little movement but give great strength. The joints between the vertebrae where the intervertebral cartilage is placed are cartilaginous joints. The limitation of movement here is crucial in absorbing both the shock from, say, jumps and jarring to the skull and brain. These joints are characterised by the presence of the connective tissue called cartilage between the bones. Cartilage contains water and acts to cushion the pressures between the bones.

Fibrous joints

These allow little or no movement; for example, the flat bones of the skull. Imagine what would happen to your brain if these joints moved around! Everyone needs to stretch their minds, but not their skulls. The bones are closely connected by seams of tough, fibrous connective tissue.

Synovial joints

These are the most mobile, so in dance these are the ones that are of greatest concern – e.g. the hip joint (ball and socket – see Figure 1.10), shoulder, fingers, toes, knees and ankles (hinge joints), which all allow a range of free movement.

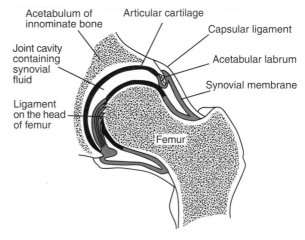

Figure 1.10 The hip showing features of a synovial joint

Of all the joints, the synovial ones are the most complex in structure, having the following structural characteristics:

- a joint cavity (a space inside the joint);
- articular cartilage, which covers the bone, reducing friction and allowing smooth movement;
- a capsule, which surrounds the joint, holding together the bones and enclosing the cavity. Ligaments and tendons also cross and strengthen joints to protect from strain or dislocation;
- synovial membrane, which lines the joint;
- synovial fluid, which fills the joint cavity and lubricates the joint.

As we can see, these different joints either allow or restrict movement, according to their structure. The point here is to know which movements are suitable for which joints, and to be able to move within the body's potential, thus avoiding injury. It is important to recognise your own limitations. Forcing or twisting a joint in directions for which it is not structured will cause injury. Therefore, it is helpful to know not only the joints' structures but also their correct movement range – see Figure 1.11.

Generally, joint movements include a range from the following:

- flexion: bending a joint;
- extension: straightening a joint;
- abduction: motion away from the centre line;
- adduction: motion towards the centre line;
- rotation: motion around the joint axis line;
- circumduction: a combination of the above involving motion in a circle.

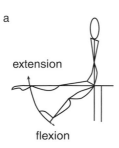

Figure 1.11 Movements possible in the joints

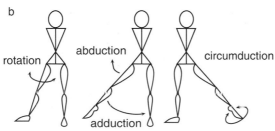

Now try Task Eight.

TASK EIGHT – *A Joints Jigsaw Puzzle*

KEY SKILLS Working with others
Problem solving

🕐 10 to 20 minutes

In groups of three or four, use sitting, standing and lying positions.

1 Experiment with bending and stretching all the joints in varying degrees – 45°, 90°, 180° – noticing which joints are more or less mobile.
- Work on circling, rotational movement in the joints.
- To music of your choice, put together a phrase to be performed in unison which contrasts rotations with bends and stretches, and uses different joints.
2 It may be fun to use chance procedures to make the phrase by writing down on separate pieces of paper the names of different joints and turning them face down. Select at random the joints, and perform the phrase in the order that you chose them.

The body and joints move through planes and axes (see Figure 1.12). An axis is the meeting point of two planes. Reflecting on the task, consider that different joints can be classified by their correct movement range, as follows:

- non-axial: linear movement only;
- uniaxial: movement in a single plane around a fixed axis;
- biaxial: motion in two planes around two axes;
- triaxial: motion in all three planes around three axes. This joint is sometimes also called a ball and socket joint.

Table 1.3 classifies the main joints in this way. Joints have sacs of fluid between the tendons and bones called bursa. These allow the smooth movement of tendon over bone. If over-used, joints may become inflamed, and this is known as bursitis.

Table 1.3 Classification of joints by type and movement range

Joint	Joint type	Movement range
Shoulder Hip	Ball and socket, synovial, triaxial	Adduction, abduction, flexion, rotation, extension and circumduction
Wrist	Biaxial, synovial	Adduction, abduction, flexion, extension
Atlas	Pivot, uniaxial	Rotation
Knee Elbow Ankle	Hinge, uniaxial, synovial	Flex, extend. Some rotation when not weight bearing
Foot	Non-axial	Linear only

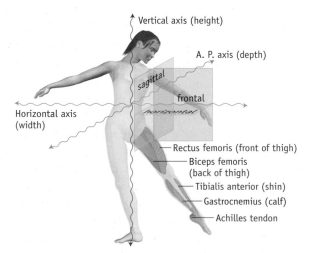

Figure 1.12 The three body planes: In *battement tendu*, which plane of movement is the dancer's left leg moving through?

Answer: The Horizontal Plane.

Table 1.4 shows how the three axes and three planes work together to produce movements. Rudolf Laban's names for the three planes are shown in italics, as well as the anatomical names.

Table 1.4 Movements that arise in the three planes and axes

Body Plane	Axis	Movement IN a plane	Movement around an axis
Sagittal Plane Divides body right to left (*Wheel Plane*)	Anterior-Posterior (AP) Axis Back to front	Travelling forwards and backwards (Advance retreat)	Side bends and leans
Frontal (or Coronal) Plane Divides body back to front (*Door Plane*)	Vertical Axis Up to down	Rise and fall – jumps	Spin, headshake 'No'
Horizontal (or Transverse) Plane Divides body top from bottom (*Table Plane*)	Horizontal Axis Side to side	Open and close – spins, turns, twisting from waist	Forward bends from waist, head nod 'Yes'

The hip/pelvis – the power generator

A useful image for dancers is to see the pelvis as a bowl. The rim of the bowl tilts during movement, and any small shift of the angle affects the body's alignment in stillness and movement. Try visualising a tilting pelvis – tilting forwards (stick out your tailbone), backwards (tuck your tailbone under) and centred may help you to feel the correct position of vertical placement. The hip/pelvis (see Figures 1.10 and 1.13) is the strongest joint in the body due to its heavy net of ligaments and strong musculature. The ball and socket are deeply set to give greater stability. At the same time, the top of the head of the femur stands out from the pelvis, giving a greater range of movement in all directions. Consider this the next time you are performing *ronds de jambe en l'air*, an exercise which increases hip flexibility.

The turn-out associated closely with classical ballet depends on the 'Y'-shaped ilio-femoral ligament and the angle at which the femur is set in the bowl of the acetabulum of the hip socket. The powerful ligament holds the femur, and if gently stretched at an early age, it can become more elastic and so increase the range of motion in the hip. While the gluteal muscle group (buttocks), with the abdominals, holds the pelvis in place, the six smaller deep rotator muscles are the 'movers and shakers' of the rotation of the thigh bone in the hip socket. *Gluteus maximus* is the largest muscle of the group and it extends the hips, for example in jumps when you extend legs in the air or in landing recovering after the *plié*.

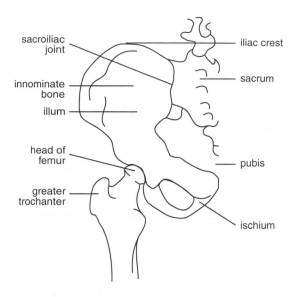

Figure 1.13 Bones of the right side of the pelvis

sacroiliac joint

innominate bone

illum

head of femur

greater trochanter

iliac crest

sacrum

pubis

ischium

An important muscle group of the hip area connecting the pelvis and spine to the legs is the *iliopsoas*, which is the main flexor muscle of the hip. Three muscles make up this group: *psoas major, psoas minor* and the *iliacus*. Their origin is on the vertebrae and they insert on the top of the femur bone (see Figure 1.13). When the *iliopsoas* is in good condition it can improve flexibility in the hip, core stability and turn-out. Also, it is the only muscle that, if sufficiently strong and supple, can lift the leg over 90 degrees.

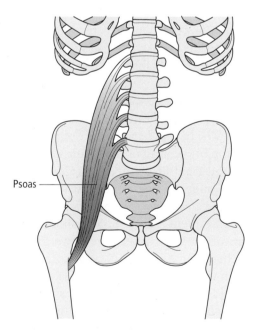

Figure 1.14 Iliopsoas

Psoas

If the pelvis is held out of alignment for prolonged periods, say with continual forcing of turn-out, the muscles around it will compensate and tighten or loosen,

losing their usual balance. Once the muscles lose their usual balance the spinal curves will also adjust. For example, a forward tilted pelvis produces a 'hollow back' in the thoracic curve, abdominal muscles weaken and back muscles tighten. And that's not all – the ribcage will stick out forwards and breathing will be restricted. When moving, this shift of the pelvis affects the vertical axis so that the dancer's lower back muscles try to compensate and extending the legs is restricted. Now try Task Nine – this will help you feel the proper alignment of the pelvis.

TASK NINE – *Hips in the Right Place*

KEY SKILLS Problem solving

🕐 10 to 20 minutes

1 Stand in a narrow parallel position, bend knees, and imagine holding an iron bar that passes through your hips with your hands. Rotate the bar backwards and it tilts the pelvis forward, sticking out your *sacrum* (tailbone). Reverse. Repeat this forward and backward tilting and feel when the abdominal and back muscles contract. Your *sacrum* is now moving, nodding forwards and backwards in the Sagittal Plane and around the Horizontal Axis. Describe the muscles action to a partner to see if you both have the same answer.

2 Repeat this but put one hand on the *sacrum* and the other slightly above it. Try to feel the tension that your nodding sacrum is causing in the muscles and how the curves of the spine alter. This will affect the spine's ability to absorb shocks when moving.

3 Now take your hands away and feel how the pelvis sits in a neutral position. Try to feel how the bowl of your pelvis sits balanced on the slight contraction in the *gluteals* (buttocks) and the top of the hamstrings.

Postural problems/injuries – the pelvis

Tight musculature and ligaments around the hip can affect the back and create misalignments around the body. Forcing turn-out, insufficient warm-up and misalignment are all possible causes of injuries such as strains to the *rectus femoris* or *iliopsoas*. The correct tilt of the pelvis is essential in order to support the normal curve of the spine. 'Sticking the tailbone out' will increase the hollow of the back and must be avoided.

Some dancers with too-loose ligaments may feel their hip go out of joint. Over time, this may lead to deterioration in the joint. The musculature must be strengthened in order to avoid this condition which, in time, can develop into osteoarthrosis of the hip where the joint narrows and the bone surface wears away – this is very painful. Many dancers trained in the Graham Technique in the early days forced the opening of the hips and have suffered such deterioration as a consequence.

Men who begin training later than most women usually develop less hip flexibility.

Figure 1.15 A dance class in the style of Martha Graham, as taught by Robert Cohan at I. M. Marsh College, 1974.

The use of the hip in different dance genres

One of the best-known characteristics of classical ballet is the turned-out position of the hips, legs and feet. Other dance genres also use turn-out to different degrees to help free movement such as in tap and ballroom dancing. Turn-out starts with *movement*, a rotation of the femur in the hip socket, along with the whole leg, ankle and foot. It needs a balance of strength and flexibility. It increases the range of motion, freeing the hip socket by moving the head of the greater trochanter back and out of the way. Therefore the following are made easier:

- leg extensions
- changing direction
- balance.

Forcing turn-out at an early age by twisting the hips will over-stretch the musculature of the spine and lead to injury of the lower back, groin and knees. In *tendu* the pelvis stays mainly square, but in high leg raises it will tilt slightly in response to the rising leg. The spine too will shift to compensate for a 90-degree or greater leg lift. There should be no collapse in the waist or ribs. Thoracic and lumbar spine should stay long and extended. Similarly in arabesque the pelvis tilts forward slightly, supported by strong abdominals.

Jazz dance and modern dance, by contrast, sometimes use an inward rotation of the leg and hip. This uses the muscle *tensor fasciae latae* in the leg (see Figure

1.4.). The inward rotation, or turned-in legs and feet, of Nijinsky's 1913 choreography 'The Rite of Spring' was an early example of modern rebellion against some of ballet's traditions.

Figure 1.16 *Le Sacre du Printemps,* 1913. Choreography: Vaslav Nijinsky for The Ballet Russes

In the jazz and modern genres, a more 'natural' parallel hold of the hips is preferred. This originated in the work of Isadora Duncan and the early ballets of Nijinsky as a rebellion against artificiality of ballet. Later, Martha Graham used it with greater emphasis to give her choreography a hard-edged look in combination with flexed hands and feet.

The mobility of the hips really comes to life in jazz dance. Hip isolations emphasise flexible movement with a strong sudden dynamic. The pelvis shifts side to side, backwards and forwards, as well as combining these directions in rotations and swinging through diagonals. These isolations are performed with walks and other combinations to express confident 'cool'.

Remember the planes of movement? Using Figure 1.12, can you answer the following questions? Do the movements as you work out your answers. Stand in a wide parallel position and move your hips in isolations:

■ From side to side – what plane are you moving in?
■ Back and forth – what plane are you moving in?
■ Rotate through side, forward, side, back – what axis are you moving around?

Answers:
Horizontal Plane.
Sagittal Plane.
Vertical Axis.

The knee bone's connected to your thigh bone!

'Knees over toes!' How many times have you heard this? To be accurate it means, for example in *plié*, that the knee should align directly with a line extending forward from the middle toes. Any inward rotation of or excess weight into the knee (for example sitting into a grand *plié*) will strain ligaments.

The knee joint (see Figure 1.17) is potentially unstable, but the cruciate ligaments hold the femur on the tibia, making it strong and robust. Also, two semi-lunar cartilages help to deepen the joint and circulate the synovial fluid, assisting shock absorption. These do not take weight, but if the knee is twisted whilst weight-bearing, they can be trapped between the femur and the tibia and will tear.

The kneecap (patella) protects this joint and acts to increase the action of the big thigh muscles (quadriceps) by serving as a point of attachment of the tendon and thereby increasing leverage for the movement of the joint.

The quadriceps extend the knee. The hamstrings flex the knee with help from *gracilis*, *sartorius* and *gastrocnemius* (calf). When the knee first starts to flex, it uses its very own muscle, the small *popliteus* on the back of the knee.

Postural problems/injuries – the knee

Most knee injuries occur when bearing weight in flexion, because this is when the joint has least stability. Many such injuries result from repeated twisted misalignment, which will loosen ligaments. Such misalignment often arises during *pliés*, when there is a failure to maintain the line of the patella directly over the midline of the feet (which extends out from the middle toe). If the knee is allowed to 'screw' because of inadequate hip flexibility, the medial ligament will take undue stress, and there will also be excess strain on the inside of the knee. Foot-rolling may also be a factor.

The maintenance of a straight, secure knee joint with minimal rotation during movement is the main way to protect it. After a knee injury, attention should be

given to the quadriceps muscle group in order to compensate for the loss of strength due to lack of use. This muscle group wastes quickly (atrophy) and so needs exercise, as do the hamstrings (the pair muscle group to the quadriceps), which provide the necessary eccentric contraction as the quads contract concentrically. This give-and-take relationship of muscle pairs is called reciprocal.

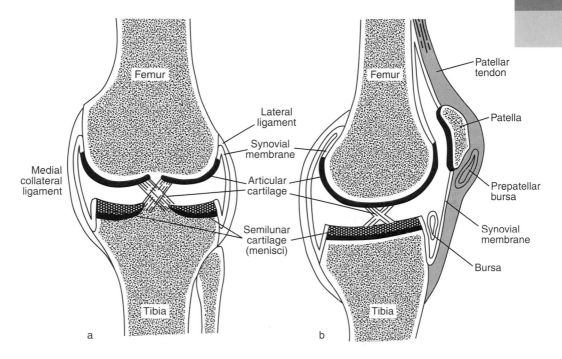

Figure 1.17 The knee joint (a) anterior, (b) from the side

Table 1.5 Injuries/problems of the knee

Injury	Symptoms	Causes	Treatment
Torn cartilage	Pain on bent leg, when weight bearing, on inside of knee. Knee locks if bent.	Incorrect *pliés* alignment – knee drops inward. Poor turn-out in hip.	Rest/operate if badly torn. Exercise quads/ hamstrings.
Bursitis (Housemaid's Knee)	Pain on either side of patella – swelling.	Excessive bending – bursa inflame.	Rest/ice/ ultrasound.
Jumper's Knee	Pain in *plié* and jumps, tender on patella under tibia when pressed.	Over-use during jumping.	Massage/ ultrasound/ stretch/ strengthen quads.

Postural defects of the knee – hyperextension

'Swayback' knees, although useful in classical ballet because they give a long, aesthetically pleasing look, are a sign of weak quadriceps. Over-stretching of the hamstrings and locking of the knees should be avoided. Knock knees, bow legs and tibial torsion also impair alignment and safe movement.

> **QUICKFIRE QUESTIONS – Test yourself**
> 1 What are the two functions of the *patella*?
> 2 Which muscle group extends the knee?

The ankle – anatomical architecture

> **FASCINATING FACT**
>
> On landing from jumps, the ankle can absorb up to eight times the body weight.

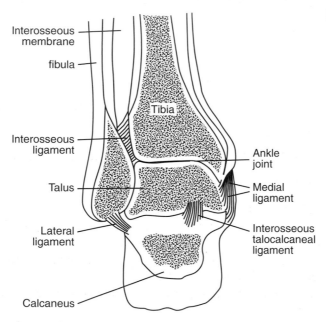

Figure 1.18 The ankle joint

The ankle joint (see Figure 1.18) lies between the tibia, the fibula and the talus. The ligaments on the outside and inside are the main means of support. The ankle joint is very stable, but is also the site of large stresses, therefore

Answers to Quickfire Questions
1 Protect the knee joint and increase action of the thigh muscles to extend the leg.
2 Quadriceps.

ankles need to be strong but also have enough flexibility in the ligaments to allow:

- safe turn-out in *plié* (eases stepping and landing);
- sufficient extension for take-off in jumps.

The ankle and foot are extended and flexed by complex layers of muscles in the lower leg. See Figure 1.19 for the main ones. Contraction of the powerful *gastrocnemius* (calf) muscle extends the ankle (*plantar flexion*) for rising on the toes (*relevé*) and jumping.

Postural problems/injuries – the ankle

The most commonly injured part of the ankle is the outside lateral ligament. It can happen from faulty landings causing the foot to sickle inwards as it rolls over on its outside edge. The ligament is then twisted and may tear. Treatment entails ice, rest, elevation and, if severe, a plaster or strapping. Recovery can take up to six weeks.

QUICKFIRE QUESTIONS – Test yourself

1 Name the three bones that intersect where the ankle joint is located.
2 Which ligament of the ankle joint is most commonly sprained?

Now try Task Ten.

TASK TEN – *Quiz*

KEY SKILLS Improving own learning and performance

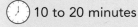 10 to 20 minutes

Look at Figure 1.20 and answer the following questions.

In the dancer on your left:

1 Choose from rotation/flexion/extension.
   (a) What two anatomical actions are her right hip performing? (2 marks)
   (b) How are the actions in the knees of supporting legs of the two dancers different? (2 marks)
2 (a) Which muscle group is mainly responsible for extending the knee? (1 mark)
   (b) Which muscle group is mainly responsible for flexing the knee? (1 mark)

Answers to Quickfire Questions
1 Tarsus, tibia, fibula.
2 Lateral ligament.

Revision Map – Introducing Muscles of the Lower Leg and Foot

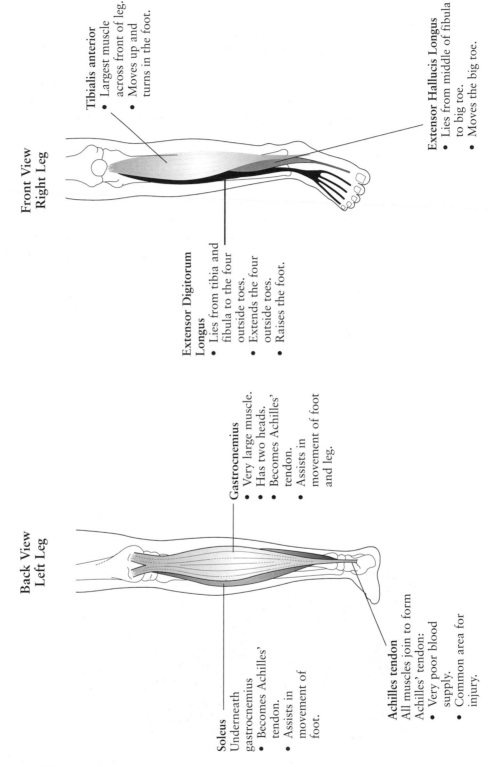

**Front View
Right Leg**

Tibialis anterior
• Largest muscle across front of leg.
• Moves up and turns in the foot.

Extensor Hallucis Longus
• Lies from middle of fibula to big toe.
• Moves the big toe.

Extensor Digitorum Longus
• Lies from tibia and fibula to the four outside toes.
• Extends the four outside toes.
• Raises the foot.

**Back View
Left Leg**

Gastrocnemius
• Very large muscle.
• Has two heads.
• Becomes Achilles' tendon.
• Assists in movement of foot and leg.

Soleus
Underneath gastrocnemius
• Becomes Achilles' tendon.
• Assists in movement of foot.

Achilles tendon
All muscles join to form Achilles' tendon:
• Very poor blood supply.
• Common area for injury.

Figure 1.19 Muscles of the lower leg and ankle

3 (a) What type of joint is the hip? (1 mark)
   (b) How many axes can it move on? (1 mark)
   (c) What name describes this range of its movements? (1 mark)
4 Choose from plantar flexion/dorsi flexion.
   (a) What action is her support foot performing? (1 mark)
   (b) What action is her foot in the air performing? (1 mark)
5 (a) Which anatomical action is her neck performing? Choose from extension/flexion. (1 mark)
   (b) What is the name for this part of the spine? (1 mark)
   (c) How many vertebrae are in this part of the spine? (1 mark)
   (d) Why is this area of the spine vulnerable to injury? (1 mark)
6 (a) The dancer's spine is rotated or twisted. Which curve of the spine does this action start in? (1 mark)
   (b) How many vertebrae are there in this curve? (1 mark)
7 The flexible spine is possible because of the intervertebral discs.
   (a) Where are these discs? (1 mark)
   (b) What are they made of? (1 mark)
   (c) What is the other function of these discs? (1 mark)

Answers are on page 333.

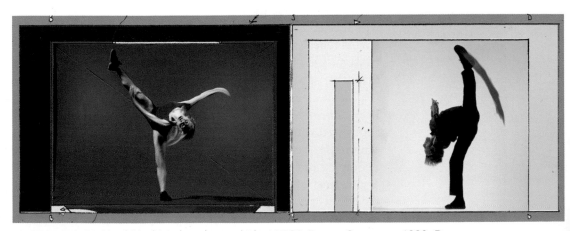

Figure 1.20 'And Nothing but the truth' by V-TOL Dance Company, 1998. Dancers Chris Devaney, James Hewison. Photographer: Chris Nash.

Stretching – a feel-good factor

Flexibility is improved by stretching. This action lengthens the muscle along the direction of the fibres (*eccentric contraction*). When stretching there should be a pleasant sensation inside the muscle. Breathing out (exhaling) deeply during the stretch will make it more effective. There are several benefits to regular and safe stretching in terms of preventative practice:

- improves alignment;
- releases muscular tension;
- increases the muscle temperature, making muscles more flexible;
- makes joints and muscles more elastic;
- helps to prevent and aids recovery from injury;
- increases concentration;
- releases toxins from the muscles after heavy physical exertion and so helps safe recovery from exercise.

There are a number of ways to stretch correctly which may overcome the blocking effect of the *stretch reflex*. This is a natural protective reflex which makes the muscle contract immediately after a stretch, so that in the case of a sudden fall or twist, the muscle is prevented from over-stretching to the point of injury. There are three methods of stretching:

- The **ballistic method** is not recommended. This alternates eccentric and concentric contractions of the muscles by bouncing, which may tear the muscle fibres. For this reason, ballistic bouncing stretches are ineffective, unsafe, and may cause soreness.
- The **static stretch** is a long, sustained stretch and hold method, using low force. During a slow action, the brain can override the stretch reflex. With conscious control, this stretch can be sustained and gravity can be used to increase the extension for at least 30 seconds, or what is comfortable. Let the muscle 'hang off the bone' and 'nudging around', feel as though the muscle is elongating. This is the most commonly used method of stretching. It starts with relaxed muscle, then stretches slowly so it does not need to overcome the stretch reflex (see below). There should be no pain. Combined relaxation and constant breathing through the muscles and between joints can reach spots that other stretches do not. This relaxed type of stretching is featured greatly in post-modern anatomical release work.
- **Proprioceptive neuromuscular facilititation** (PNF) starts with a fully contracted muscle and moves through a joint's full range of movement to achieve the stretch. Then the muscle must be fully relaxed to recover. This is a complex and time-consuming method and is riskier than the static method. Trying to stretch a muscle while it is in any state of contraction will reduce the effectiveness of the stretch and may tear the muscle fibres. However, when using *reciprocal inhibition*, the maximum contraction of one muscle will temporarily inhibit the stretch reflex in its opposite muscle. So, if you wanted to stretch, say, the hamstrings, a consciously held contraction of the

quadriceps for 20 to 30 seconds first would then allow greater stretch in the back of the thigh. After the contraction, the hamstring stretch should be held for a further 30 to 60 seconds. For this principle to work, both muscles have to be of similar mass. A bonus of the reciprocal method is the strength gained due to maximal contraction.

Both of the above recommended stretch methods use reflexes which are activated at a spinal level by a release of chemicals.

The Golgi tendon reflex is another protective reflex, but one which acts as a reaction to pressure. The Golgi tendon organs are sited at the point where the tendon meets the muscle, and they are sensitive to pressure. They totally relax the muscle when the tendon is about to pull off the bone, and they block the stretch reflex for a longer time. A word of warning, though, to dancers who think, 'Ah! I'll use this to stretch more' – the severity of the pull required to activate the Golgi reflex makes it a dangerous way to increase mobility. During intense stretching, if the reflex is experienced, there is a feeling of warm, total release. The muscle goes to jelly and the range of motion is increased noticeably. The safest way to reach this point is very slowly and carefully, after an adequate warm-up.

When the dancer holds their own body part being stretched, that is called *active* stretching. *Passive* stretches involve outside resistance, such as another person, or equipment such as a theraband, to help move the dancer into the stretch and hold them there.

TASK ELEVEN – *Some Stretches to Try*

KEY SKILLS Improving own learning and performance

10 to 20 minutes

1 Passive stretch for hamstrings with a partner using reciprocal inhibition. Dancer 'A' lies on their back and raises the right leg towards the torso (knee bent). The partner kneels next to the left shoulder and places hands on the bent knee and the quadriceps muscle of the dancer's bent leg. Dancer 'A' contracts the quadriceps muscle by pushing against the resistance of the partner's hands. Hold for 20 seconds in full contraction. The partner lets go and Dancer 'A' extends the leg, relaxing quadriceps and hamstrings and holds for 30 seconds. The partner continues to assist with the stretch by moving position to kneel straddling dancer 'A's straight leg and gently applying a downward pressure on the stretching leg with the hands placed on calf and just above the back of the knee.

2 Active stretching. Check a partner's flexibility:
   ■ For tightness in the back: one dancer kneels down with feet flat and curls forward. Look for flat places on the spine – these are points of tightness. Swap over.
   ■ For tightness in the front of the shoulder: raise an arm in abduction until it is parallel to the floor, then take the arm behind. Look for difficulty in this movement – this indicates tightness.

If any tightness has been found, now do the appropriate corrective stretch from below:

1 For the lumbar area: kneel as before, but stretch out the arms, breathe out and hold for 30 seconds. Apply the long, sustained stretch.
2 For the whole back: standing, drop from the head and curve down, lifting the abdominals; keep the legs soft and bent. Curl up again and repeat three times.
3 For the pectorals (the front of the shoulder area): make one arm reach directly behind you. Repeat with the other arm.

Generally speaking, the following guidelines should be used to sequence an exercise programme effectively:

1 Start gently and gradually build up to a more vigorous level. Do an all-over warm-up for 5 to 10 minutes first. This should raise the body temperature 1 or 2 degrees and make the muscle more elastic so that stretching is safer and deeper.
2 After the exercise of one muscle group, take time to undo the bad effects or to notice the good. For example, after a maximum contraction for strength, stretch out in the opposite direction. Or vice versa.
3 Before doing a major stretch, do a maximum contraction of the opposite muscle group.
4 Pinpoint the exact muscle or group that needs stretching/strengthening. Stretching three times a week should be adequate.
5 Find a quiet place for you to feel relaxed in.
6 See if closing your eyes assists focus and visualise imagery.
7 Vary your routine, such as the number of sessions weekly, the length of the session, the parts stretched, the duration of the stretches, to reach your target flexibility.
8 Listen to your body! Do not strain, avoid over-stretching and twisting of joints (especially the knee) and avoid compressing joints such as the discs of the spine.

Flexibility – summary

Improving mobility in the joints is crucial if the dancer is to maintain muscular balance in the body. This will also help alignment, safe working methods and avoidance of injury. You should learn what proper stretching techniques feel like when you do them, and so avoid unsafe methods.

Any muscular tightness you may have can be lessened by stretching, but any structural limitations of bone and ligament will not be affected by stretching, so all dancers should learn to work within anatomical restrictions and their personal range.

The next section is concerned with strength, and it is important to note that only when the muscles which control a joint are strong, can a full range of mobility be achieved through gradual stretching. Weak muscles should not be

stretched. When flexibility and strength are balanced the dancer can more easily reach and hold a position, for example, high leg extensions.

Strength and stamina

Strength – fitness is specific

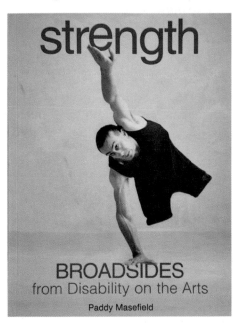

Figure 1.21 Front cover of *Strength – Broadsides from Disability on the Arts* reproduced with kind permission of Trentham Books Ltd. Photograph © Hugo Glendinning.

When combined, increasing levels of flexibility, strength and stamina form a policy of preventative training (prevent injury).

Strength is the capacity to exert a muscle contraction against resistance. A strong body moves freely, efficiently and above all safely. The aim is all-round strength, not the over-development of certain muscle groups. To build strength, muscles must reach maximal contraction.

Strength supports preventative practice in dance training in several ways. It:

- reduces risk of injury
- improves flexibility
- improves co-ordination & performance
- enhances muscle mass & the toned 'look' of the body

However, the look of muscle may mean that you actually weigh more, so be sure not to confuse weight gain with obesity.

Myths

- Building strength = bulk.
- Dancers should not use weights.
- Building strength = loss of flexibility.

The main concerns are types of muscle contraction and muscles.

Types of muscle contraction

During exercise, there are two types of contraction: isotonic and isometric.

Isotonic contraction

This involves a dynamic resistance during which the muscle changes in length but tone is constant. Machines can help in passive stretching to maintain tone in the muscle. Isotonic work may be either:

- concentric – muscle shortens, e.g. hip abductors (*gluteus medius*) of the gesturing leg as it is raised to the side (abducted);
- eccentric – muscle lengthens, e.g. hip abductors of the gesturing leg to control lowering it to the ground.

Strengthening exercises should be performed, in the full range of motion of a joint, in sets of 10–15. Repetitions slowly build to two or three sets. By adding weights, self-resistance (such as another body part), pulleys or elastic bands, overloading may be increased gradually and strength increases. The training of tap dance and film star Eleanor Powell (1910–1982) provides a great example of overload. Her teacher, Jack Donahue, hung two sandbags on a belt around her waist to develop the skill of tap that stayed low to the ground. Although Donahue insisted that tap was executed by the feet, the sandbags would have had the effect of strengthening Powell's legs and abdominal muscles, as she had to work harder in order to lift and free the legs, ankles and feet.

Isometric contraction

This involves a static resistance during which muscle tone increases but does not change length. For example, when a leg is raised to the side, holding it there means that the hip abductors have to work in static or isometric contraction to resist gravity. A weight-training programme for male dancers of the Birmingham Royal Ballet was devised by Yiannis Koutedakis at the University of Wolverhampton. The dancers used free weights and machines set at high resistance for a low number of repetitions. After the programme, the dancers felt that their physical appearance had improved.

To increase muscle strength, isometric (static) work as seen in Task Thirteen is useful, but the muscles will tire easily so frequent rests are needed. In Task Thirteen you could increase the frequency by increasing number of repetitions as your muscular endurance improves. Isotonic contraction, as seen in Task Twelve, is the most effective work to increase strength, and in this task as your

KEY SKILLS Improving own learning and performance

10 to 20 minutes

Perform the following isotonic exercise to strengthen hip abductors (*gluteus medius*). If a dancer has weak hip abductors and tight external rotators, *grand battement* and *battement tendu* will be performed with hip flexed and externally rotated, rather than in abduction.

1 Lie on your side, with legs straight and feet together.
2 Internally rotate the top leg and abduct the hip through the full range of motion.
3 Repeat ten times.
4 Build gradually to a maximum of three sets of ten. Allow 2–5 minutes' rest between sets.
5 When three sets are possible, perform the exercise standing with an ankle weight starting at 1 kg.

TASK THIRTEEN – *Isometric*

KEY SKILLS Improving own learning and performance

10 to 20 minutes

Perform the following isometric exercise to strengthen the lateral trunk flexors and correct scoliosis and an uneven hip tilt.

1 Lie on your side on a mat, with legs straight and feet together.
2 Rest on one forearm and extend the other arm to shoulder height.
3 Raise the hips sideways off the mat as far as possible, and hold for 10 seconds.
4 Repeat, then change to the other side.

With the above in mind, the principle of progressive overload to build strength can be identified. This involves increasing:

■ frequency: increasing the number of repetitions or the speed of a movement;
■ intensity: adding more and more resistance, as with weights;
■ duration: increasing the length of time a movement takes, or the number of sessions weekly.

strength improves the intensity is increased. Eccentric work should be included if muscles are weak or injured, or to increase flexibility. Targeting specific muscles for strengthening or flexibility, or the speed of execution of a movement such as fast, high leg kicks (*grands battements*), applies the principle of *specificity*. For example, you may need to strengthen the hip flexor, the *iliopsoas*, in order to improve abduction for high leg extensions.

TASK TWELVE – *Isotonic*

> ### QUICKFIRE QUESTIONS – Test yourself
> 1 What do you understand by the term *strength* in relation to the dancer?
> 2 What is the difference between eccentric and concentric contraction of muscles?

Muscles – in a duet of balance

Myth: muscles change to fat if exercise stops. This is not true at all. The strength of the muscle will reduce and it will feel softer if exercise stops, but muscle and fat are completely different tissues.

I have a big feeling about muscle – to have a muscle, to feel a muscle, to have a muscle warmed up and toned and ready to do something, it's a marvellous, sensual feeling.

(*Edward Villella in* Dance from Magic to Art, 1976)

Muscles are the meaty part of the body and there are over 600 of them. In dance, it is the striated or skeletal muscle which is of concern. This is controlled by the nervous system which sends electrochemical energy impulses, causing the muscle fibres to contract and the joints to move. The fibres in the muscles respond to nerve endings and detect the speed and amount of contraction that is required, so a jump that requires fast contractions and extensions in the legs will need the fibres to respond quickly. There are two different types of fibres in muscles:

- *slow-twitch fibres* (red fibres) contract slowly and can sustain tension over a long period. These are used for endurance, such as holding balances in dance. They work aerobically and are important for stamina. You will read more about this in the next section;
- *fast-twitch fibres* (white fibres) contract rapidly and tire easily. These are used for jumping, fast travelling sequences and similar actions. They work anaerobically.

Answers to Quickfire Questions
1 The ability to use muscles powerfully against resistance such as lifting and lowering a leg against gravity.
2 Eccentric lengthens muscles and concentric shortens them.

Strength and power in a dancer are most important during jumping, such as seen in the male solo in the ballet *Le Corsaire* (1837, Albert). The *danseur's* dazzling display of jumping culminating in a circle of soaring leaps requires strong muscles, especially white fast-twitch fibres. Individual dancers are genetically disposed as to the amount of fast-twitch fibre they have, but can increase strength through training. The other factor which influences the height of jumping is the ratio of power to the body weight. The strength of ligaments and tendons in the legs and arches of the feet is also important. Just like bones, muscle shape varies according to function. Shorter muscles, such as the biceps of the arm, give more strength.

Muscles are attached by tendons to the bone at each end: (a) the origin – this stays still; (b) the insertion – the end which pulls and moves.

Muscles can pull only (i.e. contract) and movement is brought about by pulling on the bones so as to turn these bones into levers. The structure of each such lever has three main parts:

1 the load or weight;
2 the fulcrum (balance point) of the joint;
3 the muscle action producing the effort at the point of the muscle insertion.

There are three types of lever: first-order, second-order and third-order, depending on the position of the fulcrum.

In Figure 1.22, F = fulcrum, E = effort and W = weight. An example of a second-order lever is shown in Figure 1.23.

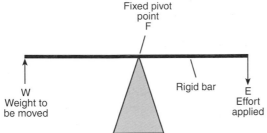

Figure 1.22 First-order lever

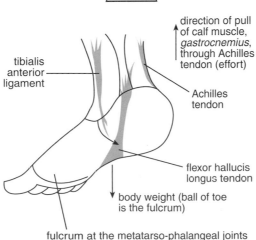

Figure 1.23 Second-order lever in rising onto one toe

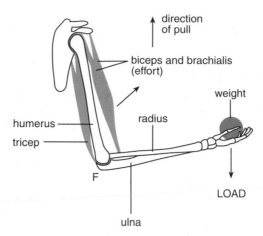

Figure 1.24 Third-order lever action of the arm

Most common levers in the body are third-order, where the 'effort' moves a shorter distance than the 'load'. This has the advantage of allowing a large movement to be made with only a slight contraction/shortening of the muscle (see Figure 1.24), thus making it a more efficient movement.

To dance without injury, a muscle needs a high level of efficiency in the antagonistic action of its pair muscle. This means that while a muscle is contracting, its opposite muscle must extend smoothly, in a harmonious duet. Muscles work in reciprocal pairs – like a *pas de deux*. Poorly trained or tired muscles do not tend to act antagonistically and they strain easily. Other muscles assist the prime moving muscle (*agonist*) by fixing parts of the body. These *fixators* and *synergists* contribute to the *agonist*'s work. For example, during hip abduction the *fixators*, the deep hip muscles, will prevent pelvic rotation, making the effort of the abductors more efficient. Meanwhile, the *synergists*, the torso side flexors and abductors on the opposite side of the hip, stabilise the core and standing leg. This clever balancing act is how muscle balance and the crossed-extensor reflex work in action.

So, for example, in raising a leg forward the quadriceps are the agonists, i.e. they concentrically contract to produce the raising movement. The hamstrings are the antagonists, on the opposite side of the joint. They relax and lengthen in eccentric contraction to allow smooth control. Similarly in *plié*, the quadriceps eccentrically contract, then in raising the body back to standing they contract concentrically to resist the force of gravity.

Muscle pairs include:

- biceps (front upper arm) and triceps (back upper arm);
- *rectus abdominis* (front torso) and the long muscles of the back;
- tibialis anterior (front lower leg) and gastrocnemius, soleus (back lower leg);
- thigh adductors (inside thigh) and gluteus medius and others (outside thigh);
- quadriceps and hamstrings.

Injuries – muscles and tendons

The stronger the dancer, the less the risk of injury, e.g. stronger hamstrings may reduce the risk of lower back injuries.

Muscles are attached to bones by the much stronger tendons. Both muscles and tendons are liable to injury. If a tendon is irritated by over-use, tendonitis may occur. Rest is then essential. The Achilles tendon is particularly prone to tendonitis. The symptoms are tenderness and crunching, particularly when plantar-flexing the ankle. Careful stretching of the soleus and gastrocnemius (lower leg) when cooling down reduces the likelihood of tendonitis.

Muscles and tendons are usually injured by too sudden a movement, or by a recurring strain on weak muscles from poor technique or over-use. Vulnerable muscles include the groin (iliopsoas, *rectus femoris*, adductors), the hamstring group and the calf (gastrocnemius). A thorough warm-up will help to reduce muscle and tendon strains, as it will for joint sprains. This preventative practice is the first line of defence. However, if you do injure yourself, the following is a good guide – PRICED is easy to remember:

P = prevent further injury
R = rest
I = ice
C = compress (bandage/support)
E = elevate (raise)
D = diagnosis, see a doctor

Once an injury has occurred, especially if it is major, you should seek diagnosis from a medical practitioner. As soon as you have injured yourself cold therapy will decrease the blood flow and bruising, which damages soft tissue. It limits swelling by lowering the muscle's need for oxygen and thus relieves pain. Apply ice for no more than 10–15 minutes, and repeat if necessary every few hours until the swelling, local heat or bruising stop. Bandaging and raising the injured limb will both help to lessen swelling. After two days, alternate between cold and hot in order to stimulate blood flow to the injury and encourage healing. The ice should not have direct contact with the skin – a bag of frozen peas works! Heat sources could be in spray form, an infra-red lamp or heat packs. Only a qualified physiotherapist should apply ultrasound. An appropriate exercise routine should be followed to maintain uninjured and injured parts alike.

Depending on the severity of the injury the dancer may need to rest for up to six weeks and should maintain treatment as advised.

Stamina – staying power

Dancing should look easy; like an optical illusion. It should seem effortless. When you do a difficult variation, the audience is aware that it is demanding, and that you have the power and strength to do it. But in the

we are huffing and puffing, CO_2 is being expelled more forcefully from the alveoli in the lungs out of the body. This removes the CO_2 from the muscles, making an exchange for O_2 possible in the capillaries, and in this way, exercise may continue (see Figure 1.25).

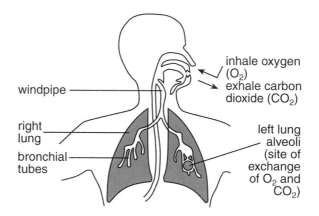

windpipe

inhale oxygen (O_2)
exhale carbon dioxide (CO_2)

right lung

left lung
alveoli (site of exchange of O_2 and CO_2)

bronchial tubes

Figure 1.25 Elements of the respiratory system and gaseous exchange

The rate of breathing is controlled by nerve cells in the brain. These detect the levels of O_2, CO_2 and acidity in the blood and stimulate an appropriate increase or decrease in respiration.

Carbon dioxide is a relatively harmless waste gas because it is displaced easily by oxygen in the haemoglobin. However, carbon monoxide, as produced by smoking cigarettes, is extremely poisonous because it combines with haemoglobin to exclude oxygen. It therefore deprives the body of a basic requirement, so smokers are less able to provide muscle with the necessary increased oxygen as demanded in dancing. Dancers who smoke will have less ability to maintain high-quality performance over long periods, and may be more prone to injury.

The ribcage protects the lungs. Attached to it are the muscles which control the expansion and contraction of the thorax cavity. These are the intercostals, the serratus group and the diaphragm. The lungs have no muscular power of their own.

The overall level of fitness for any sport or dance is something specific to that activity. However, the cardiovascular system does need a basic level of aerobic fitness, whatever the activity. An increase in the delivery of oxygen to the muscles by the heart, blood vessels and lungs is improved by slow and steady exercises, such as cycling or swimming, which gradually increase in intensity – in other words, through aerobic exercise where muscles work using oxygen. The American College of Sports Medicine defines aerobic activity as follows:

Aerobic activity is that requiring continuous, rhythmic use of large muscle groups at 60–90 per cent of the maximum heart rate and 50–85 per cent of maximum oxygen uptake for 20–60 minutes.

The main effects of aerobic exercise are:

- an increase in muscular endurance/stamina;
- an increase in cardiovascular endurance/stamina;
- a reduction of fat deposits (weight loss);
- a maintenance of bone mass.

Muscles can continue to work without oxygen, and this is called anaerobic activity. Anaerobic exercise begins when the muscle's oxygen consumption stops increasing, despite an increased performance. At this point, an oxygen debt is accumulated and waste lactic acid, which the muscle produces, can be tolerated only to a certain level before exhaustion – i.e. before a point is reached where the muscle can no longer contract. This is when the importance of cooling down after vigorous exercise kicks in, because gentler exercise and stretching remove toxins from the muscles. Aerobic exercise improves long-term endurance while anaerobic exercise improves short-term endurance. Dance tends to use mostly anaerobic activity – during technique class, performing repetitive movements will improve muscular endurance. However, some choreographers may also place vigorous demands on the dancers' aerobic endurance. This will result in progressive overload on the muscles and cardio-vascular system.

Preconditioning/preventative training for building up the stamina of the cardiovascular system is therefore advisable. In the event that the dance class is not providing sufficient training in this respect, the dancer should once again invest in some supplementary training. This supplementary type of work was noted earlier in this chapter in the Birmingham Royal Ballet's programme for male dancers, which aimed to increase upper-body strength and power. The programme focused on developing muscle fibres quickly by encouraging anaerobic activity through the use of free weights and machines set at high resistance for a low number of repetitions. But there were also exercises for slow muscle-fibre development in the form of aerobic sports such as cycling or running. You could consider walking or cycling to dance classes once or twice a week to improve your fitness and lessen your carbon footprint at the same time.

Recovery periods are needed after anaerobic exercise so that the oxygen debt is paid back and a normal chemical balance is resumed. Often, after such exercise, the muscles may feel sore or stiff. This may be caused by mild inflammation in the muscle fibres, which often occurs after new exercises or when adapting to new techniques. This condition reduces flexibility and causes general discomfort when dancing.

TASK FOURTEEN – *Quiz: Check It Out!*

🕐 10 to 20 minutes

1 Give two examples of the benefits of a strong, well-conditioned dancer's body.
2 Describe one method of progressive overload.
3 When lowering a leg from a high position at the side of the body, how do the hip abductors contract?
4 What force does the strength of the hip abductors overcome during this slow lowering of the leg?
5 Which end of a muscle *pulls* the bone of a joint, the origin or insertion?
6 Muscles work in reciprocal pairs. What is the muscle called that contracts to pull on the bone?
7 Why is stamina important for dancers?
8 What is the difference between aerobic and anaerobic activity?
9 What are the two organs that make up the cardiovascular system?
10 What gas does the body take in and send to the muscles?

Answers on page 334.

Table 1.6 Muscular functions and problems

Location	Muscle names	Function	Problems/injuries
Feet	Intrinsic muscles	Strengthen arches and keep toes long when foot is plantar flexed.	If toes keep curled, increases stress on Achilles tendon.
	Hallucis longus tibialis anterior	Dorsi flex foot (flexed).	
	Plantaris	Plantar flex foot (point).	
Leg Lower	Gastrocnemius mover muscle for travelling, jumps etc.	Plantar flex foot – a 'white' fast-flexed, knee straight. Reduces risk of tendonitis in Achilles tendon.	Stretch out after use, with ankle
	Soleus	Maintains plantar flexion, in *relevé*, pointe work – red holding muscle.	After a class with lots of adagio or balances, stretch it, with ankle flexed. Knee should be flexed and legs parallel.

Table 1.6 *(continued)*

Location	Muscle names	Function	Problems/injuries
Knee	Quadriceps group	Extend the knee by increasing leverage.	In any knee injury, the quads waste/weaken during recovery.
	Hamstring group	Strengthen alignment of knee over centre of tarsus. injure patella. Flex knee and extend hip.	Pronation (knees over-rotate)
Hip	Small rotators	Externally rotate femur and stabilise hip.	Imbalance between rotators tightens buttocks and pinches sciatic nerve.
	Iliopsoas	Medially rotate femur and flex hip.	Can appear 'duckfooted'. Cause of lumbar lordosis, lumbar back pain.
	Adductors	Laterally rotate femur (inner thighs pull together), stabilise pelvis when acting against the abductors when standing on one leg.	
	Abductors	Stabilise hip by supporting contraction on weight-bearing side.	If too weak or tense, will affect hips or knees.
	Gluteus maximus	Extends hip. Feel it contract when lifting from being flexed at hip.	Low back pain if excess lordosis (sway-back). May 'buck' during jumping.
Torso	Sacrospinalis, quadratus lumborum, *rectus abdominis* obliques, transversalis	Extend spine. Flex spine.	Strong abdominals help to protect lumbar spine.

Warming up and cooling down – wise up!

Warm-up before and cool-down after class are advisable in order to reduce the risk of injury. Dancers do not always warm up adequately before class. Do you? It is generally accepted that class is where dancers learn and improve technique skills for performance, but consideration of body conditioning for safe practice must be included in the dancer's routine. Dancers should take responsibility to allow time for their own warm-up to prepare before class or rehearsal. This applies to all genres of dance, but especially ones that require gymnastic and fast-moving sequences that put the body in positions where injuries are more likely, such as some hip-hop and break-dance moves.

Warm-up is a gradual physical and mental preparation for greater exertion which increases:

- breathing and heart rate;
- the deep temperature of the muscles – thereby improving their contractibility and flexibility;
- the flexibility of tendons and ligaments – so reducing the chance of injury;
- reaction speed;
- blood sugar and adrenalin levels.

The warm-up should include exercises which raise the pulse rate, such as moderate aerobic whole-body exercises, mobilise the joints and use the big muscle groups to raise internal body temperature quicker, and stretch the muscles (simple stretches). It is preferable for some warm-up exercises to relate to the dance movement that will follow, so that dancers are prepared physically and psychologically. If you know what your class or rehearsal will expect of you, your personal warm-up ritual may mark some of the movement that you already know, and you can use some visualisation of the moves too. As a dancer, your body is your responsibility and so a personal warm-up may have a few exercises prepared for specific muscles that need some extra t.l.c. Remember – fitness is specific and so is warming up. Stretches as the main means of warming up are unsafe and the body temperature must be raised before stretching can be safely performed. Now try Task Fifteen to devise your own warm-up ritual.

Cool-down is the gradual slowing down of the circulation in order to safely return to a resting heart rate. This promotes blood circulation to remove waste products from the muscles and helps prevent soreness. Stopping exercise too suddenly can cause the pooling of blood in previously active areas such as the lower limbs, and this can cause soreness, fainting and dizziness. Walking 'out' can work well, or marking gently some movements that you are learning can be productive too. This can also give you time to work on memory of new movement phrases and reflect on challenges from the learning experience. After a few minutes of slowing down, some gentle stretching or breathing for about five minutes is advised, and this is your chance to work on those weaknesses and capitalise on the warmth of the muscles and joints. The wearing of warmer

TASK FIFTEEN – *MY WARM-UP RITUAL*

KEY SKILLS Improving own learning and performance

45 minutes to an hour

Prepare your own warm-up ritual of 15–20 minutes along the following lines:

- 5–10 minutes easy pacing/jogging either in place or around the space;
- a light, easy moving of joints building to swings;
- gentle stretches;
- some 'technical' exercises, or a rehearsal of the dance about to be performed – this is important for mental readiness and the avoidance of injury.

clothing will help to avoid pulls and aches, and if you are going to take a few moments to relax and rest, will keep you warm.

Strength and stamina – summary

A healthy, well-conditioned cardiovascular system will provide the dancer with sufficient endurance to maintain safe, expressive and efficient movement throughout technique classes, rehearsals and performances. This system, however, works only in tandem with an equally well-conditioned respiratory system.

Strength and muscular endurance are related in a number of ways. If the muscle is strong, it can continue activity for longer. In progressive overload, which conditions for muscular endurance, the fatigue level rises and the last few repetitions can be 'maximal'. Such overload can thus serve to build strength and stamina.

Generally speaking, prevention is better than cure when it comes to injury. Technique classes and rehearsals are not always considered adequate conditioning to build a body which is 'dance fit'. The level of conditioning in any training programme must take into account the individual physical system.

Rest periods, although beneficial and necessary, can be a problem. 'Mostly the dancers are worried about getting some stamina together. After a very lovely week off, my body feels as if I've had two weeks off. Well we just have to . . . do the runs (of the whole show), daily to build it up.'

These most basic physical attributes – alignment, flexibility, strength and stamina – are all under the control of those most fascinating parts of the body, the brain and the nervous system. These are attuned to respond to the ever-changing conditions of our body and surroundings. They are the instruments which fine-tune the high degree of co-ordination and skills which dance demands. It is to this control tower that we now turn our attention.

Co-ordination – fine tuning!

The skills of balance, control of energy and accuracy of action are the subjects of co-ordination in dance training. In order to increase skill levels, the nervous system must be finely tuned. Through repeated practice in class, skills will improve. This may – for example, in balance – involve a decrease in the weight-bearing area. Greater speed will result if the pace of an exercise is gradually increased. You may have noticed that your teacher gradually increases the complexity or length of phrase, or the speed of an exercise. This will help to gradually improve your skills. Co-ordination requires negotiating the direction of forces in the body so that complex dance skills and combinations can be performed safely and expressively.

The function of daily class is to practise technical skills. By movement repetition, dancers build a link between commands and muscle memory. Gradually, as small memory pictures (engrams) are stored in the brain, skills become more automatic. Once these are memorised the dancer can focus more on the nuances of expression for performance. Computer software such as Life Forms can be used to aid memory. Choreographer Merce Cunningham uses it to store class exercises in a computer which dancers can check for clarification of co-ordination and sequences. Research has shown that it can take up to 180 repetitions to establish a new muscle memory, so technique learned in jazz class may not be helpful in a contact improvisation class, because the engrams acquired in one dance style may not be relevant to other styles. The nervous system consists of:

- the nerves/neurons;
- reflexes and receptors;
- the brain.

Together, these engage in a complex communication system which controls all human interaction in the internal and external environments.

There are two parts to the nervous system:

1 The autonomic nervous system regulates involuntary functions of digestion, hormones and cardiovascular activity.
2 The somatic nervous system regulates both movement itself and our perception of movement.

Both systems are controlled by the brain via neurons – there are millions of these individual cells capable of sending messages to and from the brain and the rest of the body. There are two types of neuron:

1 Sensory neurons transmit messages about tension in muscles, tendons and ligaments, and about hot, cold, pain, orientation in space and co-ordination to the brain.
2 Motor neurons pass impulses from the brain to the muscles.

The two types together allow you to put your finger on your nose without having to look at it.

The brain and neurological centres – communications networks

The brain can lose up to 100,000 cells a day and, just like flexibility, reduces after the teenage years.

The centres comprise:

- **the midbrain**: the primitive control centre regulating physical reactions like sweating and cardiovascular activity;
- **the cerebral cortex**: the centre of fine motor control, involving decision making for initiating and arresting motion. When new movement combinations are being learned, the new information may cause a feeling of awkwardness. Gradually, in dance, most movement becomes reflex as motor memory develops;
- **the cerebellum**: this transmits information to the midbrain and cerebral cortex regarding the status of the body. It is crucial in maintaining upright posture and balance. When you miss the last step on the stairs, it is because the cerebellum has been misinformed by the eyes and so sends the wrong messages, and in turn, the wrong amount of muscle contraction required for ascent or descent is then executed.

Receptors and reflexes – incoming and outgoing messages

In order for the centres in the brain to function, receptors must send information from muscles, tendons and joints about tension, co-ordination and spatial orientation. The brain then reacts by sending messages via motor neurons so that appropriate adjustments are made. Earlier in this chapter in the section on flexibility, the spinal reflexes affecting stretching were mentioned. These are muscular reflexes which are designed to protect the joints and muscles. There are three other such reflexes, as shown in Table 1.7.

There are also reflexes relating to the senses of sight, touch and hearing (*proprioception*): receptors in the eyes, skin and ears react to stimuli from the outside and send messages to the cerebellum, and appropriate adjustments are made on command from the brain. These reflexes are known as the righting reflexes (see Table 1.8) because they are primarily concerned with maintaining balance and orientation, and they comprise the aural, skin and visual righting reflexes.

The psychology of dance training – mind over matter

As the explanations above demonstrate, there is a definite connection between mind and body: the mind can affect the way the body feels and reacts. In dance, where the focus is such a personal one as your own body, there is a need to avoid

Table 1.7 Muscular reflexes

Name of reflex	Action	Applications
Flexor reflex	All flexor muscles contract when one is powerfully accompanying it with flexors for hands, feet, knees – as activated.	Increases intensity of abdominal contraction as seen in the style of Martha Graham. When learning new skills, sometimes powerful flexions are accompanied by unwanted tightness in neck, shoulders etc.
Extensor reflex	Stimulates all extensor muscles when one is powerfully activated.	Explains 'bucking' when beginners start to jump. The powerful contraction of the extensor muscles of the feet, ankles, knees and hips causes an overflow of neural activity to the extensors of the spine, and the head and shoulders are thrown backwards.
Crossed extensor reflex	Activates the contracting muscle of the diagonally opposite limb, and facilitates the antagonistic muscles of parallel limb.	For balance, when the right hip flexes, the left hip extends; and when the right shoulder extends, the left shoulder flexes. This is active in all balance and travelling (see Figure 1.20 for Task Ten). In Graham Technique spiral exercises. In opposition – e.g. skips. Often, beginners flop about. The wise teacher may not mention arm position, but allows the body to 'take over', thus allowing the natural reflex to establish itself as the norm without the conscious control of the cerebral cortex.

unhelpful, harmful practice when learning new co-ordinations. The concerns involved here are:

- tension and stress;
- kinesthetic sense;
- the use of imagery/feedback.

Tension, stress and the dancer – cool under pressure

One look at a beginner's dance class will tell you how much of an increase in the overall tension level there is in order to achieve a desired movement. As we

Table 1.8 Righting reflexes

Name of reflex	Action
Aural righting reflex	Organs of balance in inner ear. Three semi-circular canals are filled with fluid and have hairy linings. As the fluid moves, the cilia (hairs) interpret messages to adjust balance. When infected, say, during a cold, there is a distortion in the feedback sent to the nervous system, and a loss of balance may result.
Skin righting reflex	Receptors called exteroceptors are sensitive to pressure and send messages on where the body weight is placed. Whether lying or standing on feet or hands, the receptors in the skin are active. They can be of help to dancers on stage under blinding lights who may not be able to rely on visual righting sensations. These reflexes can be improved by practising movements with eyes closed.
Visual righting reflex	We depend on these mainly to maintain balance. Try standing on one leg with eyes closed. Activation of visual reflex is attempting to keep both eyes on the horizontal. This is not so appropriate during tilting, so then the other reflexes may be of more use.

know, the cerebral cortex activity and other muscular reflexes are the reasons for this. It is incredible that students can move at all when trying to use such high levels of tension to perform relatively easy tasks. In addition, localised tension in fingers, face, shoulders, etc interferes. Known as 'beginner's paralysis', this does lessen as the dancer's general skill level and co-ordination increase. The ability to inhibit undesired movement in one part of the body is necessary in order to focus on a new skill. The paralysis may return with each new difficult skill, but gradually tension is lowered. In this trial and error process, the dancer may try different muscular combinations, and may encounter blockage in motor learning and co-ordination. Eventually, with enough practice, a dancer is not always relying on feedback about the position of, say, a foot or when to bend the leg, and even in the most complicated sequences they control their dancing so that it looks smooth and 'natural'.

You cannot help facing movement blocks that will stand in your way. No one can remove these blocks except you yourself, and only when you are able to remove them will you eventually discover yourself. This is the only way to improve . . .

(Hanya Holm in The Vision of Modern Dance, 1980)

Movement blocks to co-ordination vary and are due to any of the following:

- specific weakness in the musculature, e.g. an inelastic antagonistic muscle;
- variations in potential according to body type (somatotype): mesomorphs, ectomorphs and endomorphs have preferences for different types of movement. The mesomorph prefers faster turns and jumps, whereas ectomorphs prefer a slower pace. All have different areas of weakness. Mesomorphs need to stretch their heavier muscles, whereas ectomorphs work to improve strength and stamina. Endomorphs work to improve their endurance and may need to control their weight. Similarly, males, with narrower hips and a more direct connection between the femur and the pelvis than females, tend to be able to run faster but have less of an outward hip rotation. Other individual anatomical differences include different lengths of torso and legs: those who have long legs and a short torso easily allow their limbs to reach out around them, whereas the long-torso and short-legged dancer would be more mobile in the torso and have a greater range of tilt, curve and bend;
- stylistic blocks: unfamiliar patterns between techniques – say, between release style and classical ballet technique.

Whenever possible, the emphasis should be on relaxing and allowing natural reflexes to guide the way. Once the conscious use of the cerebral cortex cuts in, the intuitive powers of the dancer have less of an influence, and stress and tension start to mount. Sometimes, taking some rest can even help you to remember movements because the brain keeps on processing new movement memories for up to five hours after class ends.

How you treat your body can influence your thoughts and feelings. Regular exercise makes one feel good, builds body awareness and should generate confidence and an overall sense of health and well-being.

Constant demands for utmost physical control result in high muscular tension, sometimes in specific parts of the body. This can cause muscular imbalance, pain and a subsequent spread of the tension. The specific demands of dance can increase levels of neuromuscular tension for dancers, making this a major cause of injury in dance training. An over-anxious dancer may have high levels of neuromuscular tension, and this may have any of the following effects:

- There is more injury than usual (the accident-prone dancer).
- The dancer starts to imagine injury and then feels actual pain.
- A dancer pretends to be injured in order to avoid a stress situation.
- There is a loss of flexibility.
- There is a loss of smooth, co-ordinated movement.
- There is an increase in the heart rate and blood pressure.

A relaxed dancer will have better co-ordination, circulation and respiration. Tight muscles can constrict blood vessels and so impede blood flow, cutting down the exchange of O_2 and CO_2. Any long-term effect of anxiety which impedes performance – like pretending to be injured – needs firm handling.

Pre-performance nerves, butterflies, breathlessness, nausea, dry mouth and a need to sit on the lavatory are all normal nervous responses associated with an increased release of adrenalin into the blood. Once the dancer is on stage, however, the fear vanishes and the show goes on.

Sometimes, after a long intense period of training or rehearsal or a tour, dancers become stale. All the hours of repetition and practice are suddenly gone, and fatigue and depression follow. A dancer may be injury-prone at this time.

Injury itself may cause further anxiety. Injured dancers, instead of treating symptoms early on, may continue to work until eventually they have to stop completely.

Dancers are afraid of being seen as lazy or unworthy . . . Injuries should be seen as a positive opportunity to resolve the problem, not as purely negative.

(A dancer in Fit to Dance?*, 1996)*

Symptoms such as a loss of appetite, weight loss, depression, tiredness and digestion problems are common. A change of routine or environment or a few words of support may be simple but effective anecdotes to aid the recharging of the emotional batteries. Eighty per cent of learning difficulties are said to relate to stress.

Often, a dancer will be unaware of neuromuscular tension until they actually feel pain: it will have been gradually building up, allowing the nervous system to tolerate its presence. Until the tension is released, the dancer will not even be aware of its presence – it has been successfully hidden for so long because it would otherwise have interfered with progress in training.

There are certain areas of high tension which are most difficult to release:

- An habitual posture is a learned habit often adopted in order to over-achieve in a specific skill (leg higher/more turn-out, etc.).
- The tension has become part of the expected feedback during dancing, and changing it can cause real feelings of disorientation and disturbance.
- Emotional or physical pain from the past is often cloaked in neuromuscular tension, so reducing it can cause fear, often related to a loss of control. This may manifest itself as nausea, weeping or exhaustion, and needs careful handling. The need for relaxation techniques such as yoga, 'release' and the Feldenkrais® and Alexander techniques is now widely recognised.

Let us take an example of neuromuscular tension in the shoulder joint. Raising the arms and keeping the shoulders down is a learned co-ordination. Naturally, the scapulae (shoulder blades) will rise. In training, this involves constant contraction of the antagonistic muscles, so the tension level may build. It is the *latissimus dorsi* muscle which holds down the scapula. Careful stretching and relaxation will lessen the tension.

The shoulder joint (see Figure 1.26) is an area of great mobility, and special conditioning is needed before such skills as lifting are taught. There is perhaps more concern here for male dancers, although post-modern work makes this a potential danger area for females too.

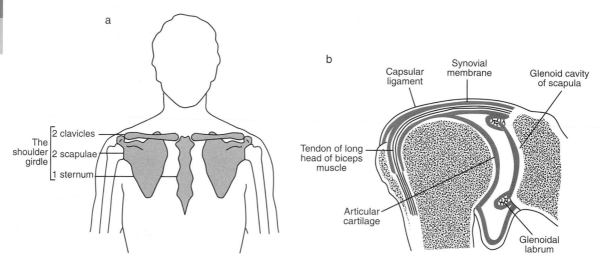

Figure 1.26 (a) Shoulder girdle (b) shoulder joint

Figure 1.27 To show lifting: Nina Sorokina and Mikhail Lavrosky of the Bolshoi Ballet in *Diana and Acteon*

A general strengthening of the following muscle groups should proceed by progressive overload to a point where more weight is being lifted than will be lifted in performance:

- the flexors/abductors of the shoulder: deltoid, trapezius, serratus anterior, rhomboid major and minor, *latissimus dorsi*, pectoralis major;
- the torso generally;
- the upward rotators of the scapula: subscapularis, teres minor, infraspinatus;
- the extensors of the knee and hip.

Six basic principles for safe lifting in dance are as follows:

1 Maintain proper alignment.
2 Apply force close to the centre of gravity of the person to be lifted.
3 Apply force as close to the vertical as possible.
4 The lifter should lower their own centre of gravity with a *plié* in order to harness the powerful force from the knee and hip.
5 The lifted dancer should be kept as directly above the lifter's centre as possible.
6 Use the muscles of the leg, but the torso/back must also be strong and stable during the lift.

When lifting a partner above head height, abduction and flexion of the shoulders is important. There should be no backwards tilt in the lumbar spine. If the elbows or wrists are swayback (hypermobile), there may be an increased vulnerability to injury. In order to avoid injury, greater strength is needed. Restriction of the dorsi flexion of the wrists may also cause lifting problems.

Problems/injuries of the shoulder joint

The constant contraction increases tension deep in the muscle and as a result the scapula will be pulled forward and eventually the muscles will go into spasm. This is known as pectoralis minor syndrome, and it may be painful to rotate the neck. There may also be numbness in the fingers and arm (on the ulna side). When the muscle is very tight, the nerve is pressed, in a way similar to sciatica in the hip. The source of the problem is mainly in the front in the pectoralis minor. Deep-pressure massage can relieve the pain, though it would seem that it takes considerable time for the posterior muscles – i.e. the trapezius and the deltoid – to get the message that they can finally relax. Pectoralis minor syndrome is common in dancers because of the demands to keep the shoulders down. However, non-dancers such as typists, swimmers, flautists and string players are also susceptible.

Clearly, there are some complex co-ordinations and timings to be learned in order to acquire correct lifting techniques. Any co-ordinations in dance have traditionally been taught through verbal instruction, 'monkey-see-monkey-do', and touching the dancer. This approach has been tried and tested over centuries of dancing. Relatively recently, however, a new school of thought has introduced

alternative approaches which put more emphasis on the inner self. This holistic approach involves seeing life as a whole, with mind and body together, and is an altogether more internal approach, starting from the inside out.

The kinesthetic sense, sensory feedback and imagery – pictures in your mind

The mind can work in a negative way in training, as we have read. It is only common sense, therefore, to assume that it can also be put to positive use – namely, by allowing our minds to use pictures and images that affect every cell in our bodies through sensory feedback. You may have already tried this in some of the tasks in this chapter. In the traditional list of the five senses – touch, taste, sight, hearing and smell – the forgotten sixth one is the kinesthetic sense. This involves the perception of motion and of position, and it depends on the proprioceptors that are in the skin, muscles, joints, tendons and sensory organs involved in the righting reflexes. These send information to the central nervous system regarding muscle contraction, relaxation, joint position and speed of motion. Accurate kinesthetic perception requires the integration of this information with the perception of spatial co-ordinates, and it operates in the skills of balance, accuracy and the control of energy. Without proprioceptors you would have to look at your body every time you wanted a part of it to move!

The proprioceptors on the skin can be useful for teachers when they use touch to correct and guide their students. Touch can help dancers to locate a muscle that should be working in a certain way and at a given time, and this can help to improve alignment, balance or give support to a part of the body. Dancers can also find massage useful for tired and stressed bodies, and use touch on their own muscles to improve specific movements. For example, try Task Sixteen.

TASK SIXTEEN – *Inside Out*

KEY SKILLS Improving own learning and performance

10 to 20 minutes

Ensure that you are warmed up thoroughly first. Stand at the barre in a comfortable first position and brush the leg out to the side, keeping it long, off the ground, three times. You are abducting the leg (*grand battement*). Try not to think about how high the leg is going but work to feel stable in your torso and hips. Repeat on the other side. Start again, but this time place your hand at the top of the leg, just under the gluteals, and as you brush slide the hand down the leg and in time with the leg lengthening; let the hand direct the energy out along the leg, to waken up and lengthen the hamstrings. Work until you have the timing of leg with hand. Repeat on the other side. The leg should feel freer and longer with the hand.

Start again and with the hand add the breath – exhale and fill the leg with air as you brush. Again the movement should be feeling easier and more controlled if your co-ordination is well timed.

Finally, ask someone you trust to give your shoulders a soft massage. Now return and with the hand, breathe and feeling the shoulder blades (scapulae) softly dropping down your back like a waterfall, repeat the brushes. Write down any differences you felt throughout this exercise.

When a dancer is under pressure in class to perform there is the risk that they may pick up bad habits in the way that they do certain movements. These habits then have to be 'unlearned' and the muscles reconditioned so that a new, more appropriate muscle balance replaces the previous one. This can take time and the use of imagery can be most helpful here in establishing correct, safe engrams. Often when beginners who have had a great deal of ballet experience start to use parallel position, they comment that it feels 'wrong'. This is typical of the difficulties dancers encounter when learning new ways to balance the muscles. Parallel position is *not* easier than turn-out and the use of the leg muscle, *tensor fasciae latae*, may come as a surprise to dancers who are unaware of it. This muscle helps to secure the head of the femur bone in the hip socket. You can try this visualisation to help connect legs in parallel: close your eyes and visualise pulses of light running up and down the back and sides of the leg, connecting your heels to under the gluteals and the *talus* (ankle) to the head of the femur. This is an anatomical image that, if used regularly, may help to put in place an appropriate engram so that the parallel position becomes automatic and no longer feels 'funny'.

When the kinesthetic sense is operational, it can act as a link between mind and body in order to improve co-ordination. Functional Magnetic Resonance Imaging measures the blood flow in the brain and has shown that the pre-motor cortex in the brain can be activated by watching dance, just as if the muscles were dancing. The receptors and brain centres can link up and use imagery to cause changes in, and to deepen the dancer's understanding of, movement. The post-modern dancer Remy Charlip called such release work 'bone meditations'.

Take an image, let it hang in the mind, let the sensation of the thought dissolve through the body. Let the movement inside of the body . . . move the outside.

(*Miranda Tufnell in* Body Space Image, *1990*)

■ Kinesthetic imagery involves using feelings that accompany body movement, so that when a movement is performed correctly, it has a certain feel. For

example, when doing foot 'pushes', as in Task Six, use the image that the floor is covered with sharp pins to improve the use of the intrinsic muscles of the foot and the articulation of the arches and metatarsals. This exercise increases strength and mobility in the feet.

- Visual imagery involves a mind picture, maybe of a rainbow, which the fingertips may draw in the space above your head as you do large side-to-side triplets. It must relate to a desired shaping or placement of body parts, and be an image which you can hold in your mind's eye. Visual imagery can also be helpful for relaxation exercises. Set a scene in your mind which will be clear to you – say, a deserted, beautiful beach where a warm, soft breeze blows and the waves lap gently at the shore.

- Anatomical imagery can help with alignment, and as with all images, returning to the same picture or feelings each time a certain movement is executed should trigger the same muscle response, thereby improving accuracy and safe practice. Anatomical imagery is based on a sound understanding of body structure – of the size and shape of bones, joints and muscles, as in Task Eighteen.

TASK SEVENTEEN – *Chill Out*

KEY SKILLS Improving own learning and performance
Working with others
Communication

10 to 20 minutes

In pairs, play some soft music in a warm, quiet space. One person reads out the task slowly and quietly for the other, who is lying in the constructive rest position:

'In a relaxed state, surround the head with a cushion of air, and let the jaw hang softly. Allow the brain to rest lightly in the bones of the skull. The brain is a control tower of information, sending and receiving, quietly humming, pouring, sifting. The brain sends messages that flow out into the spinal chord, down the spine and out to all over the body, networking to the six senses. Relax and listen to the world around you. Let the sounds and sights be felt and reflected through your body.

[Allow time here for the dancer to absorb these thoughts.]

'Open the body through the senses. Allow the body to move out amongst these sensations. Send these feelings back to the fluid-filled corridors of the mind where over 10 billion cells await the arrival of the information. Repeat this feeling of to-ing and fro-ing from brain, to body and outside a few more times.'

TASK EIGHTEEN – *Kinesthetic, Visual and Anatomical Imagery*

KEY SKILLS Improving own learning and performance

🕐 10 to 20 minutes

Read and visualise this. Standing, let the shoulder girdle rest on a rounded ribcage. See the shoulder girdle like a ring circling, opening. See the scapulae like a pair of rafts floating on the ocean of the back. The arms hang from the scapulae. Imagine the scapulae as a pair of ears opening . . . listening out to the tips of the shoulders . . . down in the lift to the basement of the spine.

(Based on an image in *Body Space Image*, 1990)

Now try visualising the following. Stand in second turned-out, close your eyes, arms by your sides. You are going to slowly raise your arms to second, breathing out without opening your eyes. As you do this, first use the anatomical image of the muscles of your *latissimus dorsi* on your back (check with Figure 1.5 if unsure). You can see these muscles broadening across your back and energy flowing from the tip at the bottom of your back out towards your arms. Lower the arms.

Repeat and add in the image of your scapulae bones sliding down your back. Keep using soft breath to support your movement.

Finally, repeat a third time and see the *latissimus dorsi* like a powerful pair of angel wings sending light through your hands out in front of you. You may need to repeat these images a few times to benefit and build solid engrams that are safe and reliable.

This visualisation should help you to raise your arms without putting tension in the wrong parts of your shoulder girdle. One image may work better for you than another, so choose which one you prefer or make up your own.

- **Body image:** these days, the stereotyped image of the dancer's sylph-like body is gradually being eroded away. Yet anorexia nervosa and related illnesses are still common. Dancers who have a negative body image, or who block out parts of their body that displease them, may be on the road to injury, failure and illness. A complete, clear and accurate body image is required for dance work. Too often we are bombarded with media-approved images of men and women. While we know anyone can dance well, and while our teacher may encourage all the politically correct attitudes, there are still the magazines, television programmes, etc. contradicting what we want to believe.
- **Mental rehearsal:** this is an imagery technique that uses the body image to improve motor skills. You review the performance of an action in the mind. The aim is to see yourself executing the desired move effortlessly and

accurately, e.g. a pirouette. Many believe that this technique releases impulses over the neuron pathways and taps into natural movement. New co-ordinations result as appropriate muscles are triggered. Research has found that this technique produces action potential in the muscles.

■ **Movement memory**: this is separate from the kinesthetic sense. It is stored in the cerebral cortex and assisted by the kinesthetic sense. Motor memory is developed by repeating movements in class or in rehearsal. As with any repetitive activity, the ability to pick up a movement quickly improves, as a larger and larger storehouse of movement pictures (engrams) to draw from is developed. Memorising of several different aspects of dance can help co-ordination build from simple to complex moves and should include order, action, timing, orientation in space, and dynamics, as well as techniques specific to a single dance genre or style.

The mind is a muscle.
                    (From the dance of the same name by Yvonne Rainer, 1966)

Dance skills become second nature as they are repeated and memorised. So, just like the training of a muscle, the more you use the memory, the fitter it becomes. Indeed, the physical senses of experienced dancers are so well tuned to their minds that they can later reproduce a movement learned by observation only. This is one reason why repetition of movement in class is so important.

Physical skills in dance training – bare necessities

The concept of co-ordination in dance training is a complex one. It takes into consideration the many aspects of the nervous system in the psychology of dancers, as well as psychological strategies which can improve the quality of training. What are the actual skills which a dancer may improve by adopting such strategies? A general heading of 'co-ordination' covers a number of individual skills. These are listed below, and along with each is a task which adopts the use of psychological strategies as mentioned earlier. The skills are:

■ control of energy;
■ balance;
■ accuracy.

Control of energy – may the forces be with you

The image of energy flowing from the centre of the body outwards is a vital one for dancers. In classical ballet, the lifted centre is the accepted norm. Learning to lift the weight up from the centre of the body, away from the pull of gravity, gives a look and feel of lightness, and also enables you to move, stop and change direction easily. (Do not hold the breath here.) Movements such as *plié*, falls, turns and jumps are all performed more safely and effectively with a lifted centre. In a fall, the centre keeps lifting as the body drops. This prevents too hard a landing and enables recovery for the next move (similarly for a jump).

Dancers are often required to show changes of character, mood or emotion and will need to be able to have control over a wide range of dynamics. You can read more about the dynamic range later in Chapter Three.

A swing requires the dancer to drop with gravity on the downward phase. Too much tension/resistance will prevent the arc of the swing from giving in to gravity. Swings are useful for warming up too, because they promote blood flow to the muscles in a low- to medium-impact movement range. Now try Task Nineteen.

TASK NINETEEN – *There is Nothing like a Swing!*

KEY SKILLS Improving own learning and performance

🕐 10 to 20 minutes

Standing, swing one arm back and forth. Notice how energy is required to lift your arm, but that gravity takes over on the downward phase. Try swinging other parts of the body – the leg, hips, upper body from the waist. Too much resistance, as you will see, will block the natural swing.

Figure 1.28 To show balance. Bedlam Dance Company 'In the Third Person', 1997.
Dancer: Rachel Krische.
Photography: Chris Nash.

Balance – delicate and solid

This has to do with:

- alignment and stability;
- directing energies through the body.

Balance is developed as a dance skill through training. Stability is decreased by lessening the base on the floor – thus, balancing on, say, one foot makes it more difficult to keep the centre of gravity over the base. Energies are directed out from the centre through the extremities of all the limbs, and whenever one body part reaches away from the centre, an opposing part has to be stretched in the opposite direction in order to maintain balance. For example, on a rise (*relevé*), balancing is easier if you think about pressing down smoothly into the floor whilst sending energy up through the centre.

Make a drawing copying the figure in the photograph of Rachel Krische (Figure 1.28). Fill in arrows which show the direction that energy is being directed to maintain balance.

As mentioned earlier, the crossed extensor reflex is a natural muscle co-ordination. It is crucial to maintenance of balance in many movements. Look back to the dancer on the left in the photograph (Photo 1.2) for Task Ten and you can see it in action. Her left arm and shoulder are in diagonal opposition to her right hip and leg. Often beginners in dance class can become so confused and tense that they lose touch with this natural reflex, so you can see walking actions take on a rather awkward robot-like look. As the cerebellum overloads with too many new co-ordinations, movement becomes over-conscious and contrived, cutting out the usual natural reflexes. Similarly, dance styles may deliberately cut out such reflexes for expressive effect. This occurred when Nijinsky used parallel actions to give the two-dimensional look in his 'Rite of Spring' (1913) and required the dancers to 'unlearn' their trained oppositional skills.

Dancers mainly use the eyes to maintain balance, e.g. when spotting turns, but blinding stage lights may lessen their effectiveness. This is when the other righting reflexes come in handy. The aural organs and the skin exteroceptors are both essential to good balance. In class, try doing some movements with eyes closed in order to sharpen your awareness of the other righting reflexes. The balance mechanisms of the inner ear are delicate and that is why if you have flu and your ears are affected you should not dance because your sense of balance will be impaired.

Being centred is crucial to achieving good balance. Centring is both a physical and a psychological concept: it refers to the physical centre of gravity and, psychologically, to the satisfying feeling of being whole and grounded.

In ballet and tap, the placement of the centre is fairly stable in order to enable fast footwork, multiple pirouettes and so on, but in the modern genre the centre shifts more frenetically as the body tilts, curves, falls, bends and extends

continuously. In technique for contact improvisation, when partnering consists of building trust during counterbalancing, catches, support and lifts, the physics of aligning the lifter's centre under that of the dancer who is being lifted in preparation for the lift makes lifting safer and easier. If this positioning is executed with accurate timing, the body does the work for the dancer, with less need to use 'brute strength'. Some ideas on how to make a start on this are given in Chapter Six.

Accuracy – nail it!

The dancer must be able to move not only well but also accurately. This comes about with the ability to reproduce movement that has been seen in a demonstration. Beginners need to see movement in terms of placement, shape and direction. As dancers become more experienced in co-ordination, they are able to see more of a whole picture and yet at the same time be sensitive to detailed positioning. A good example of this is the skill of spotting turns. As mentioned earlier, when you turn, the fluid in the inner ear starts to circulate and, after several turns, builds up momentum. When you stop turning the fluid continues and fools your brain into thinking that you're still moving – you feel dizzy! Flicking the head around in the skill of spotting keeps the fluid relatively still and so the dizziness may be only momentary, allowing the dancer to maintain balance during the turn and continue dancing accurately after it too.

Dancers also need to develop sensitivity to changes in dynamics and spatial orientation, so that these may also be performed accurately each time. For dance, the fullest movement potential of each individual dancer should be developed, and whatever the genre, this entails controlling movements more efficiently, harmoniously and expressively. This makes performance more pleasing to watch for the audience, safer for the dancer and presumably allows the choreographer more probability of expressing the intentions of the dance.

The use of breath with the movement can help accuracy. It also adds vitality and reduces tension in the body. It further assists with the control of active muscles and with the relaxation of those not required. The overall effect is to give movement an effortless look and a greater expressive quality – in phrasing, rhythm, balance, jumping and stretching. Restricted breathing will limit both the movement of the thorax and stamina.

Task Twenty offers a few things to try which show how breathing can either enhance or restrict movement.

Well-timed breathing also reduces stress and tension, which are major causes of injury in dancers. Relaxation techniques can play a crucial part in safe practice, and it is ultimately each dancer's responsibility to ensure adequate rest and relaxation for themselves. This may be a regular daily routine attached to a class or rehearsal schedule, or participation in yoga or meditation or some other relaxation-based technique. A lack of it can produce staleness and proneness to injury (real or imagined).

TASK TWENTY – *Take a Breath*

KEY SKILLS Improving own learning and performance

 10 to 20 minutes

1 Lie with arms above head, but half-bent, and legs relaxed. Check with your hand to see how much arch there is in your thoracic/lumbar spine. Breathe in through the nose, stretching your arms away from your feet. Breathe out forcefully, making a hissing sound, allowing arms, legs and back to relax. Imagine your lungs to be two balloons emptying and filling. Repeat three times. Check to see if the spine arch has lessened – i.e. relaxed.

2 Stand with your weight on both feet, arms abducted to your sides. Lift one leg directly in front of your body to a comfortable height and exhale at the same time. Release the breath beyond the toes.

3 Improvise and compose a short original phrase of movement. Practise it until you have memorised it. Repeat, trying out different patterns of breath until you find one which is most suitable for the movement.

4 From standing, collapse down and exhale. Rebound up and inhale. Repeat a few times. Now reverse the breathing pattern and choose which of the two worked best for you. (Note: in general, dancers inhale when a movement suspends and exhale when giving in to gravity.)

TASK TWENTY-ONE – *Find a Path of Least Resistance*

KEY SKILLS Improving own learning and performance

 10 to 20 minutes

Work in pairs. Lie down flat and close your eyes. Allow your partner to take one arm; do not resist or assist as it is lifted a little by the hand. Allow it to be moved up, down and sideways and rotated, giving the full weight to your partner. Where resistance is met, this is a likely point where you hold neuromuscular tension.

Repeat with the other arm and legs, and as you work, note where points of tension are discovered in your body.

Co-ordination – summary

In training, the dancer is clearly engaged in a complicated day-to-day workload, not least of which is to improve the many complex co-ordinations of the

nervous system as demanded by any dance style or genre. Be it ballet, modern, post-modern, jazz, tap, street, ballroom, African or South Asian, all ask a great deal in terms of co-ordination. Control of energy, balance and accuracy are all essential when performing any dance actions.

TASK TWENTY-TWO – *Quiz: Check It Out!*

 10 to 20 minutes

1 Name two important foundational physical skills for dance.
2 What is an engram?
3 Why is the cerebellum important for dancers?
4 Give an example of a picture that you may use for visual imagery, and describe the dance movement that the image relates to.
5 Name two righting reflexes.
6 What are two aspects of being centred for a dancer?

Answers on page 334.

General body maintenance – domestics

To be fit for dance, all the aspects mentioned in this chapter are essential. What is required is a balance of exercise, training in skills, rest and relaxation, and finally an adequate diet.

Diet – nutritious habits

You are what you eat.

So what are you then? A can of diet coke? That means you're sweet but go flat too quickly. A chocolate bar? Fatty and satisfying but prone to constant cravings. A fresh mackerel? A cool alert customer. Recent research has proven that eating oily fish regularly provides the right chemicals to improve transmission between brain cells. So the old wives' tale that fish is brain food is true! Therefore, if you wish to improve your co-ordination in dance training, cut out the junk food and settle for the fish.

Dancers are notorious for food abuse, and possibly even more so for pretending that it is not happening. Mention the word 'diet' to a dancer and the response will be cloaked in terms of eating less. 'Diet' should be a term which implies eating a sensible range of foods adequately. Enough calories, vitamins and minerals, etc. must be consumed to keep you healthy now and in later years.

Basic considerations are:

■ what to eat   ■ when to eat   ■ how to eat   ■ eating disorders

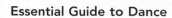

Table 1.9 Essential components for a healthy diet

Nutrient	Sources	Needed for	Amount per day	Lack of: the effects
Proteins	Lean meat, fish, dairy, bread, cereals, beans	Muscle and tissue development and repair. Normal metabolism	40g per day = 400g bread or 200g meat	Loss of muscle. Illness – e.g. flu – causes loss of protein
Carbohydrates (sugars, starch, cellulose)	Sugar, potatoes, wheat, rice, cereals	Energy	50–60% of food intake	Fatigue – weakness, headaches, irritability, poor co-ordination, nervousness
Fats	Dairy, meat, eggs, oily fish, cooking oils/fats	Improving the taste and feeling full. High energy source = high calories! Carry vitamins A, D, E & K		Too much is more the issue: heart disease, high level of cholesterol in blood
Vitamins	Most foods, particularly vegetables	Proper body functioning	Small daily amounts; e.g. 30g vitamin C, 1g vitamin B12	Vitamin D: rickets, bones soften. Vitamin C: scurvy. Too much: vitamin A: harms eyes; Vitamin D: upsets metabolism
Minerals	Most foods	Producing enzymes and hormones which control a number of functions in: blood, bones, teeth	Some, like calcium (in dairy products), are needed in large amounts. Others, like	Lack of iron (18g): anaemia. Lack of iodine: low metabolic rate, energy loss, weight

Table 1.9 *(continued)*

Nutrient	Sources	Needed for	Amount per day	Lack of: the effects
			zinc, sodium, potassium, in smaller amounts	gain. Lack of calcium (1200mg daily): long-term brittle bones
Water	Water! Tea and coffee are diuretics and increase fluid loss. So does alcohol	Physiological processes, e.g. flush waste from kidneys, maintain blood volume, sweating	Drink plenty daily	Dehydration, muscle fatigue, cramp, injury, exhaustion

> We need to re-educate dancers and get them to establish good nutritional habits. They should be eating carbohydrate and eating every three hours. We want the dancers to be slim, but with healthy, strong muscle tone so that they can resist injury.
>
> *(Tony Geeves in* New Scientist, *25 December/1 January 1994)*

Appearances can be deceptive. You may look thin, but snack-based, high-fat diets produce underdeveloped muscles which leave space for a substantial layer of fat on a seemingly slim body.

What to eat

An ordinary person with a quiet lifestyle needs 1,500 calories daily just to maintain normal body functioning and minimum activity. It is only reasonable, therefore, to assume that dancers need more in the region of 2,000 calories daily. About two-thirds of calorie intake is needed just to maintain the normal functioning of muscles, organs and body temperature. The rest of the day's activities – eating, walking, dressing, working – need about 800 calories. The equation is easy – whatever calories we use up day to day come from food. If you consume more calories than you use, you put on weight. If you consume fewer calories than you need, you lose weight.

The following are essential components of a healthy diet:

- proteins – for building up the body;
- carbohydrates – to provide energy;

- fats – for energy and flavour;
- vitamins – small but essential;
- minerals – for bones and blood;
- water – for basic physiological functions.

The reduction of specific fatty areas, like under the upper arm, can be brought about by certain strengthening exercises for targeted spots. For example, lots of abdominal curls will remove fat from the abdomen, and similarly with strengthening exercises for the hips, thighs and upper arms.

Starvation diets are dangerous and unlikely to succeed. They cause dehydration and long-term damage to basic body tissues and functioning if followed regularly. Similarly, the spot reduction of weight in specific sites such as the thighs is not helped by wearing plastic trousers. These do not reduce fat and in fact promote a loss of fluid that cause dehydration and heat stroke; they are useful only for keeping warm. The best way to lose weight is a calorie-controlled diet in combination with aerobic exercise. Burning off fat from all over the body by breaking it down for use as energy is the result of aerobic exercise.

Losing weight is a long-term process: it takes months. It should be a carefully monitored affair. Height and weight tables are not the best way to gauge whether you are over- or underweight. The use of skin-fold callipers to measure fat on, say, the triceps is recommended and the fat here should not exceed 8–10 mm in women and 6–8 mm in men.

Remember, the calories required for energy will vary with the individual metabolic rate. Muscle tissue burns off calories more quickly than other forms of tissue because it has a higher metabolic rate. It is also heavier than fat tissue. There is a possibility of confusion here. Through exercise, muscle tissue builds up and therefore weight increases. Weight loss is thus not an indication of fitness. Although muscle weighs more, it also burns off more calories, so weight loss is easier! With regular exercise, dancers who burn calories slowly can become high-calorie burners (there is a general increase in the metabolic rate as muscle increases) and fat stores are reduced more rapidly. More muscle and less fat results in an improvement in body shape and general fitness, but not necessarily weight control.

There is nothing nutritionally wrong with being vegetarian; in fact, nutritionists favour such diets. However, the recommendation is to eat foods from all food groups. Eating more carbohydrates or protein than fats will ensure fewer calories and more energy.

When to eat

An important consideration here is that when the body is digesting food, the blood flow moves away from muscles to the digestive system. Obviously, this would not, therefore, be a good time to be exercising. Eating too soon before class or a performance will cause increased blood flow to the digestive system and so deprive the muscles of an essential supply. Pre-performance eating needs careful scheduling. A small meal at least two hours before the show gives enough time for digestion. Foods like pasta or a sandwich, containing complex carbohydrates, are best because they will allow a steady release of energy throughout the performance. Concentrated sweet fluids are to be avoided because their absorption is too slow to enhance energy levels. These fluids may produce a peak of glucose in the blood (the body will release a burst of insulin to deal with this) and then a fall and a trough (see Figure 1.29) below the normal level, which will make the dancer feel fatigued. Obviously, a tired dancer is one prone to injury. The daily rush and demands on a dancer can create a tendency to skip meals. Several small meals daily – 'grazing' – is an effective eating regime to accommodate such schedules.

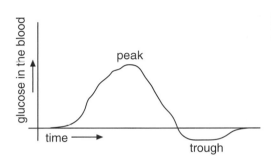

Figure 1.29 Changes in blood sugar level after drinking sweet liquids

TASK TWENTY-THREE – *Food Glorious Food!*

KEY SKILLS Communication

 Several hours

Make a large (A3-size) poster which gives advice to dancers on what to eat. Use drawings, magazine cuttings, food labels, etc. Make it bright and informative. Research the calorific values of food to include on the poster.

TASK TWENTY-FOUR – *Dear Diary*

KEY SKILLS Improving own learning and performance

Keep a food diary over two weeks of all the foods that you eat, and their weights. From this you can work out the total calories taken in and divide this figure by 14 to obtain your daily intake. Compare your food diary with an activity diary for the same period. You can then work out the daily expenditure of calories per 24 hours. Then you will know the average number of calories you will need daily to maintain your present weight. If weight loss is desirable, decrease your daily intake by 500 calories – which comes to a weight loss, per

week, of 2lb or 900g. If weight gain is required, add 500 calories daily to give 2lb or 900g weight gain per week.

How to eat

A balanced daily intake of all food groups is the best` way to eat. Also ensure that when your dance schedule is at its busiest you eat and drink enough water to maintain safe energy levels. Weight loss and weight gain are often concerns for dancers, and this reflects the preoccupation with abnormal thinness that permeates today's society. Gymnasts, models, some athletes and more and more men are targets of this 'look'. The eating disorders which arise from these unreasonable demands will be discussed below.

The definition of a 'good' dance student may be considered dangerous and harmful to methods and aims of dance training. The stereotype of the slender sylph, with a wraith-like figure, is still dominant in people's minds when they think of dance. Even the words 'sylph' and 'wraith' are actually names for sprites and ghosts and it is easy to overlook the romantic roots of this image. After all, dancers are only human and the last time I looked there were no elves or goblins – not real ones anyway. So why do dancers still allow themselves to be stereotyped in this inhuman way? Why is there this illusion, or delusional way of seeing dancers as romantic princes and princesses?

What do princes (or princesses) look like? Whose choice is it? Who is it 'up to', if not each individual dancer? Should a dancer consciously choose to become anorexic? These romantic images are loaded with serious, and on occasion life-threatening, implications.

Eating disorders

Research has found that ballet dancers had a notoriously high incidence of anorexia and bulimia. Anorexia nervosa is self-starvation and bulimia is a related disorder involving binges of eating and then vomiting, the abuse of laxatives or diuretics, or fasting. Both of these disorders will disrupt menstruation and give a long-term risk of osteoporosis (thinning of the bones). The first conference about osteoporosis was held in 1993. Many findings were brought to light. Here are some of them:

- Poor nutrition may be a contributory cause to hormonal imbalance, and when hormonal imbalance is combined with intensive exercise, the menstrual cycle may be upset. Any dancer weighing less than 47kg (7st 6lb) is at risk.
- In adolescence, 50% of the bone mass is acquired. Loss of bone density correlates with missed periods. Adequate nutrition is essential if stress fractures are to be avoided. As always, prevention is better than cure. Taking extra calcium and avoiding smoking, drinking and drugs are advised.

Oestrogen therapy for younger dancers can help alleviate loss of period and fragile bones later in life. Some dance experts look ahead and even foresee a time when dancers may sue their companies and teachers for exposing them to food abuse under health and safety legislation.

In extreme cases, these eating disorders can be fatal. If you think that you have such problems, or that a friend does, then it is important for you or your friend to talk about it and seek help. Some symptoms are obsessive preoccupation with weight, guilt about eating, unrealistically high expectations of oneself.

TASK TWENTY-FIVE – *The Dot Method Discussion*

KEY SKILLS Communication
Working with others

⏱ 10 to 20 minutes

In small groups, discuss what a dancer should look like and why. Discuss the health benefits and threats of certain images that are imposed on dancers. One member of the group should be the notetaker and keep a bullet list of points as the discussion progresses.

After 5–10 minutes the whole class come back together and make a compilation list of all the groups' ideas, on a white board. Then each student is given five dots to 'spend' how they like. If they think that being thin is *the* most important 'look' for dancers then they can give all five dots to that. Or they could give two dots to one issue and three to another and so on. At the end, when everyone has spent their dots, adding them up should show what the class thinks is most important.

Diet – summary

The food you eat should be organised to give you:

- maximum energy;
- minimum body fat;
- enough variety to ensure efficient body functions and so avoid injury.

A dancer's domestic duties

To finish Chapter One, here are a few thoughts on the responsibilities of being a dancer and making a positive commitment to working with others in class and rehearsal.

friend to help you monitor changes. You should evaluate how effective your programme is.

Area targeted for improvement	Describe strategy	Needs improvement	Working towards	Achieved
E.g. Flexibility of hamstrings	– A regular routine of reciprocal stretching. Monitor improvements regularly.	✓ 2nd Sept. Unable to touch toes. Hands at calf level.	✓ 2nd Nov. kept to routine once every two days. Hands now a little lower – lumbar spine feeling more relaxed.	
Copy this table into your own portfolio. Select and enter three target areas.			✓ 2nd Dec. Didn't keep up routine regularly so not much more progress.	
Strength of				
Stamina				
Alignment of			✓ 2nd Jan. Christmas – Blew it! New Year's Resolution – to keep to routine.	
Co-ordination				
Control				
Balance				
Accuracy				
Motor memory				
Attention to:				
■ warming-up				
■ cooling-down				
Diet				
Smoking				
Understanding and safe use of Technical terms e.g. turn-out				
Safe practices; clothing/floors .... treatment of injury			✓ 29th Feb. I am writing this whilst stretching. Mission accomplished!	

References and resources

Books and articles

Berardi, G., *Finding a Balance*, New York and London: Routledge, 1991

Brinson, Dr P. and Dick, F., *Fit to Dance?*, London: Calouste Gulbenkian Foundation, 1996

Chmelar, R.D. and Sevey Fitt, S., *Diet for Dancers; a complete guide to nutrition and weight control*, Pennington, NJ: Princeton Books, 2002

Clippinger, K., *Dance Anatomy and Kinesiology*, Champaign, IL: Human Kinetics, 2007

Dick, F., 'Fit but fragile', *Dance Theatre Journal*, vol. 11, no. 2, 1994 (article about osteoporosis)

Dyke, S. (ed.), *Your Body Your Risk*, London: Dance UK, 2001

Ellfeldt, L., *Dance from Magic to Art*, Iowa, IA: William C. Brown Company, 1976

Foley, M., *Dance Spaces*, London: Arts Council of England, 1994

Foulkes, J., *Modern Bodies: Dance and American Modernism from Martha Graham to Alvin Ailey*, Chapel Hill, NC: University of North Carolina Press, 2002

Franklin, E., *Conditioning for Dance*, Champaign, IL: Human Kinetics, 2004

Geeves, T., *New Scientist*, 25 December 1993/1 January 1994

Koutedakis, Y. and Sharp. N.C.C., *The Fit and Healthy Dancer*, Chichester: Wiley & Sons Ltd, 1999

Laws, H., *Fit to Dance*, London: Dance UK, 2005

Morrison Brown, J. (ed.), *The Vision of Modern Dance*, London: Dance Books, 1980

Olsen, A., *Body Stories: A Guide to Experiential Anatomy*, New York: Station Hill Press, 1991

Solomon, R., Solomon, J. and Cerny-Minton, S. (eds), *Preventing Dance Injuries*, Champaign, IL: Human Kinetics, 2005

Tufnell, M. and Crickmay, C.A., *Body Space Image*, Dance Books, 1990

Volianitis, S., Koutedakis, Y. and Carson R.J., 'Warm-up: A brief review', *Journal of Dance Medicine & Science*, 9(1), 2001

Wessel-Therhorn, D., *Jazz Dance Training*, Oxford: Meyer & Meyer Sport, 2000

Video and DVD

dancebooks.co.uk – on this site there are many jazz, tap and ballroom film resources

The Erick Hawkins Modern Dance Technique, 2000, DVD

Tools for Modern Dance, Y. van der Slik, 2007, DVD

■ For anatomy/injury treatment, causes and prevention

www.eskeletons.org – interactive learning with human anatomy, great fun!

www.cmcrossroads.com – Stretching and flexibility – everything you ever wanted to know, Brad Appleton.

www.foot.com – for foot health

www.footphysicians.com – for foot and ankle information

www.iadms.org – The International Association for Dance Medicine and Science.

■ For 'alternative' techniques to improve safe and effective movement:
www.alexandertechnique.com
www.feldenkrais.com – for information on the Feldenkrais Method
www.pilatesfoundation.com – The Pilates Foundation
www.skinnerreleasing.com – The Skinner Releasing Institute

■ For general interest in health, safety and preventative practice in dance
www.danceuk.org – Dance UK
www.intute.ac.uk/artsandhumanities – dance photography by Chris Nash

2 THE DANCER IN PERFORMANCE

As well as the technical necessities of the physical skills of dance training, a dancer in performance needs other important skills. A dancer must be able to communicate and express the overall intention of the dance. In order to do this, certain skills of interpretation and expression are a necessity. The great ballerina of the Romantic era, Marie Taglioni, was greatly admired for such performance charisma. In this description of her by an actress of the time, we have a feel for that inspirational quality that she had dancing the lead in *La Sylphide* (1832), the first romantic ballet.

What was it then? It was, once again, the ideal Beauty that radiated from depths of the soul into this body, animated it, lifted it with such power that something marvellous took place before our eyes as we saw the invisible made visible.

(Maxine Shulman in *Ballet and Modern Dance*, 1992)

As a natural presence on stage, the ballerina Taglioni is well known, but there must also be training beforehand, and she was no exception. She kept a record of the daily regime that included two-hour sessions of each of the following: strengthening for legs and feet, balance and centring, and steps and jumps. But we know that the physicalities of training are rigorous and virtuosity alone is not enough. In the end, it is the expressiveness of a performer which must be right for a particular dance. Jean Georges Noverre, the great reformer of ballet in the eighteenth century, remarked that the corps de ballet should harmonise their feelings with their movement. He believed that only then would they be able to express the emotions of the dance and give life to the dance.

A true dancer has a temperament which directs him to express feelings and ideas through moving the body in space. This instinct must be greatly enhanced by training so that he not only has a strong and co-ordinated instrument, but an immediate impulse to translate his comments and reactions into rhythms, muscular dynamics and spatial arrangements.

(Louis Horst in *Modern Dance Forms*, 1961)

Many famous dancers have captivated audiences down the years with their charismatic stage presence and highest quality performances. Fred Astaire (1899–1987) made 31 musical films over 40 years, such as *Top Hat* (1935) and *Swing Time* (1936), as soloist and partner to equally accomplished dancers, such as Ginger Rogers, Cyd Cherise and Judy Garland. He had impeccable timing and elegant ease of technical execution in tap and social dance. He was renowned for his striving for perfection and worked closely with his dance director, Hermes Pan, to achieve dances that demanded physical daring. His physical skills are legend, but if you watch any of the dance sequences in the films, there is that extra special star quality that stands out on stage. Astaire's focus is always in the right place, his occasional looks to camera, cheeky smiles and romantic demeanour all fit the role he is playing and are captured on film for audiences to enjoy today, decades later.

Figure 2.1 Fred Astaire plays John "Lucky" Garnett and Ginger Rogers plays Penelope "Penny" Carroll in the musical number "Pick Yourself Up" in the 1936 film *Swing Time*.

Dancers such as Taglioni and Astaire showed star quality. You can improve your performance skills and the next section identifies some ways to help your interpretation of ideas, themes, images, moods and styles as you rehearse or perform.

Developing the dancer's interpretative skills

The nuances of the dance content are likely to be a part of the exchange between dancer and choreographer in rehearsal. The dancer must be capable of tricky

technical adjustments and yet keep the flow and expression of the movement. The dancer should be clear about the intentions of the dance, whether choreographed *on* them by a choreographer or if choreographed by the dancer him/herself.

The choreographer should be aware of how to make the most of a dancer's interpretative skills so that the appropriate ones are prompted. Interpretative skills include:

- projection;
- emphasis;
- group awareness;
- musicality;
- involvement of the whole self.

Projection – energy beams

Projection involves throwing the energy out from the body so as to give a quality of life to the movement. As you dance, you should try to extend from your centre all the way through to the fingertips and toes. When a dance is performed technically correctly but lacks projection, it is unlikely to reach an audience in a significant way. Projection enables the dancer's movement and energies to reach out beyond the body and 'touch' the audience's feelings. In this way, it makes dancing come alive. There should be an awareness in the dancer that is part of each movement and can spark off various corresponding tensions and muscular reactions in observers. Recent research has found 'mirror neurons' that stimulate the brain to simulate seen movements. In class you use this to improve your physical skills, but the audience are also using this as they watch performances, even though they are not moving.

Dancers' physical skills of accuracy, co-ordination, movement memory, balance and dynamic control lay the foundations for clear expression in performance. These basic skills require that when you perform you work to improve your use of the following:

- Efficient and correct use of energy contributes to projection. Isadora Duncan was one of the first to talk about energy flowing from and to the centre of the body and the extremities. She believed that this enabled the feel of the movement to travel across space. Irek Mukhamedov is a dancer highly praised for his projection. Choreographer Kim Brandstrup describes Mukhamedov's skill:

> Like Sinatra he can whisper into 2,000 ears at once. He works from the inside out. He finds out why he does things. If you know what the feeling is you can enhance the feelings rather than the gesture.
> (In interview with Louise Levin, *The Telegraph*, 1999)

- Correct breathing also aids projection. The technique of breathing through the movement should be practised first of all in class.

■ Appropriate use of facial expressions is also important. Muscularly, the face is a very complex part of the body – full of expressive potential. For many styles of dance, such as ballroom, a calm, pleasant, open face will help to animate a performance – and it takes fewer muscles to smile than frown, so your dancing can be energy efficient. Cheesy grins, however, are often inappropriate, and likewise downcast or stressful expressions can kill a dance stone dead for an audience. This was observed as a problem when executing the very difficult fouettes of classical ballet. The great choreographer Mikhail Fokine did not favour dancers showing virtuosity for its own sake. He believed that the movement should serve as part of the expression of the dance, and that 'tricks' like the fouette, undermined the projection of feeling:

> The fouette . . . is the most hateful invention of the ballet. The dancer expresses ecstasy and joy, but her face – what does that express? Quite the opposite. She seeks for balance and her whole face proclaims it. The face betrays her losing her balance . . . unity of pose and movement is a law which, to my regret, is not felt by everybody.
>
> (Mikhail Fokine in *Mikhail Fokine and his Ballets*, 1945)

Sometimes the themes and content of dances would not require any smiling if the dance was about despair, distress, anger or loss. Look at the photograph from the DV8.

Figure 2.2 To show the face in use in performance. 'My Body, Your Body', 1987 by DV8. Dancer: Liz Ranken. Photographer: Chris Nash.

- Focus is also an important element of projection. Traditionally, this is thrown out to the back part of the auditorium. This is particularly necessary when the audience is seated above the stage looking down. A dancer who continually looks down may not be delivering a convincing performance because this has the effect of cutting the audience out of the action. An outward projection is not, necessarily, appropriate in post-modern dance. For example, the choreographer Yvonne Rainer describes the performer as a 'neutral doer'. She believes performance to be something artificial, and an unnecessary display of technical virtuosity. This 'problem' of artificiality is addressed by:

> . . . never permitting the performers to confront the audience. Either the gaze was averted or the head was engaged in movement. The desired effect was a work-like rather than exhibition-like presentation.
>
> (Yvonne Rainer in *Trio A, The Vision of Modern Dance*, 1980)

Focus can accent a line or an emotion. A wandering focus can show that a dancer lacks confidence or is not fully concentrating. Occasionally, students can be so concerned about how they look that they watch their teacher, peers or even the audience and this distracts the attention from what everyone should be thinking about – the dance! Finding focus appropriate to the expression of each dance is key. Students can be helped by peer and teacher evaluations, such as in Tasks Two, Six and Seven, because the dancer is less likely to be able to see the problem. Alternatively, personal evaluation can be achieved by reflecting on video footage from class, rehearsal or performance.

Sometimes focus relates more to the overall intent and demeanour of a dancer. The modern dancer Martha Graham was renowned for her intensity of focus in performance that was well suited to the serious intentions of much of her choreography, such as found in solo performances of *Lamentations* (1930) and *Frontier* (1935). These solos, and other seminal works of Graham, pioneered early American modern dance and were part of a legacy for later developments all over the world. One of her ex-dancers, Robert Cohan, became the founding director of *London Contemporary Dance Theatre* in 1967. He imported Graham technique, mixed with American jazz dance, to Great Britain and founded a breeding ground for new British dance ideas from the 1960s to the present day. Cohan required less intense focus from his dancers than Graham. His choreography was wider ranging in dramatic content, from the comic *Waterless Method of Swimming Instruction* (1974) to the cool of *Cell* (1969) which explored ideas and images of individuality.

- In addition, the dancer should correctly orientate the dance to the audience, ensuring that body facings are accurate and that the audience sees movements and body shapes at their most expressive angle. These facings and angles will have been determined by the choreographer, but the dancer must make sure that their reproduction is accurate. Now try Tasks One and Two. For more on where a dancer is focusing and how this can determine expression, see Chapter Three.

TASK ONE – *Focus and projection*

KEY SKILLS Problem solving
Working with others
Communication

45 minutes to an hour

In groups of four, each choreograph an 8–16 count phrase of movement to music. Music suggestions: Kronos Quartet *Purple Haze*; Les Baxter *Roller Coaster; The New Groove 2, Here We Go.*
  Take it in turns to be the outside 'eye' for the improvisation that follows. Three dancers dance their own phrases next to each other and the outside 'eye' asks the dancers to use different focuses and facial expressions from the list below:

- outward projection;
- inward projection;
- focus on a fixed-distant point, e.g. high right diagonal;
- focus on other dancers;
- focus with the movement, e.g. on the leading body part;
- focus against the movement, e.g. against the direction;
- with calm, 'neutral' facial expression;
- with intense, powerful facial expression;
- with natural, relaxed smiles;
- with big grins and projection on audience throughout.

After each different arrangement the outside choreographer describes to the dancers what the effect was in terms of the feelings, ideas, themes, images and possible content that were observed. Sometimes the outcome may be serious, other times humorous or disturbing and so on. Be as clear and articulate as you can in describing what you see.

TASK TWO – *Facings*

KEY SKILLS Problem solving
Working with others
Communication

45 minutes to an hour

Work in groups of at least five dancers. Using a short phrase learned in technique class, dance it:

- in unison, facing the same way as each other;
- in unison, facing different ways from each other;

- in canon, facing different ways;
- dance the phrase, starting at different points within it, so some may start at the end and others in the middle and so on.

If possible, take turns to watch to check the dancer's accuracy and sensitivity to the group timings and facings.

The dancer must realise the need for a high energy level throughout the performance – in the quieter moments, as well as in the faster, stronger sections of the dance. Being generous with your gestures and movements when dancing will also help an audience to enjoy the performance more. This serves to engage them in the dance and make them feel that they are interested to know more about what they are looking at. This is particularly so in classical ballet, whereas in modern dance the choreographer's intent may involve a more closed feeling. Either way, the dancer must use the appropriate focus and projection. The choreographer should know what type of projection is appropriate and, in rehearsal, cue the dancer to make the right choices.

Emphasis – colouring expression

Emphasis involves knowing what aspects of energy, space and time to accent at different moments throughout the dance. The dancer is responsible for giving a clear performance to the audience. This involves colouring the movement with the right kind of expressions, namely those which the choreographer intended. The dancer must be able to direct energy impulses, and to emphasise space and time in the way laid down by the choreographer. Energy impulses may be directed between dancers, or to a certain fixed point on stage. They may sometimes have an inward, thoughtful feel, directed in at the dancers themselves. The shading of the dynamics and qualities by the dancer is vital to the expression of the dance.

This process of understanding the physical emphasis begins in rehearsal, and it can be a tiring affair. It is important, however, for the dancer to keep energy levels up throughout for two reasons. First, the choreographer often needs to see the dance performed fully to decide if it really works. Second, the dancers themselves need to repeat the movement over and over again so that they too know intimately what is required. This may involve discovering what kind of quality a particular role or character needs, or it may involve acquiring a feel for where the movement phrases begin and end. If a dance requires a particular highlighted moment, then you could try working without the music so that the dynamic emphasis that is needed can be worked on more specifically without the interrupting influence of the music's phrasing. Or the climax of the piece may need a very specific timing or position on stage which is crucial to the expression. Many small, subtle details thus need close examination and practice.

Dancers need to be skilled in emphasis in different styles of social dance, involving factors such as the difference in the dynamics and use of sharp angles in the pathway of the dramatic tango, in contrast to the free flowing and curving floor patterns of the waltz. The moods of these two dances are quite different in their interpretation of the feelings of 'love'.

Dancers differ in their personal emphasis when they perform identical dance phrases. Next time you are in technique class, or if you are ill and have to sit out, watch how different dancers use their weight differently or demonstrate subtle changes in timing or line, without any incorrect movement that detracts from the sequence.

Sometimes the dancer, as choreographer, creates a special personal style of movement. When a dancer performs their own choreography, a special signature movement may emerge. One such dancer is Siobhan Davies, better known as a choreographer, but in her early work with London Contemporary Dance Theatre she created solos for herself as a way to break out of the Graham technique and find her own personal movement style. This was noticeable in *Sphinx* (1977), which emphasised a fluid, sensuous rippling of energy through torso and limbs, and set the tone for her later choreographic development. The images danced in *Sphinx* were catlike and human at the same time, and emphasised energy differently than Graham's explosive outwards contractions, by substituting a contemplative inward pull, more sinuous and feline. Although, when dancing in Cohan's choreography in 1974 Davies' versatility as a performer was obvious when she danced the comic role of a woman trying to put up a deckchair and change into her swimming costume in *Waterless Method of Swimming Instruction*.

When a role is danced by different dancers the emphasis of phrasing, timing and dynamics may change. This would alter the expression so that varied interpretations may be seen between performances over time. This tradition, of dancers moulding roles to suit their temperaments and strengths goes back a long time. Carlotta Grisi, the first ballerina to dance the lead in *Giselle* (1841, Coralli and Perrot) danced the final mad scene with a forlorn gentleness. In contrast, Fanny Elssler's later interpretation of the role used a greater dramatic emphasis in the use of energy, and in fact, set the trend for how the role is emphasised by dancers in the present day.

In Sir Frederick Ashton's (1904–1988) *Cinderella* (1948) the leading role was meant to be danced by Margot Fonteyn, but an injury meant that Moira Shearer took over. Shearer emphasised lightness and was technically exquisite. However, when Fonteyn returned in 1949 she brought a different emphasis bringing the dramatic character to life with a range of feelings, from sad, sweet and frightened little girl through to playfulness, when she dances with the broom pretending to be at the ball.

Emphasis can also rely on the expressions of the face. The enormously expressive faces of classical Indian dancers are a fine example of finely tuned facial muscles, and should convey *bhava* (mood) and *rasa* (sentiment). In *angik abhinaya* (the technique of the use gestures of the body) the facial gestures alone

include seven movements of the eyeballs, nine of the eyelids, six each for the nose, lips cheeks, seven each for the eybrows and chin and thirteen gestures of the head.

Classical Western character roles, such as the Ugly Sisters in Ashton's *Cinderella*, rely heavily on the use of facial expression to interpret their roles as you can see in photograph. Danced by Ashton and Sir Robert Helpmann, using the English Victorian tradition of pantomime dame, they danced *en travesti* (men dressed as women) in a comic double act, played to perfection. Helpmann's domineering leer lauded it over Ashton, the scatterbrained one of the two sisters. The role of the forgetful sister, that Ashton adopted, had a highly practical start as the role was put together in a rush and so allowed him to hide any real losses of memory during performance. Another aspect of emphasis needed in the roles as Ugly Sisters in order to produce comic effects would have to be timing between their actions and reactions.

Figure 2.3 Sir Frederick Ashton and Sir Robert Helpmann (1952) as the Ugly Sisters in *Cinderella*

Through rehearsal and practice, the dancer will build a secure knowledge of the emphases that occur in a dance. This will provide support and help the dancer to remain calm during those last few moments before the performance begins when stage fright may be a problem. Being able to focus clearly on the movements and expression, marking these through calmly, will take your mind away from yourself, and your nerves, and put it exactly where it should be: on the dance for the audience, not on your ego.

TASK THREE – *Phrasing, emphasis*

KEY SKILLS Problem solving
Working with others
Communication

45 minutes to an hour

Using the same phrase as in Task Two, dance it to different pieces of music. Let the music affect your phrasing, emphasis, dynamics. Add to the phrase in improvisation, exploring the different possibilities for each piece of music. (Suggested music: The Chieftains, *Tennessee Waltz /Tennessee Mazurka*; Philip Glass, *Dance VIII*; Elvis, *All Shook Up*; Dave Brubeck, *Take Five*; Tchaikovsky, *The Dance of the Reed Flutes* from *The Nutcracker*; Dean Martin, *Cha-Cha d'armour*.)

Group awareness – teamwork

When dancing in groups, the dancer has to think not only about the content of the dance but also about movement cues which may come from others. Peripheral vision, i.e. what you see from the corners of your eyes, is useful here and avoids any inappropriate turning of the head that is not part of the choreography. A useful tip, which works most of the time, is to identify the 'lead' dancer as the one that the rest of the group can see, although of course everyone still has to know their own movements and not rely on others to copy. Some

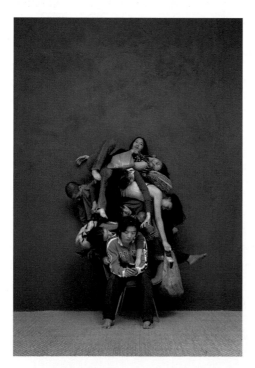

Figure 2.4 Group awareness – group dancers Akram Khan
Photographer: Hugo Glendinning

dancers have a 'sixth sense' or a 'third eye' which helps them to feel where others are in relation to themselves even if they cannot actually see the others. Of course, these responses also have to do with good timing in relation to others, and they make for accurate unison, canon or action–reaction relationships.

Having a sensitivity in performance to other dancers' use of space and timing is also a safety factor in avoiding collisions. Learning the correct names for specific parts of the stage, such as 'up' and 'down' stage, will help you to be more professional in your use of the space. In musical theatre and *corps de ballet* large group unison dance sequences, accurate spacing, counting and timing are key for the required look and style of such works.

My company is fortunate; it's not very large, but it is nonetheless filled with people who are willing to take responsibility, not just for themselves, but for every other member of the company, which means that a dancer doing one of our pieces not only knows her own part, but knows everyone else's part who is working at the same time, and knows how that fits into the whole work . . . it's something few dancers seem to take seriously. Musicians are much better about it because harmony is easier to hear than it is to see.

(Twyla Tharp in *The Dance Makers*, 1980)

Awareness of others in contact improvisation and social dance is also important for risk management. 'Listening' to others, as you take or give weight, so as to maintain a sensitive and safe rapport with other dancers, will help to ensure a quality performance. A good example of this is the partnering of ballerinas as they pirouette on pointe. The man has to be sensitive to how much help the dancer may need to spin by a push–pull motion of his hands on the ballerina's torso. Also he has to take care to apply even pressure so as not to push the dancer off her centre.

Now try Task Four.

TASK FOUR – *Birds-of-a-feather*

KEY SKILLS Problem solving
Working with others
Communication

45 minutes to an hour

 In groups of five or more, decide on how to make the following group formations:

- wedge
- close cluster
- a diagonal line
- straight line side by side
- scattered cluster
- outwards facing circle

accents of the music need to be used appropriately with the body, voice and sometimes props add to the sound, such as canes. Tap dance uses the feet as part of the musicality too. The famous solo in the rain from *Singin' in the Rain* (1952) by Gene Kelly (1912–1996) is a superb example of a dancer's musicality. Kelly dances as he sings, taps, uses the umbrella and the sounds of splashing through the puddles to accent or counterpoint the music. His athleticism also enables him to make the most of the set, such as swinging on a lampost, to further enhance the mood of the music and the scene's portrayal of someone head-over-heels in love.

Dancers need to keep an open mind about all music and try to appreciate different syles, even if they do not like it! Developing your listening skills is important. You could try to pick out instrumentation of music so that you can *dance* the drum beat, or the bass guitar, or the cello or the voice, or any of the instruments that make up one piece of music. Try listening to something new regularly and be on the look out for fresh sounds. Sometimes, just by changing channels on your TV or radio you can find some unexpected music that you have never heard before. Of course, there is always the Internet. Always write down who the musician or composer was. A good idea is to keep a special notebook of new music as you find it.

Involvement of the whole self – in the zone

You can do the steps with muscle memory, but once you get up on the stage, it's not about steps at all. You really have to reason why you're doing it. You can't just go through the motions; it has to involve your whole self.

(Alvin Ailey in *The Dance Makers*, 1980)

Moving from the centre of the body is an important physical sensation necessary for the correct execution of movements. However, the involvement of the whole person is just as crucial: without this, the performance would be uninteresting and dull for the audience. The dancer needs to focus both on the content of the dance, and on the movement in giving an expressive performance. This involvement of the whole dancer in performance has to involve a response to the style of the dance.

Irek Mukhamedov describes how he approaches this:

You know somebody made up that fairy story from real life . . . Maybe it's the schooling I've had. To put your emotions through your body, through your fingers. Not just to go, 'I-Love-You', (and he mimed the three classic gestures), but to finish the phrase through . . . the whole body, eyes, even lips. Then it's not just signs – the audience will understand what I'm saying.

(Interview with Ismene Brown in *The Electronic Telegraph*, May 1998)

Training in Bharatha Natyam has similar challenges. Learning the expressive skills of *abhinaya* is demanding and only possible by the dancer's belief in and identification with characters and situations. The subtleties of expressing love and loss must come from deep within if they are to convince an audience.

TASK FIVE – *View and respond – characteristic features of Christopher Bruce's dance style*

KEY SKILLS Improving own learning and performance
Problem solving

Several hours

This task is linked to Task Six. You will need to use self-directed study time to complete this task. Repeated viewings of recordings of the dance excerpts will be needed. You are advised to watch as many excerpts from the following dances by Christopher Bruce:

- Section 1, 2 and 6 from *Ghost Dances* (1981, premiere, Ballet Rambert at Bristol Theatre Royal. Video performed by the Houston Ballet Company). Theme: the suffering of people who are victimised and oppressed. This theme was continued in his later *Swansong* (1987).
- Sections 2, 8, 9 and 10 from *Sergeant Early's Dream* (1984, premiere, Ballet Rambert, Marlowe Theatre, Canterbury. Theme: migrating to a new home; feeling displaced and nostalgic for the old life.
- Watch each excerpt once without taking notes. Then write down your first impressions.
- During subsequent repeated viewings you can stop and start the video as you record what you see. Select one or two of the categories in Table 2.1 and tick off movement characteristics as you see them.

Music and DVDs for both of these dances are listed at the end of the chapter. Both recordings of the original music are commercially available.

Below is an additional task to use with the Bruce viewing. Choose two different excerpts from your viewing and complete the sentence starters for each one:

1 In this section the dancers play the characters of. . .
2 This section of the dance describes how. . .

Table 2.1 Some characteristic features of the dance style of Christopher Bruce as required by dancers in their interpretative skills

Characteristic movement features	Ghost Dances – section 1	Ghost Dances – sections 2 and 6 Sergeant Early's dream – sections 2, 8, 9 and 10
✓ **below**	Imposing, powerful presence.	Enjoyment of dance and life
1 Projection: ■ energy	Hold body tension and control Deliberate Wild – unpredictable Steady outwards gaze Sudden changes	Natural, relaxed with some tension occasionally
■ focus characterisation	Vigilant, looking out for victims	Out and down (natural)
■ phrasing	Nonmetrical, breathy and also with the beat	Natural with the music phrasing
2 Emphasis ■ dynamic range	Strong but gradual change from slow to sudden Free flowing but with interruptions and containment of energy	Lively, quick, light, bouncy Some stronger, downward weight into the ground
■ style	Breathy to insistent range Use of Graham-like flexed foot, contraction and release of torso Bird imagery (also used in *Swansong)* Special emphasis in use of masks on two-dimensional inhuman creatures	Combines ballet, folk and modern dance genres. Use of flexed foot in folk style Dance styles used to represent human life as a struggle or lament and as a celebration of hope, strength and dignity
3 Musicality	Movement in near silence Gradual increase in tempo Move with and in counterpoint to the musical phrasing. At first movement phrasing glides over the music	Using a right-left-right step pattern to accent 1st beat in music. Counting – & **1** & **2** On the beat and with the time signatures of the music Gestures reflect meaning of lyrics

Table 2.1 (continued)

Characteristic movement features	Ghost Dances – section 1	Ghost Dances – sections 2 and 6 Sergeant Early's dream – sections 2, 8, 9 and 10
4 Involvement of whole self ■ images and characterisation	Figures representing violence and death Slithery, menacing Puppet-like-controlling Hovering bird of prey	Ordinary people, share love – vulnerable Some humour Enjoy life but struggle to resist the threat of loss and are pulled back to face reality

5 Accuracy
■ physical demands
■ body/actions travelling
	Strength, stamina, flexibility
	Dynamic alignment
	Flexible torso:
	  – walks, rolls, slides
	  – weight on hands
	  – folk dance step, grapevine
		Stamina and co-ordination of feet and arms
		Dynamic alignment
		Upright posture
		  – steps, walks, runs (lifting back foot), skips, gallops folk dance steps – quick, precise footwork; heel and toe steps; Irish; tap; Hornpipe.

Stillness	Hovering balances on one leg Head – tilts, rotations	Sudden pauses when 'captured'
Isolations/ Gesture	Arms – elbows, shoulders, folding into body Feet and legs – flexed	Arms – natural, counterbalance and enhance steps
Falls	Athletic drops, one to one knee and from jumps and sudden falls	Feet and legs – high knee lifts
Jumps	Explosive, weighted	Heavy drops
Turns	Frequent	
■ Space	Use space expansively	Turning in walks, jumps and runs
Directions	Forward advancing in Sagittal Plane and sideways in Horizontal Plane. Together these combine to express threat and otherworldly creatures	Use space expansively Multi-directional Use diagonals and curving pathways Mostly medium level
Floor pattern	Direct pathways	
Level	Abrupt high and low	

Performance is, for many dancers, the most exciting reason for learning to dance. Once you're in the lights or in an informal sharing you should be dancing with every bit of energy and commitment that you have. On a stage this involves dancing at the split second that you enter and being completely in the moment as you exit, not stopping until you are in the wings.

The whole person, body, mind and spirit must be totally involved in the moment of performance. In the following description, Isadora Duncan reveals what she believes dance could be. You may be struck by the total involvement of the dancing child being the thing that captivated and transfixed Duncan's attention. It is a strong memory recalled with great impact.

I gazed across the vast expanse of surging water, wave after wave streaming past. . . . And in front of it all, the dainty figure

. . . dancing on the edge of the measureless sea. And I felt as though the heart-beat of her little life were sounding in unison with the mighty life of the water

. . . she dances because she can feel the rhythm of the dance throughout the whole of nature. To her it is a joy to dance; to me it is a joy to watch her.
(Isadora Duncan in *The Dancing Times*, April 1926)

Reaching the moment in performance when you can dance confidently, comfortably, expressively and safely brings you as a dancer to a milestone of a journey of preparation. Your technical classes, body conditioning, rehearsals and studies all prepare you for the moment when you can express whatever the choreographer has composed. Committing your whole self at all times during this preparation process should bring you as a dancer, your choreographer and the audience to a fulfilling and rewarding performance.

Now try Task Six.

TASK SIX – *Your performance skills solo* (continues from Tasks 1, 2, 3 OR 5)

KEY SKILLS Communication and improving own learning and performance

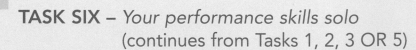 Several hours

You can use the characteristic movement style of Christopher Bruce that you observed in Task Five for this task or use any of the movement material from Tasks One, Two or Three. Make a short solo, between 2 and 3 minutes. Perform it for your group. Use the sheet below to help you evaluate each other's solos in how successful they are in their interpretative performance skills.

This sheet can also be used to evaluate performance in group dances by adding a category for group awareness skills.

Name			
Title of dance			
Evaluation of solo dances – interpretative and performance skills ✓ the columns			
	Needs improvement	Mostly effectively achieved	Consistently / imaginatively
Evaluate success in: 1 Projection – appropriate: ■ energy/extension ■ breath control, ■ facial expression, ■ focus ■ facings 2 Appropriate expressive emphasis ■ use of dynamics ■ style 3 Movement memory 4 Musicality 5 Involvement of whole self 6 Accuracy in emphasis of ■ actions/body ■ use of space ■ use of time			
Comments and suggestions based on the above: Set targets for improvement:			

Appreciation of a performance as dancer – reflection

It only demands the dance be a moment of passionate, completely disciplined action, that it communicate participation to the nerves, the skin, the structure of the spectator.

(Martha Graham in *The Vision of Modern Dance*, 1980)

A dancer's concern is to evaluate their accuracy and expressivity of performance. During the performance a dancer may encounter unforeseen problems of execution of movement phrases, timing, spacing or interpretative skills. The usual process is to feed these back to the choreographer, who may have noticed them too, and proceed with correction in the studio. This can be an ongoing process.

Similarly, if the choreographer has refinements to make post-performance, it is back to the studio to put the new improvements into practice. In your preparation for examination performances you will be involved in an ongoing process of feedback, reflection and feedforward as to how to improve your performance in solos or group dances. This process will include evaluations and constructive criticism by yourself, as well as from your teacher and peers. Useful tactics that you can use to help you improve performance and set goals include the following:

■ written journals;
■ evaluations of video footage.

A SWOT analysis of your evaluation sheet from Task Six could be helpful. SWOT stands for:

STRENGTHS
WEAKNESSES
OPPORTUNITIES
THREATS

Your SWOT analysis can be used in combination with feedback from peers and teacher. See Task Seven.

TASK SEVEN – *Your solo evaluations*

KEY SKILLS Problem solving
Improving own learning and performance

Several hours

This task is like a series of mini-performances with evaluations and is designed to carry on from Task Six, but you could apply it to any solo work that is going to be assessed.

From the evaluation sheet of Task Six prepare a SWOT analysis in your journal. Once complete, select three main areas to target for improvement and record them in your journal. During your self-directed learning time, when you reach a point where you think that your targets have been achieved, film your performance and watch the video to evaluate your progress. Once you are happy that your goals have been reached, ask a peer and the teacher to watch your improved version and ask them to comment on the progress that you have made with the three goals that you set. As you listen to their critique make brief notes in your journal so that you can record what has been achieved and what may be your next target area for improvement.

TASK EIGHT – *Crossword*

KEY SKILLS Problem solving

🕐 10 to 20 minutes

Finally, to end this chapter complete the crossword and see how much you can recall about Chapters One and Two.

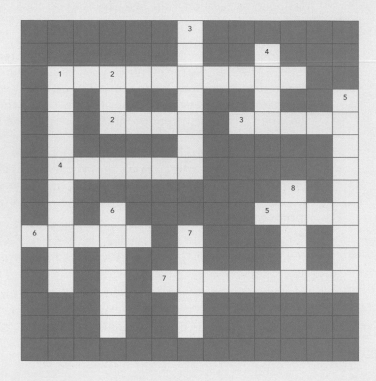

CLUES

Across

1 When a dancer sends out energy through the fingers and toes to an audience (10)

2 In ballet the legs (4) & 2 down (3)

3 Humerus (5)

4 The hip (6)

5 See 4 down

6 With other dancers you need (5) & 5 down (9)

7 Different dancers perform roles, such as Cinderella, with different . . . (8)

Down

1 You use this type of vision to see other dancers (10)
2 See 2 across
3 When dancers show body shapes and different angles to an audience they change their. . . (7)
4 You should always do this after class (4) & 5 across (4)
5 See 6 across
6 The vulnerable curve of the spine, with five vertebrae (6)
7 Thigh bone (5)
8 Where a dancer is looking (5)

Answers to be found on page 335.

References and resources

Books

Anderson, J., *Ballet and Modern Dance: a Concise History*, New Jersey: Princeton, 1992

Au, S., *Ballet and Modern Dance*, London: Thames & Hudson, 2002

Crisp, C. and Clarke, M., *Making a Ballet*, London: Studio Vista, 1974

Horst, L. and Russell, C., *Modern Dance Forms in Relation to Other Modern Arts*, New York: Dance Horizons, 1973

Kurth, P., *Isadora: A Sensational Life*, New York: Little Brown, 2001

Mazo, J., *Prime Movers*, London, Adam and Charles Black, 1977

McKim, R., *The Essential Inheritance of the London Contemporary Dance Theatre*, 2004

Rogosin, E., *The Dance Makers*, New York: Walker & Co., 1980

Video and DVD

From www.dancebooks.co.uk

A wide choice of Hollywood musicals and films

Three by Rambert Dance Company – *Lonely Street, Lonely Town* (North), *Intimate Pages* (Bruce) and *Sergeant Early's Dream* (Bruce)

From Amazon.com

The Houston Ballet – *Ghost Dances* (Bruce), *Images* (Stevenson), *Journey* (Bruce)

Websites

www.theplace.org.uk
www.rambert.org.uk
www.houstonballet.org

Articles and reviews

The Electronic Telegraph: www.telegraph.co.uk

Music

The following CDs all have a range of music for improvisations.

■ The following are recommended for Task One.

Kronos Quartet *Released: 1985–1995*. Nonesuch, 7559-79394-2, 1995

Benedict, B. (Producer), *Cocktail Capers*. Ultra-Lounge: Bachelor Pad a-Go-Go.
  Capitol Records 7243 8 37596 2 0, 1996

The New Groove 2, Polygram Records, 1998

■ The following are recommended for Tasks Three, Six and Seven.

Benedict, B. (Producer), *Volume nine Cha-cha De Armor*, Ultra-Lounge:
  Bachelor Pad a-Go-Go. Capitol Records 7243 8 37595 2 1, 1996

Dave Brubeck, *Take Five*

The Chieftains, *The Special Guest Collection*. RCABMG, 74321 717402, 1999

Glass, P., *dancepieces*, CBS MK 39539 (01 039539 10), 1987

Tchaikovsky, 'The dance of the Reed Flutes' from *The Nutcracker*

■ The following are recommended for Task Four.

Andreas Vollenweider, *Down to the Moon*, CBS 57001, 1986

Janos Balint and Nora Mercz play, *Romantic Music for Flute and Harp,* NAXOS,
  8550741

■ For Task Six music for the Christopher Bruce solo.

From www.dancebooks.co.uk

Incantations with the Sergeant Early Band

3 THE CONSTITUENT FEATURES OF DANCE: MOVEMENT

> With every new ballet that I produce I seek to empty myself of some plastic obsession and every ballet I do is, for me, the solving of a balletic problem.
> (Sir Frederick Ashton in *Dance from Magic to Art*, 1976)

Composing dances may be said to be a process of problem-solving. Dance training prepares the body for the physical demands of dance and improves co-ordination skills. The next step may be making your own dances. Using the physical intellect imaginatively to compose dance involves learning about the components that make up a dance. Making dances, as outlined in Figure 3.1, is the focus of this chapter. The rehearsal process is further examined in Chapter Seven.

As the choreographer, you must be able to make clear for your dancers exactly what movements you require. This will help you to collaborate with the dancers and bring out their best in performance. Therefore, you need to be able to observe and analyse in order to find the most appropriate and successful movements. Task One will help you with this.

Figure 3.1 Process of composing a dance

Idea (content)
Research
↓
Experiment with putting ideas into movement (improvisation)
↓
Select the most appropriate movements
↓
Refine and organise the structure and form a cohesive whole
↓
Rehearse, perform and evaluate success

This section identifies the building blocks of how to break down and improvise with movement so that it can express what the choreographer has to say. Analysing and explaining movement is *basic* to what you will need when making your examination solo and group compositions. It will help you make appropriate decisions as to the movement that best expresses your ideas and to

describe to your dancers, in movement and verbally, how you want them to move. Learning terms that identify specific aspects of movement material will also help you to write your choreographic journal. These basics not only apply to you as a student of dance but can be observed in professional choreography too, so you can use the vocabulary you learn in this chapter with your own dance composition and when you study professional repertoire for your examination. Just like professional dancers and choreographers, you need a sound knowledge of the rules – even if only to go on to break them successfully and safely. Choreography is still limited by consideration for the safety of the dancers. That is why Rambert Dance Company's physiotherapist Cathy Barrett attends rehearsals of new repertoire because:

Behind every 'innovative' choreographer, you will often find a rather nervous physiotherapist!

(Rambert Student Information Pack)

TASK ONE – *Dare to be different*

KEY SKILLS Problem solving
Working with others

 10 to 20 minutes

(This is a good task to do if you happen to be injured or ill.) Watch a class of dancers perform a taught phrase. Choose three of the dancers and make notes on:

■ individual differences in how they perform the phrase;
■ individual differences in how successful they are in performing the phrase.

In addition, evaluate why some are more successful than others and suggest how those who are less successful can improve their performance.

Figure 3.2 is a mind map showing the various constituent features that all dances, of any genre, possess:

■ the movement components;
■ the dancers;
■ the physical setting;
■ the accompaniment (the aural setting).

The last two features will be discussed in Chapters Four, Five and Six. Let us now analyse the movement in detail, as it relates to the craft of choreography.

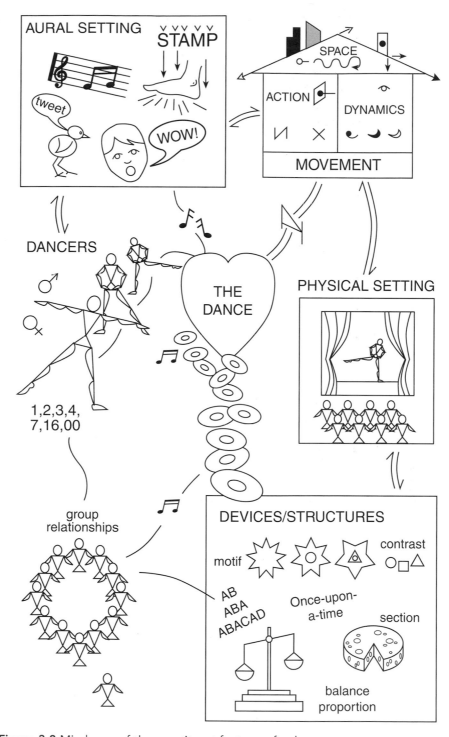

Figure 3.2 Mind map of the constituent features of a dance

The six dance actions

There are three basic anatomical actions that the body is capable of performing: flexion, extension and rotation (see Chapter One). The dancer in training will use these three basic actions in endless combinations to produce the six dance actions. These are:

- travelling (locomotion);
- elevation;
- turning;
- gesture (isolation);
- stillness;
- falling.

Travelling (locomotion)

Walking is a fundamental human activity, one which takes us from A to B.

Every time you step you fall only to catch yourself from falling . . .
(Laurie Anderson from the album *Big Science*)

The natural human walk places the heel down first. The endless other possibilities – rolling, knee walks, sliding, crawling, etc. – are where choreography begins.

TASK TWO – *Just walking?*

KEY SKILLS Problem solving

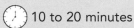 10 to 20 minutes

- Walk slowly, feeling the moment of loss of balance as your centre shifts forward.
- Gradually accelerate to a fast walk – feel the natural walking action of heel down first (dorsi flexion).
- Change to a stylised dance walk: toe down first (plantar flexion).
- Carefully explore and experiment with different walks: on heels; on toes/balls of feet (metatarsal arch); on the outside of the foot (inversion); on the inside of the foot (eversion).
- Walk on different levels.
- Walk in different directions.

Walking involves an even rhythm. The ankle must extend to push off the back foot and shift the body weight forward. The centre needs to pull up to maintain a smooth, even quality. The eyes should focus on eye level, not downwards, and the arms should work naturally in opposition to the legs.

A parallel walk is more common in modern dance, while walking with turn-out from the hips is more usual in classical ballet – although the famous classical dancer and choreographer Vaslav Nijinsky caused a sensation by breaking this rule when he used a parallel walk in *L'Après-midi d'un Faune* (1912). Nijinsky wanted to give a look of classical Greek friezes in two-dimensions. So he used parallel legs and arms also unnaturally parallel to the leg action. At its première, the audience at the Paris Opera rioted!

Running is a fast walk using a greater extension of feet and legs, and the emphasis here is upward and forward. Running also involves an even rhythm.

Runs, triplets and prances are all variations of walking. Triplets are in a 3/4 waltz time signature, with the accent on the first downward step. Prances are runs which emphasise the upward knee lift sharply with a sudden extension of the foot.

TASK THREE – *Busy feet*

KEY SKILLS Problem solving

 20 to 30 minutes

Using any of the following: walking, runs, triplets, prances, skips, long and short steps, taps, pauses:

- Combine them to make a phrase which can be repeated on alternate sides continuously. Keep it simple – i.e. no arms, jumps, falls.
- Practise the phrase until you have it very clear and accurate.
- Repeat it four times.
- Find a way to record your phrase in your choreographic journal.

Music suggestions: Traveling Wilburys, *Poor House*; Bacon de Gaia, *Sakarya*; Goldenhorse, *Telephone Call*; Kronos Quartet, *Scherzo*; Dean Martin with Kevin Spacey, *Ain't that a Kick in the Head*.

When a number of steps are patterned together, they become recognisable dances. Sir Frederick Ashton's use of folk steps in *La Fille Mal Gardée* (The Unchaperoned Daughter, 1960) includes clog dance, maypole dancing and a Morris dance. In *Cinderella* (1948), Ashton's famous 'Fred step', based on the step that ballerina Anna Pavlova often performed in her *Gavotte Pavlova*, appears in Act One. As the gavotte music starts, the Dancing Master 'teaches' the step to an Ugly Sister and then fun ensues as the Sisters pursue their studies with lacklustre achievements and contention between them. Later, Cinderella picks up the step with aplomb as she reflects on the Sisters' dancing lesson, and continues straight into a series of *développés* in *relevé*. She repeats the step on the other side of the body and puts the finishing technical touches to it by adding a pas de chat and a jump.

Matthew Bourne often uses social dance steps and styles. In the *'Country'* section of his *Town and Country* (1991), he makes a reference to Ashton's *La Fille* when peasants do a clog dance. Bourne's is humorous satire of the upper classes who hunt and shoot around the peasant dance and the whole parodies the unrealistic, romantic view of nature. In *Late Flowering Lust* (1994 for BBC television) he used Morris Dance and social dances of the 1930s such as the Charleston and the Turkey Trot. Christopher Bruce also uses social dance steps in his work, such as the use of court dance in the *Lady Jane* section and the jive in *Not Fade Away*, in *Rooster* (1991).

Social dances, such as waltz and quickstep, travel and twirl around the dance floor and evoked romance in the Hollywood musicals and films of the 1930s and 1940s, 'Depression' years. The swirling waltz, first made popular in the Romantic era of the nineteenth century, was re-cycled by stars such as Fred Astaire and Ginger Rogers in films typified by *Top Hat* (1935, RKO Radio Pictures). Such dances as the waltz sprang from peasant society and were considered by some at first to be immoral. Jane Austen's novel *Pride and Prejudice* was written in 1813. In the 1940 film of the story it is claimed that the waltz should be banned! The closeness of the man's hand on the waist of the woman and the facing relationship of the couples was quite provocative at the time, but proved to give such pleasure in the freedom of movement around the room and indulging in anothers' company that the waltz soon became fashionable. The original European waltz in 3/4 time was a symbol of elegance, control and man leading woman, an important moral code of Edwardian times. By the start of the twentieth century, the waltz was the dance of choice of the social dance scene and became popular with all classes of society. No longer the sole property of the European aristocracy, the waltz began to develop a new look from the New World – North America.

Out of North America came the Boston, a slower waltz that took four bars of music to turn rather than the old-time quicker two bars, and related more to the melody of the music than the beat. This, plus the increase in the closeness of the couple now dancing hip to hip, intensified the romantic intention of the dance. The enhanced social intimacy, conveniently reinforced the romantic stories of Hollywood films' basic plot – boy meets girl, boy loses girl, boy wins her back. The plot may have been predictable, but it won the hearts of the audiences of the time, allowing them to escape the horrors of the real events in the world. Even today, many dance films use this plot successfully. Perhaps, it is not only the plot that carries audiences away to a feelgood place, but also the swirl and the intoxication of the travelling, quickfooted social dances. These early dance films paved the way for later successes, such as one of the most famous *West Side Story* (1961, choreographed by Jerome Robbins).

The North American minstrel shows of the mid 1800s mixed Irish jig, clog dancing and a new style of step dancing – the soft shoe. As leather soled shoes replaced the wooden of the clogs, techniques developed to make the most of the new texture's contact with the floor. The soft-shoe technique was more graceful and used lighter taps. Irish-American George Primrose (b. 1852), one of the most admired soft shoe dancers, created many new steps. One of the most popular styles, the Virgina essence, used a gliding, forward travel across the stage. The dancer would go 'through the foot' with straight legs. Think of a 1980s Michael Jackson's *Moonwalk* and you have the idea.

The travelling tapping of Fred Astaire was a characteristic feature of his technical skill. In *Top Hat*, Astaire's solo, a late night celebration of his bachelorhood, 'No strings (I'm Fancy Free)', combines tap shuffles in place, building to travelling steps, quick-fire heel dabs and finally covers the space of the whole set (a hotel suite) with very loud tapping and beating the furniture. The only thing that finally stops him is the interruption by an irrate Ginger Rogers, having been woken up. Astaire realises that he finds her quite attractive, when she is cross. This was a ploy used in several films to push along the romance of the stories.

Other types of travelling, such as walking on the hands, are used in more contemporary theatre dance. A characteristic of Martha Graham's dance vocabulary was a shuffling walk on the knees. In *Strange Fish* (DV8, 1992), a male dancer walks on his hands rising to the challenge of his macho identity. Rolling and sliding are used to travel by the ghost characters in Christopher Bruce's *Ghost Dances* (1981), to express that they are creatures of the underworld.

Figure 3.3 To show travelling on the hands: V-Tol Dance Company in *'And nothing but the truth'* (1998)
Photographer: Chris Nash

TASK FOUR – *Shall we dance?*

KEY SKILLS Problem solving
Working with others

🕐 20 to 30 minutes

Some of the steps from this task may also help with the earlier solo in the style of Christopher Bruce.

1 With a partner, try some traditional dance steps. You can find your own, add hops, runs, walks and try these:

Schottische – travel on a diagonal line slide onto left foot (long step), close right underneath (short), slide & step left again (long) right leg staying low at the back as you hop. Repeat to other side. (**L**RLL, **R**LRR) Pattern long/short/long/hop – 4 counts.

Waltz – step forward low right foot (long step), high forward left foot (long step), high underneath you right foot (close). Repeats other side. Down, up, up – 3 counts.

Grapevine – going to the right sideways - step side right foot, cross behind with left foot, step side right foot, cross infront with left foot. Repeat as many times as needed.

Mazurka – lively one this! Travel to the side or diagonally forward, glide step right, cut underneath with left and hop on left. Repeats on same foot each time (**R**LL).

2 With a partner, compose a short duet which uses a variety of contacts and steps – e.g. ballroom hold, link arms, hold waist, hands on partner's shoulders, skater's hold (side-by-side, arms infront crossed over right hand to right and left to left). You can have a bit of fun with this improvisation so some of the music suggestions have a lively tone, others are more traditional to reflect the social dance theme.

Music suggestions: Malcolm Arnold's Dances; Chieftains with the Corrs, *I Know My Love*; Elton John & Kiki Dee, *Don't Go Breakin' My Heart*; David Bowie & Mick Jagger, *Dancing in the Street*; Eliza Carthy, *Pretty Ploughboy*; Gotan Project, *Santa Maria (del Buen Ayre)* this is a tango.

Elevation

Elevation involves rising from the floor, such as in a jump or in *relevé* on a half-toe or *en pointe*. This is an exciting part of any choreography.

Here we are again with both feet planted firmly in the air.
(Hugh Scanlon, British Trade Union leader)

Every human movement has three phrases:

1 preparation
2 action
3 recovery.

These are particularly clear in the action of jumping:

1 Preparation: bend knees; lift centre, rib cage and head.
2 Action: extend feet and legs strongly and suddenly to take off – lifting arms may assist upward thrust; breathe in; lift focus.
3 Recovery: for safety and the protection of the Achilles heel, always land 'through the foot' – i.e. toe-ball-heel to floor; bend knees; maintain alignment and lift from centre on landing. Extend legs to standing.

As noted in Chapter One, sometimes beginners, in an effort to take off, over-contract the muscles of the body, and a 'bucking' effect is seen in the air. Encouragement to relax in the air is needed here.

Jumps can be identified by whether the take-off and landing are on one foot or both. Two feet limit the permutations to:

■ hop: take off from one foot, land on the same foot;
■ leap: take off from one foot, land on the other foot;
■ jump: take off from two feet, land on the two feet;
■ *sissone*: take off from two feet, land on one foot;
■ *assemblé*: take off from one foot, land on two feet.

Figure 3.4 'Bread' by Bedlam Dance Co. (1997)
Photographer: Chris Nash

Other details – like rotation of the legs, the use of the free leg(s) in the air, flexed or extended feet, the arm position, turning, travelling and so on – give jumps endless expressive potential. Jumping can burst upwards suddenly,

propel powerfully forwards or sideways. A jump may soar, like leaps arcing through the air, or use arms swinging in opposition to legs to enhance the effect of suspension. When combined with runs, the leap has a spectacular look. Landings can differ too. A rebound into another jump gives a bouncy effect and expresses something quite different from falling to the floor on landing. (What might the latter type of landing express to an audience?)

In *Nymphéas* (1976), Robert Cohan used the Impressionist paintings of water-lily ponds, by French artist Claude Monet, to stimulate ideas for choreography. Lively two-foot-to-two-foot jumps with deep pliés on landings are used effectively in one section danced by the men, and give the impression of frogs springing between the pads of waterlilies.

Skimming jumps are seen in Siobhan Davies' *White Man Sleeps* (1988). Merce Cunningham's unusual use of jumps in *Beach Birds for Camera* (1991, music John cage, director Elliot Caplan) evokes impressions of the subject matter by using the changing of the weight of the body during jumping. These 'birds' are not creatures of the air – they look physically 'beached'. The jumps do not soar through the blue sky, but depict skitterish landings and weighted drops, almost as if this whole scene portrays a colony of seabirds on their beach nesting ground. Cunningham's characteristic dance technique uses a very flexible torso and fast footwork, both of these characteristics are clearly performed by the dancers in *Beach Birds for Camera*. The next task will help you to understand the five different jumps and how the flexible torso and emphasis of different weight in the body can be used in jumping.

TASK FIVE – *Jump around and beachbirds*

KEY SKILLS Problem solving

Several hours

This task links to Tasks Sixteen and Twenty later in the chapter.

1 Watch the black and white section of *Beachbirds for Camera* and spot the use of the different take-off and landing foot patterns in the jumps. Write them down in your journal as you see them. Did you see all five? Try to note the different types of landings – ones that drop and stop, others that bounce into another jump.

2 Watch the section a second time and note the use of the torso – how it extends upwards, bends forward and tilts to the side. Also watch carefully how the dancers emphasise different weights of their bodies when they are in the air, on landing and when turns are added into the jumps. Keep rough notes in your journal.
   EITHER

3 Compose a phrase of movement which contains the five jumps in any order into a lively sequence. Add steps and repetitions as desired. Music suggestions: Cameo, *Word Up*; House of Pain, *Jump Around*.

> OR
>
> **4** Compose a phrase of movement which contains combinations of the five jumps with a Cunningham-like flexible torso, different body weights, stillnesses and fast footwork to make a sequence that is 1 minute long. Music suggestions: Kronos Quartet play George Crumb, *God Music* (3m 03 secs.)

Turning

Turning is almost a dervish exercise with the world going around and you feeling calm and quiet.

(Hanya Holm in *The Vision of Modern Dance*, 1980)

Certainly, the dizzying effect of turning was one of the reasons that the waltz proved so popular and no doubt the dancers, and the audiences of the Hollywood films of the 1930s, would have felt swept off their feet with the romance and indulgent pleasure. The belief in the power of turning in the Sufi religion of the Middle East is so great that the dervishes' hours of spinning, they feel, connects their being to the heavens and the earth, centring them and empowering them to overcome any dizziness.

Turning strictly refers to rotating the whole body around with a change of front, or a full or multiple rotation. Twisting is also rotation, but refers to movement within a joint, e.g. turn-out of the hip. There are many different types of turn: full, half, quarter, multiple, inward and outward, jumping, travelling, on- and off-balance, pivot, spin and so on. These all require good placement and alignment to avoid a loss of balance or orientation. When beginners first start, they may feel as if their whole universe is moving, and this can cause great insecurity. Constant practice is therefore required.

The eyes must focus straight ahead, not downwards, for balance. In classical ballet, 'spotting' is often used. This involves fixing the eyes on one spot for as long as possible and whipping the head round as quickly as possible. This helps to avoid dizziness. Modern and post-modern genres sometimes deliberately remove spotting, and the skill of retaining orientation then becomes internalised, not unlike the whirling dervishes. A practical example is barrel turns, which in ballet are performed outward, leaping sideways around and spotting on a mental image of a centrally placed barrel. Originally a favourite of sailors, this is an exciting explosive jump to watch. The post-modern version may be performed inwards, with less sudden upward feel and more skimming in soft curves along a straight pathway. The deliberate removal of spotting gives an even, lifting quality.

Turns can also start in different ways. Lifting the weight onto a half-toe rise (*relevé*) or *en pointe* allows the body easily to rotate around the axis. This may be continued in multiple by using the free leg to extend and flex in *retiré*

(drawing the leg up in a bent position so that the toe touches the inside of the support leg) to give added momentum on each 360° turn. The weight of throwing an arm, leg or head may also initiate turning. The *Rose Adagio* in Marius Petipa's *The Sleeping Beauty* (1890) features multiple pirouettes. Princess Aurora turns swiftly as she accepts a rose from each admiring prince. And the post-modern work *Rotary Action* (Arnie Zane and Bill T. Jones, 1985) makes a clear use of cartwheels, rolls, turning around a partner, and the rotating of hips and shoulders in a simple but effective interpretation of the title.

Figure 3.5 Sir Peter Wright's *Nutcracker*

Photographer: Asya Verzhbinsky

Royal Ballet in the snow scene of Sir Peter Wright's *Nutcracker*.

TASK SIX – *And the wheels go round and round*

KEY SKILLS Problem solving
Working with Others and Communication

Several hours

Choreograph a trio/quartet using the idea of transport. With turning as your dominant movement theme, ideas which may be useful for improvisation will include: the wheel, the Highway Code, traffic control, behaviour behind the wheel, bicycles, trains and the behaviour of passengers in train stations or at bus stops. After each rehearsal take a few moments to record the session's process of working in your group. Your journal is important for this task. You

---

could use the action words from this chapter to help you to record movements and moments that expressed successfully. You could also use drawings, numbers or other symbols that you create yourself to record your discoveries. This is also an opportunity to describe any moments that were memorably enjoyable or difficult.

Music suggestions: Tony Allen, *Eparapo*; Duoud, *Racailles*; Michael Easton, *On the Metro & Driving in Paris* (2m 30s).

Gesture (isolation)

Graham's knee comes up to her chest, her back curves slightly forward, and now her leg, knee leading, juts inward, circles out, in, out again, while her arms swoop through the air like a bird's wings. . . . Graham speaks of the turbulent emotions lying deep within Judith's body.

(Elinor Rogosin in *The Dancemakers*, 1980)

The powerful language of gesture is all around us everyday. Waving goodbye, folding arms, pointing fingers, raising eyebrows, a nod and a shake of the head are ordinary body language which we all use to accompany speech. These everyday forms of movement are a rich source for choreography – as we note in the quotation above, where the gestures tell of the deepest vengefulness and passion. Gestural movement does not involve any transference of weight. Gestures are usually movements of single parts in isolation, or combination, and the rotation of the joints can play a significant part in subtle communication. The facing of a palm on the hand, brought about when the humerus bone rotates in the shoulder joint, can make all the difference to the expression of a movement. You can try this for yourelf in Task Seven. Similarly, rotation of the legs in the hip sockets in turn-out, parallel or turned-in opens up a range of expressive possibilities from humour to lyricism. Leg gestures can express a range of ideas. Ashton's use of quivering crossing and uncrossing legs, when Cinderella is lifted by the prince, enhance the romance of her being swept off her feet. Whereas, Cunningham's dancers use of a single trembling leg portrays the image of delicate birdlike steps in *Beachbirds for Camera*.

Gestures of the free leg in tap dance are used to make some of the syncopated sounds that are typical of the style. They counterpoint the music by crossing accents or time signatures. Tap evolved in North America, out of the soft shoe dance's innovators such as George Primrose, but it was the new style of buck and wing that really heralded what we call tap dance today. Buck and wing, as seen in the chorus routines from famous Hollywood musicals such as *42nd Street* (1933, choreography, Busby Berkely, dancers Ruby Miller and Ginger Rogers), uses the 'wing' step. This involves the gesturing leg swishing sideways to free a flexible ankle and make multiple taps. This is how tap dance began to syncopate with the music.

This film and others, such as Berkley's *Gold Diggers of 1933* and *For Me and My Gal* (1942) were made at the depth of the Depression and told the old story of struggling against all odds to make a living, being discovered and becoming an overnight success in show business. Escapism at its absolute best, and one mirrored in many more recent movies and shows, such as *Saturday Night Fever* (1977, starring John Travolta), *Dirty Dancing* (1987) and, of course, A *Chorus Line* (1975, director, choreographer Michael Bennett).

Astaire used hand gestures to embellish his famous routine with Rogers 'Let's Face the Music and dance' in *Follow the Fleet* (1936, RKO Radio Pictures). The popular Art Deco style of many 1930s figurines typically included graceful hands and Astaire used these 'Egyptian style' shapes to add interest to the steps.

Bharatha Natyam from India uses a large number of hand, arm and facial gestures called *mudras* in a complex language to tell rich narratives of myths and stories. Elements of this genre are visible in the work of post-modern choreographer Lea Anderson for 'The Cholmondeleys' (pronounced *chumleez)* and 'The Featherstonehaughs' (pronounced *fanshaws*). In 1984, 'The Cholmondeley Sisters' was founded and choreographer Lea Anderson's use of quirky hand, arm and facial gestures and sign language gave her work a characteristic detailed look. Her early 1985 works *Baby, Baby, Baby,* to music by singer Nina Simone and *The Clichés and the Holidays* signed her personal signature style in terms of her characteristic dance vocabulary. Anderson's choice of subject, often mixing humour with darker tones to smash stereotypes of the modern world, was also clear from these earliest beginnings. The 'babes' were like an all girl 1960s pop group and the gestural vocabulary communicated, like cartoon speech bubbles, their thoughts. As for the holiday clichés, Anderson's postcard of Spanish holidays and hotel Flamenco was performed to the wail of Catalan folk singing and made all the funnier by the deadpan faces of the dancers. Both of these themes, as with her vocabulary, were developed later in such works as *Cross Channel* (1991, director Margaret Williams) and *Go Las Vegas* (1995 for 'The Featherstonehaughs'). Her early programmes appeared in unusual venues for the 1980s such as pubs and clubs, and I can remember my first viewing of her work in a tiny upstairs room in a pub in Brighton. The Cholmondeleys are described here by a dance critic:

I became riveted by a single striking resemblance, which was simply their extraordinary range of gesture and facial expression. Their hands . . . seemed to have a life of their own tracing elaborate, decorative patterns in space or spinning memories; . . . while their faces had an even more eloquent repertoire of pouts, stares . . . and glances.

(Judith Mackrell in *Dance Theatre Journal*, 1986)

Richard Alston, better known for fine footwork, incorporated hand gestures like clicking fingers and clapping to show disgust or rejection in *Pulcinella* (1987). The gestures have an Italian feel such as when Pimpinella first enters. Amongst the *bourrées* and the *brisés* her hands gesticulate rapidly to her

Figure 3.6 The Cholmondeleys in *The Cholmondeley Sisters* (1984)
Photographer: Chris Nash

bothersome husband. In reply, he jumps in second position whilst tapping his forehead as if to exclaim that she is mad.

Mimetic gestures are used in classical ballet to tell stories and make clear the relationships between characters. Jean Georges Noverre (France, 1727–1810) described his thoughts on reform for ballet in his Lettres sur la Danse et sur les Ballets (1760):

. . . study how to make your gestures noble, never forget that it is the life-blood of your dancing.

(Cyril Beaumont in *Dance Horizons*, 1966)

Later, in the nineteenth century, Marius Petipa (1818–1910) used long passages of mime as a kind of sign language so that obvious meanings were clear. For example, shaking a fist meant anger, while placing the hand on the heart meant love. Other gestures were less direct, like pointing to the heavens to declare everlasting love, or circling hands and arms around each other and over the head to symbolise dance.

Mime is used rarely in modern ballets but is seen in the classics. In Petipa's *The Sleeping Beauty* (1890), Princess Aurora greets the four princes. In turn they support her in attitude and turn her as she holds the balance. When each releases her hands she raises both arms above her head to make a crown. This arm gesture means princess and it is repeated almost as a 'How do you do, pleased to meet you' greeting to each prince in turn.

Similarly, Carabosse mimes anger at being uninvited to the princess's christening in a death threat. Bringing up the arms to the side of the head and then down quickly with fists clenched so that they cross in front of the torso mimes death.

TASK SEVEN – *A movement is worth a thousand words*

KEY SKILLS Problem solving
Working with others
Communication

🕐 45 minutes to an hour

1 In pairs, experiment with palm facings as you raise an arm forward from your side, in the sagittal plane, and return. Try different arm rotations so that the palm faces upward, downward, inwards and outwards. Vary the direction and speed of the gesture – try downwards fast or diagonal and slow/fast. As you move, put expression into the movement and decide on how each one differs in what it communicates. Write down in your choreographic journal what your final solutions were. Try to use descriptive words or verbs such as generous or giving. Practising these kind of descriptions will help you in your final written examination.

2 In pairs, use as many different parts of the body as possible, isolate and improvise with gestural movements. Some of these may be recognisable everyday gestures, others more quirky.

3 In pairs, select a few everyday gestures, ones from the changes of palm facings and a few less common to create a dance entitled 'For a small space'. Music suggestions: Tomita *'Ballet of the chicks in their shells'* by Moussorgsky, from *Pictures at an Exhibition*; Penguin Café Orchestra, *Broadcasting from Home*, various tracks.

Gesture really comes into its own in the hip, rib, shoulder isolations so characteristic of jazz dance, typically found in the style of Jack Cole (1914–1974). Cole's work had both sensual and explosive dynamics and is found in his film choreography for Marilyn Monroe in *Gentlemen Prefer Blondes* (1953) and the Broadway show *Kismet* (1954), adapted for film in 1955. His style influenced Jerome Robbins and Bob Fosse. Fosse's style is immediately recognisable with the pumping hips, mobile wrists and jutting shoulders.

The African roots of jazz are clearly seen in American Alvin Ailey's dance style. Fluid hips and torso create a range of images from social dance sassy 'bump and grind', to tortured Graham-like contractions such as seen at the end of the solo *Cry* (1971), when the female dancer sinks to the ground in a gesture of her oppression. Male dancers, at the end of *Blues Suite* (1958), end in a similar manner.

Stillness

Stillness is not an absolute point. It is an ever-receding depth of understanding.

(Mary Fulkerson in *The move to Stillness*,
Dartington Theatre Papers, 1981–1982)

Being still is active! It requires strong control. There is muscle activity in a pause, a feeling of ongoing energy. Stillness contributes to rhythm, acting a little like a full stop in a sentence, and it gives the onlooker a chance to reflect on what has just been seen. It may also act to highlight what is about to happen, and it is often used as the ending for a dance.

The skill of balance may be involved if the body is being held still on a small area like the toes, and this requires strong control and co-ordination. The part on the floor pushes down whilst the rest of the body pulls upwards and sends energy outward to the extremities. This counter-tension outwards and towards your centre holds the body lightly over the base.

Good balance, say holding an arabesque or attitude, is helped by breathing and good alignment of pelvis and spine. Eyes and the balance organs in the ears help too, so do the proprioceptors.

In Richard Alston's *Soda Lake* (1981) stillness is used extensively, and is clearly appropriate to his study of the vast open spaces of the Mohavi Desert in North America. The silent, motionless 'passive landscape' (as Alston described this desert in 1983 on The South Bank Show), as presented in a minimalist set, is a perfect vehicle for stillness. Alston chooses certain shapes and positions of rest for which the dancer in performance has to allow adequate time: holding such positions as 'the big bird' and 'the sentinel position' are demanding on a dancer's stamina and sense of timing.

Alston's choreographic style has shades of influence of the work of Merce Cunningham, and this is not surprising as after initial training at London Contemporary Dance Theatre from 1970–75 Alston went to New York and took classes at the Cunningham studio. At that time he also studied ballet and found new interests in the films of Fred Astaire, as well as the works of post-modern choreographers, such as Trisha Brown and the founder of contact improvisation, Steve Paxton. Traces of Cunningham influence can also be seen in other English choreographers emerging in the 1970s and 1980s, such as Rosemary Butcher, Siobhan Davies and Ian Spink. Davies' *Sphinx* (1977) also uses animal imagery in the movement.

Stillness is a noticeable feature of Cunningham's *Beach Birds for Camera*. In the opening sequence, the dancers hold a stillness standing in a small parallel position, only interrupted by the occasional soft swaying torso and slow arm gestures. Later in the black and white section two male dancers face each other in a lunge position holding a prolonged stillness. In the colour section of the dance, a male soloist holds an arabesque for an absolute eternity, while other

dancers exit and enter and duets continue in the background. The end of the dance uses a stillness, but it has an almost temporary feel as if the duet will continue after the audience has gone. A really unusual way to end a dance – more like another beginning. Typical Cunningham – even endings are not what we expect.

Of course, many dances start and end with stillness. From a dancer's point of view control over this action is therefore crucial. Balance and stillness are maintained as long as your centre of gravity is aligned over the part of the body which is bearing the weight. This can be seen when street dancers finish a break move and they hit complicated body positions in stillness, balancing on their head or shoulders. Once balance is lost and gravity takes over, movement results and often this involves falling.

Figure 3.7 *B Girls.* Dancers from 'Into the Hoods'.
Photographer: Hugo Glendinning

TASK EIGHT

KEY SKILLS Problem solving
Working with others
Communication

🕐 10 to 20 minutes

1 *GUESSING GAME.* In pairs, one person closes their eyes while the other makes a shape. Without opening your eyes, use touch to feel your way around your partner's shape. Your partner must

> keep very still. When you think you know the shape, make it yourself and then open your eyes to see how accurate your copy is.
>
> ⏱ Several hours
>
> **2** *FEEL THE HEAT.* Find prints of paintings by the Impressionist artist Georges Seurat – either *La Grande Jatte* or *Une Baignade* would be appropriate. In threes or fives, compose a short dance which uses stillness as a predominant feature to punctuate the movement. Convey a feeling of calm and heat. (Suggested music: Claude Debussy's *Snowflakes are dancing*, from *Children's Corner No. 4*, or *Passepied* from *Suite Bergamasque No. 4.*)

Falling

In classical ballet, the high level predominates, while one of the aims of early modern dance, by contrast, was to show the effort of moving against gravity, not to hide it. This latter trend increased the use of falling and of low-level movement. I like to consider falling as the sixth dance action.

Doris Humphrey, one of the early pioneers of modern dance, regarded the struggle against gravity (suspension, fall and recovery) to be the very essence of life and action – 'The Arc between Two Deaths'.

Standing still before a mirror, I found that first the body began to sway. Then, letting myself go, three things happened. I began to fall, the speed increasing as I went down. The body made an involuntary effort to resist the fall . . . I hit the floor.

(Quoted by Ellfeldt in Dance from *Magic to Art*, 1976)

Falling requires skill and co-ordination in order to be performed safely, and like all dance actions it requires practice. There is a moment when the pull of gravity overtakes and the dancer 'intentionally' gives in to it. During this descent, the abdominal muscles must pull-up; and landing on the knees, elbows, shoulder tip or sacrum should always be avoided. There are two types of fall:

1 A collapse: a relaxed, successive giving-in which happens over the centre of gravity and tends not to rebound.
2 An off-balance fall: the centre of gravity shifts off-centre, making falling unavoidable as the pull of gravity takes over.

The moment that balance is lost was used highly effectively in Martha Graham's *Heretic* (1929). The dance depicted a harsh 'zigzag' uncertain energy, and the world was in a similar state as the stock market crashed. She cast

127

herself as the outcast rebel in *Heretic*, pitted against a chorus of female puritans who crowd around her. At one point, with the chorus either side, she performs one of her signature backward falls. Starting with a slow lean, as if to resist, but then finally gravity takes over. A characteristic of Graham's work was the use of how the moment of off-balance sent the body to travel into space. This can be seen in technical exercises such as swing falls that travel sideways down the floor. Graham was known to take vocabulary from her dances and use it in her technique class. In this way, her technique developed and for students of dance this way of developing their own movement style is worth noting. Using your choreographic journal would work well as a way to record your discoveries and to write about things that you found were not so successful too.

TASK NINE – *Walking & falling at the same time. . .*

KEY SKILLS Problem solving
Working with others
Communication

🕐 10 to 20 minutes

1 Explore the feeling of walking, falling and recovering. At the ends of falls, try out different techniques: stillness; rebound; rolls. In addition: falling in different directions: forwards, backwards, sideways and diagonally; try out both collapses and off-balance falls (see above); and try adding jumps and swings into the falling. After five or 10 minutes, join up into a large group.

🕐 10 to 20 minutes

2 Continuing to explore the above themes, select some of the more successful ideas, whilst also copying the variety of tempos, falls, shapes and rolls that the other dancers are doing.

🕐 10 to 20 minutes

3 Using landing/gymnastic mats, try to teach each other any falls and rolls which someone may have learnt in a martial-arts class – like a judo or karate session – or in a gymnastics class.

Various actions may pre-empt a fall – jumps, swings, turns – and at the end of the fall action phase, recovery may involve stillness, a roll or a rebound to continue.

Repeated falls and recoveries of a faster freer style than Graham's, are often used in the work of post-modern choreographers such as Belgian, Wim Vandekeybus. His studies in psychology and acrobatic training combine to

produce super-charged and high-risk physical partner work, where dancers express a fight for survival. Typical of his work is the dance video *Roseland* (1991), where dancers fly through the air like missiles along with bricks that are caught, thrown and dropped along with the human projectiles. In 1988, British dancers Louis Richards and Kevin Finnan started the company *Motionhouse*. They too used high-speed contact work, as typified by their depiction of the conflict and social alarm that was created by the spread of AIDS in *The House of Bones* (1990). Dancers drop off a scaffold, from quite a height, to be caught by a partner, expressing the intense emotions connected with issues in today's society. Dancers push, pull, drop and throw each other reflecting on how people can hurt each other in real life.

The six dance actions of travelling, elevation, turning, gesture, stillness and falling, which are the foundations of choreography, are further developed by using a variety of other considerations, namely the where, the when, the how and relationships. These will form the focus for the next part of this chapter.

TASK TEN – *Gravity*

KEY SKILLS Problem solving
Working with others
Communication

 20 to 30 minutes

Fall forward from a standing position, sensing the moment when your centre of gravity shifts out of the plumb line and you have to catch your weight with a step into a safe lunge position. (Lift your torso using the core stabilisers, a slight turn-out will help and check that your bent knee is properly aligned over the foot.) Repeat until you can safely go low enough to transfer your weight simply, smoothly, gradually and safely to the floor until lying flat. Then roll to stand. Practise until the phrase is very clear. Make sure weight transference is smooth throughout.

The space component – the where

'No room! No room!' they cried out when they saw Alice coming. 'There's plenty of room!' said Alice indignantly.

(From *Alice in Wonderland* by Lewis Carroll)

Designing a dance in space helps the audience to understand it, and any dance must be organised in space in a way appropriate to the chosen idea or theme. Dancers work *in* a space – i.e. a studio, gym, stage – but they also dance *with* space: it is alive, like an active partner. Mary Wigman (1886–1973) was a

The work of one of the early British post-modern choreographers, Rosemary Butcher, is characterised by strong use of floor patterns that often relate to the site where a dance is performed. In *Shell* (1980), she worked with artist Jon Groom's sculpture, emphasising its curving lines by echoing and contrasting them with the spiral and circular floor patterns. Similarly in 1982, Butcher used linear floor patterns to match the beams of light from projections by Heinz-Dieter Pietsch.

Directions

As with different patterns, different directions – forwards, backwards, sideways, circular, up, down – may also provoke different reactions. Advancing forwards is positive, assertive and authoritative, whereas the backwards retreat possibly more defensive. Jumping up is lively, while there is an opposite feel to falling down. Sideways may be seen as sneaky.

At the end of Richard Alston's *Zansa* (1986) as dancers crawl backwards a soloist rushes forward across the front of the stage. All the previous tensions and crossings of duets and soloists are echoed here by an opposite in direction and level which brings the dance to a timely and appropriate end.

Planes

Anatomically, movement in certain directions occurs in three planes, as mentioned in Chapter One. The sagittal, horizontal and frontal planes can be useful to express your ideas, images and themes.

Movement which emphasises width can appear flat, perhaps mechanical or puppet-like. This kind of movement would be appropriate when dancing in a mask, because of the inhuman, two-dimensional look which, like a mask, it conveys. The opening of *Ghost Dances* (Christopher Bruce, 1981) uses width to great effect. The dancers' tilting head gestures, sideways leaps and extensions into stillness create an unreality in our minds. They place hands on each other's shoulders and move in unison in a side-to-side folky step, presenting an image of power which is ominous and threatening to us mere mortals. These movements also serve to emphasise the death masks and the body paint which create the effect of flat skeletons hanging in the gloom. As soon as the mere mortals enter, we are drawn into the latter's more three-dimensional world – and into their vulnerability – by the way they travel slowly along the depth of the diagonal (up stage left to down stage right). By adding depth to the original movement, Bruce places these mortals in a more real, human world. The audience is drawn into a place where two worlds meet, and an accompanying sense of danger is conveyed. Merce Cunningham's use of the planes is very complex. He combines fast footwork that quickly shifts from the sagittal to the horizontal pathway and then adds on top an equally fluid torso, bending to the side, extending upwards and curving low forwards. Cunningham dancers need strong abdominal muscles to control these constant shifts in space.

Levels

Levels are an aspect of height. In classical ballet, the emphasis is often on the high level, whereas the low floor level is a feature of modern and post-modern dance. Martha Graham's earthy relationship with gravity was also a feature of the work of Doris Humphrey. We also see it in the post-modern work of Lea Anderson, for the Cholmondeleys – in 'Knees', the end section of her 1989 work *Flesh and Blood*, the dancers seem earth-bound, weighty.

From the vertical to the horizontal, from standing, kneeling and lying, her cast explore the different levels between high and low, as if making contact with the unknown.

(Ann Nugent in *The Stage*, 1989)

Ashton's *Cinderella* (1948) exaggerates the high level of ballet even more than usual when Cinderella makes her entrance to the ball. Moira Shearer's famous walk down the grand staircase, serenely beautiful, looking straight ahead *en pointe* and above all around her – the ultimate catwalk statement! In Matthew Bourne's *Swan Lake* (1995) there is an ingenious use of level playing on the set design. As the young prince lies asleep swans, as if in a dream, appear from deep underneath the oversize bed. Later in the same scene the swans gather on the bed, putting themselves higher up than the prince, who is now on the floor. They loom, menacing and dangerous, from their perch warning of the tragedy which is about to follow.

The middle level is our everyday one. Falling out of or rising above this level offer obvious expressive possibilities for choreography.

TASK ELEVEN – *Words in space*

KEY SKILLS Problem solving
Communication

 20 to 30 minutes

1 Use the words below to create short phrases of improvised movement which use direction, pattern in the air and on the floor, and personal/general space in a way appropriate to the meaning of the words. This is fun to do in a group, mixing in the the words (like a rap) as accompaniment.

- Up one minute, down the next.
- Far-reaching effects.
- Neither here nor there.
- On the straight and narrow.
- Draw the line.
- At loose ends.

 20 to 30 minutes

2 Choreographic journal

In your journal, record your floor patterns using the notation of Figure 3.9 as a guide. Show this and the dance to another student or your teacher to see how accurate your notation is.

The size of movements

Tiny hand gestures, large sweeping arm gestures, a single step, travelling all around a space – these movements will communicate different sensations to onlookers, and the contrasts involved here should be explored by all choreographers.

Again, this factor is shown clearly in the work of Lea Anderson in *Flesh and Blood*. The small movements of eyes, noses, fingers and heads which draw the letters J, O, A and N in the air are later developed by enlargement, they travel and transform into arm gestures in the second section, 'Movement choir'.

Merce Cunningham uses gestures to add detail to his characteristic footwork. The flexible torso is as expressive as the arm gestures. This is seen clearly in *Beach Birds for Camera*, as the dancers settle to rest or preen. At one point, there is a small group of dancers that wriggle or rotate their torsos back and forth or side-side, suggestive of settling on a nest – the rib cage seems bone-free almost like another limb. Also, small subtle hand and arm gestures are an important feature in the dance as they move minimally, but with a hypnotic quality.

In *Carnival* (1982), Siobhan Davies (for Second Stride) used the Saint-Saens music *Carnaval des Animaux* and produced some amusing contrast in movement size. Twelve dancers travelled fluidly and swiftly around the stage space in wide sweeping pathways in the 'Aquarium' section, reminiscent of shoals of tropical fish. In contrast the lovelorn cuckoo uses repetition of a small, restricted arm gesture depicting his beating heart. The predictable repetition to match the bird call in the music is sad but very amusing, especially when he misses a beat. The very restricted movement of the elderly tottering tortoises (danced by Davies and Ian Spink), travelling precariously across the stage, added another range to the expression and used the dancers' acting abilities too. This humorous piece, using characterisation of animals and their 'human' qualities, is not typical of Davies. It has more in common with her London Contemporary Dance Theatre (LCDT) beginnings, being more in a Cohan dramatic style. Indeed, *Carnival* was later taken into the repertoire of the larger companies LCDT and Rambert Dance Company.

The focus

This constituent feature of a dance composition can mean different things at different moments during a dance. As we saw in Chapter Two, focus is an important interpretative skill for the dancer in performance. Choreographers too use focus in different ways and it can involve any of the following:

- *where* the dancer is looking: up or down; at a part of the body; at another dancer; at the audience; with or against the direction of a movement; on a fixed spot;
- which way the body is *facing*: for example, does a certain shape look better facing on a diagonal or flat to the audience than it does facing sideways on?

In *Sergeant Early's Dream* by Christopher Bruce (1984), the dancers' focus is often thrown out to sea which is painted on the backcloth. This draws the attention of the audience to the dancers' longing for their original homeland which is full of memories and nostalgia.

Siobhan Davies often uses a soft, understated inward focus to pull the audience into looking more closely at the movement itself.

The use of focus in the ball scene of Bourne's *Swan Lake* (1995) adds dramatic tension. As the lead males, the Prince and the 'Swan', dance, their gaze is drawn to each other repeatedly. Sometimes on their dancing partner, or on the movement itself, but always drawn back to look at each other.

A similar use of focus can be seen with ballroom couples, but sometimes this is deliberately mainpulated to create the opposite effect, as in the tango's abrupt turns of the head and focus away and towards the partner. Such a sudden change of focus creates a mood of tension and challenge in the love duel of the fiery tango.

Figure 3.10 Showing volume and focus in *Etceteras* (2004)
Choreography: Linda Ashley. Dancer: Melissa Breckon, AUT University Bachelor of Dance, Auckland, New Zealand

Shape and volume

The body can create a variety of shapes – curled, straight, wide, twisted and so on – and the spaces around and between bodies also need to be sculpted. In visual art, this latter space is often called the negative space. In dance it is seen during stillness, but also in the transitions from one shape to the next, and when it is enclosed by boundaries, it creates a feeling of volume. For example, when a dancer places the arms in front of the body, as if curving them around an imaginary beach ball, the sensation of volume is clearly felt.

Different shapes have different expressive potential. In classical ballet, it is so often curving lines which are used. These have a sense of the lyrical and the romantic, and an ongoing flow and grace. In contrast, the harsh angular and straight lines of early modern dancers are hard-edged, tough and strong, and these have held the potential for expressing the social upheavals of their times.

The modern dance as we know it today came after the World War. This period following the war demanded forms vital enough for the reborn man to inhabit . . . All life today is concerned with space problems, even political life. Space language is a language we understand. We receive so much of sensation through the eye.

(Martha Graham in *The Vision of Modern Dance*, 1980)

Similarly with symmetrical and asymmetrical shapes: the former giving impressions of regularity and stability, and the latter coming over as more unpredictable and insecure.

If symmetry should be used sparingly in choreography because of its calming effect, then asymmetry, which stimulates the senses, is the area to court and understand for dancing.

(Doris Humphrey in *The Art of Making Dances*, 1959)

Humphrey's is the modern view of space with an interest in disruptive asymmetry. However, symmetry can be used to great effect and this is very clear in Anthony Van Laast's choreography for Andrew Lloyd Webber's West End and Broadway musical *Bombay Dreams* (2002). In the number *Shaklaka Baby* (music originally from the Tamil film *Mudhalvan*, 1999), Van Laast shows how inventive use of symmetry can grab the attention. In a phrase where the dancers are in a straight line one behind the other (a formation that can look dull without enough thought), the positioning of the arms of different levels is reminiscent of the many armed Indian god of dance, *Shiva*.

Busby Berkeley (1895–1976) often used symmetrical group shapes for Hollywood films. His trademark overhead camera angle first appeared in *Whoopee* (1930) and enhanced the kaleidoscopic changes in the symmetrical shapes to great effect.

Further consideration about the use of space is to be found in later sections. In Chapter Four, which deals with the physical setting, there is an analysis of how to use a stage space, and of how different physical settings affect spatial design of movement.

As we move through space, we also, of course, move through time, and this will be the next constituent feature of dance that we will examine.

TASK TWELVE – *Your film journal*

KEY SKILLS Problem solving
Communication

🕐 45 minutes to an hour

Use a camera to film short extracts of your improvisations as you work in this task. This footage can be used as part of your choreographic record and journal. If you organise your film archive on your computer using software such as *iMovie* or *Windows Movie Maker*, date and title your collection, so that you may look back and use movements in your later dance compositions.

- Individually, choose four contrasting body shapes.
- Place them in an order and link them up with travelling movements. Find a way, whilst holding each shape, of making it turn or travel, or both.
- Experiment with giving the shapes different facings so that an audience sees them from different angles – e.g. above, sideways, etc.
- Experiment with changing the focus of the eyes during both stillness and travelling – e.g. moving from a focus on different parts of the body to a focus on the room around you.

🕐 45 minutes to an hour

Using your evaluations of the video extracts that you have, choose movements to create a short solo piece entitled either:

- 'Distortions', or
- 'No way out', or
- 'Metamorphosis'.

(Recommended music: *The Big Blue* film soundtrack, by Eric Serra.)

The time component – the when

'If you knew time as well as I do,' said the Hatter, 'you wouldn't talk about wasting it. It's him . . . I dare say you never even spoke to Time! . . . Now if

you only kept on good terms with him, he'd do almost anything you like with the clock.'

(Alice in Wonderland by Lewis Carroll)

Time can seem to have a life of its own. We have all experienced waiting for the kettle to boil, and how, when we are in a hurry, it seems to take longer. As choreographer, you may alter how an audience perceives time by the way that you yourself manipulate it. Like design in space, time plays an intrinsic part in the organisation of movement for choreography. It orders and measures, but it can also be a slippery customer, so, as the Mad Hatter cautions, it is advisable to be on good terms with it.

Patterning movement in time gives it form and rhythm and makes it interesting for the onlooker; the performing dancer, on their part, requires an accurate feel for the temporal boundaries of the choreography. The analysis of time and rhythm in music will be examined in more detail later. Here we are concerned only with the simpler aspects of time as a constituent feature of dance vocabulary.

Speed and duration

Dance is concerned with a single instant as it comes along.

(Merce Cunningham in Dance from Magic to Art, 1976)

Sudden or sustained, and fast or slow, are two simple ways of analysing a movement, in terms of how much time it actually takes. Sudden movement can produce a sense of urgency in the onlooker, in contrast with an indulgent, gradual feeling that a slower and more sustained movement can create. If you compose a three-minute dance which is made up of 12 slow movements, it will have a leisurely feeling. Pack it with 200 movements, however, and the onlooker will feel rushed along at a breathless pace.

As choreographer and dancer, you need to build up your sensitivity to the duration of movement. Merce Cunningham and others often work with a stopwatch, which allows the speed and duration of a movement – which, after much rehearsal, always stays accurate – to be measured independently of the tempo of the music. One of his dancers, Karole Armitage, once said that he had taught her to recognise exactly how long a movement takes.

In composing dances, it is likely that you will mix slow and fast speeds. The way that you mix these will reflect your personal sense of time and the content of the dance idea.

A good example of this is in Alvin Ailey's *Blues Suite* (1958). It is set in a cheap brothel in the southern states of the USA where life is hard for the women who work there and for the men who visit. Each room of the house has its own story and the dance is made up of several scenes. The third section is a mostly slow tempo piece for a female trio. However, throughout all the sections faster,

desperate movement interrupts repeatedly. These frequent and sudden contrasts in tempo create a feeling that for these people fun is only fleeting and life is a struggle.

Phrasing

Single actions joined together make up phrases. Finding your own inner rhythm that will guide you to form phrases is an ongoing process which itself may take a long time. Phrases usually have a feeling of unity, logic or completeness about them. Each is a simple unit with a beginning, middle and end. The individual parts have a physical logic which connects them and makes sense. Phrases are grouped together, and build up into longer sequences and sections. In this way, their individual and group timings give a dance its form and allow the audience to find a visual sense. Unphrased movement is like a blurred photograph: very difficult to make sense of or to watch for any length of time. Phrasing occurs naturally both in life itself and in other art forms like music, poetry, painting and film.

In technique class you will learn phrases which, by challenging your physical skills as a dancer, contribute to your dance training. These are not necessarily of the same kind as phrases found in choreography which has as its main aim expression to an audience. It is important that you, as a dancer and choreographer, learn to be sensitive to the differences between these two kinds of phrase.

Phrase length

Phrase means length in time. Breath length if you're angry, it's a short breath, it's a short phrase. If you are in a love scene, like Tristan and Isolde, it goes on forever, you're in a l-o-o-ng phrase.

(Martha Graham in *The Dance Makers*, 1980)

A phrase may be of any speed or duration and there will be a mix in any one dance. When music is being used, the phrases are usually based on the underlying beat or musical form. Finding a movement's natural timing/phrasing allows you to alter it to suit whatever the expression demands. As Graham points out, breath can be a strong influence in phrase length – a forceful, sudden exhalation or panting, for example, will produce its own kind of phrase length. Increasing the depth of your breathing can give you a strong sense of where the phrase begins and ends. Each deep breath is a short phrase:

■ inhale: rise, expand;
■ hold: suspend, high point;
■ exhale: fall, collapse, release into an action.

The length of a phrase is determined by its content. If a short, punchy effect is required, the phrase will be a corresponding length.

So within one dance there will be phrases of differing lengths. Consider Richard Alston's *Soda Lake* (1981). Danced accompanied by silence, the phrase lengths are very clear as there is no sound to distract us other than noises made by moving. The phrases vary from lingering and sustained to explosive whipping releases. The phrases are punctuated by long pauses giving the whole form the feeling of the original stimulus, that is the sculpture and the panoramic sparse landscape of the Mojave desert in the USA.

TASK THIRTEEN – *Soda lake*

KEY SKILLS Communication

 45 minutes to an hour

This task asks questions which relate to the constituent features as covered so far in this chapter: action, space, time, dynamics and phrasing.

- On video, watch *Soda Lake* (Richard Alston, 1981).
- Watch the first section again. It ends when the dancer runs back under the sculpture for the second time, sinks, rolls and holds in the lying 'rest' position.
- Use repeated viewings and pauses to answer the following questions about the first section of the dance:

1 There are four different phrases in the first section, How do they differ? (3 marks)
2 Name the five different actions used in the first phrase. (5 marks)
3 In section one the dancer uses differing amounts of space at various moments. How would you describe the differing uses of space? (2 marks)
4 The action of stillness is used a great deal.
  (a) How does it shape the phrases in section one? (2 marks)
  (b) How does it reflect the idea that the dance is based on? (1 mark)
5 (a) Describe two contrasting ways in which the dancer uses focus. (2 marks)
  (b) Suggest what these may express. (2 marks)
6 Suggest three ways in which the movement relates to the sculpture. (3 marks)

Total: 20 marks – answers are on page 335.

Phrase shape

The content of the phrase determines not only its length but also its shape. Our breath phrases, for example, will differ in shape. The deep breath has a clear high point, but the panting phrase is shaped, with no real high or low points.

The shape of a phrase is mapped according to where its low and high points are. These may occur at the beginning, the middle or the end. The high point may be structured through an emphasis on any aspect of space, time or dynamics. It may be faster or stronger, or more expansive in space. And these changes can come about gradually or instantaneously.

Stillness may also be used in shaping. A catch of breath or a moment of hesitation or anticipation may provide time both to reflect on what has just happened and to heighten the impact of what is about to happen. A pause or a longer hold can help both to capture the attention of your audience and to increase their interest in your composition. In ballroom dancing, sometimes a *hesitation step* is used and this accents the hold of the breath creating a suspension that elongates the usual phrasing. The body weight is held on the supporting foot for one or more beats and this breathy moment can express a romantice carefree mood.

In Siobhan Davies' *Rushes* (1982) there is clear use of pauses that suddenly punctuate the phrases and sharpen the pace. In this way you may see how phrases, and the way that they are punctuated, can be like writing sentences and paragraphs.

Time affects the dynamics of any movement. If you change the time taken by a movement, you change the quality of that movement. And furthermore:

Accuracy of time is necessary to maintain the desired space. Change the space and the time changes, unless the speed of the particular phrase changes in order to keep the time the same. Change the time and the space and the movement changes.

(Carolyn Brown in *Merce Cunningham*, 1975)

TASK FOURTEEN – *Movementscape*

KEY SKILLS Problem solving

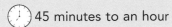 45 minutes to an hour

Using sudden and sustained speeds, stillness, and different levels and sizes of movement, make three phrases of different shapes using the following words as guides:

- melt, float, collapse;
- erupt, crawl, pulsate;
- sparkle, float, fade.

Use breath as an accompaniment when possible – it may add to the shaping of the phrase. Improvise individually on this task. You might like to draw the shapes of the different phrases, as a *Movementscape* in your choreographic journal. Be creative – use different shapes, lines, colours, symbols to record the phrases. For example melt, float collapse may look like Figure 3.11.

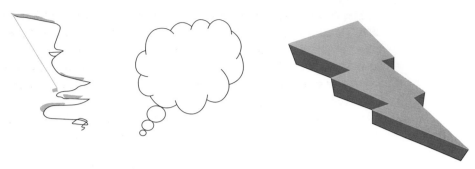

Figure 3.11 Melt, float, collapse
(Recommended music: *Diva* film soundtrack.)

The dynamic component – the how

Every moment varies dynamically along a range from light to strong. The dynamics and textures of a dance are like the colours of a painting. They create interest and contrast, as well as conveying much of the choreographer's intentions. In classical ballet, especially in the romantic tradition, the dominant dynamic is that of the sustained and the effortless. The tradition of modern dance, by contrast, emphasises heavy falls and suspended recoveries. Whatever genre is being used, the choreographer needs an understanding of the terminology and analysis involved in the dynamics of dance.

Energy is the potential for action which gives the 'Go!'. In dance training, finding the right amount of energy to perform a movement efficiently is a priority. In composing dances, the task is to find out how to use energy in a way that is most appropriate to whatever it is that is being expressed.

Energy remains neutral until a force is applied which releases it. Depending on the intensity of the force applied, the resulting movement will vary in its weight from strong to gentle. 'Weight' is a term used specifically by Rudolf Laban in his analysis of effort, but it is also a term used in the dance world generally.

When force and time act together, dynamics result, so there may be a sudden strong dynamic or a sudden light one. Some dynamics are quite specific and are named 'qualities' – like swing, collapse, vibration or percussive (sudden, strong, sharp, staccato) movement. A vibration is used for comic effect by Robert North in his all-male *Troy Game* (1974, London Contemporary Dance Theatre). One dancer is showing off his slinky cool 'salsa', so the other dancers try to stop him by jumping on him and holding onto him, but he carries on. As his knees vibrate and his head shakes, they all start to shake too!

Laban defined a wide range of specific qualities which he called efforts. These are described by the way that space, time and weight are combined – see Table 3.1. In Laban's analysis, space refers to the pathway of a movement through the air. The way in which energy flows through the *body* uses different terms – *free* or *bound flow*. The strong contractions and releases of the torso as featured in Graham technique show the 'held', bound or restrained dynamic. Whereas, in later post-modern choreographers such as, Siobhan Davies and Richard Alston, the torso is still curving but uses freer flow of energy through the body.

The broad spectrum of dynamics which is available for choreography should be explored to the full. In *Nymphéas* (Robert Cohan, 1976), sustainment and suspension are emphasised. Impressions of waterlilies floating and of the gentle movement of the water are conveyed. Contrast is then provided in the storm scene when the dynamic becomes stronger, more sudden, wild and free.

The range of dynamics can also be used to portray character. Even in the world of classical ballet, with its dominance of smooth effortlessness, subtle changes can still be used to great effect. In Sir Frederick Ashton's *The Dream* (1964), the characters are identified by the individual dancers' own inherent dynamic qualities. The original Puck, danced by Keith Martin, has robust, bouncy, driving character, well suited to the impish spirit. Ashton also used a wide range of dynamics in the 'Season Variation' from *Cinderella*, ranging from the quick, bouncy jumps and flicking wrists of spring, through summer's sustained curving arms heavy with the heat, to winter's frozen arabesques, held as if bound in ice.

Although tap dance is often thought of as mainly percussive, a range of dynamics was used to express romance in Hollywood films of the 1930s. A soft shoe sand dance in *Top Hat* provided a highly romantic scene when Astaire lulled Rogers to sleep, after he had kept everyone in the hotel awake half the night with his over-exuberant tapping.

Table 3.1 The eight basic efforts

Effort	Time	Weight	Space
Punch	sudden	firm	direct
Float	sustained	light	flexible
Flick	sudden	light	flexible
Dab	sudden	light	direct
Press	sustained	firm	direct
Glide	sustained	light	direct
Slash	sudden	firm	flexible
Wring	sustained	firm	flexible

Formal lines, like those of a corps de ballet for example, in Fokine's *Les Sylphides* (1909), are very different from the less regular formations of a dance like Alston's *Wildlife* (1984), where the concern is for the energy of zig-zags and angularity of shape.

Close masses and scattered groups convey contrasting expressions to an audience. Close masses include clusters of loosely arranged dancers, or dancers in compact geometric shapes, such as triangles, wedges, squares and circles. These group formations were used in Task Four from Chapter Two and require the dancers to be sensitive to each others' personal space. Another relationship to try, that could be added to Task Four in Chapter Two, uses a diamond formation and needs dancers to be sensitive to each other in time as well as space – see Task Sixteen.

In the entrance to the Ball in Bourne's *Swan Lake* (1995), a tightly clustered group is used for the press and autograph hunters, whereas the celebrities promenade formally in pairs. Bourne has used the groupings to successfully enhance the drama, story and characterisation here.

Siobhan Davies' characteristic use of dancers makes full use of the stage space; complex scattered groupings of dancers disperse and reform. This can be seem in the manipulation of two trios of dancers in *Plain Song* (1981). The trios work sometimes as self-contained units, or fragment into duets and solos, or unite into a sextet. Dancers strike up new relationships, mixing and matching the dance vocabulary, unpredictably gathering and scattering across the space. Similarly, in her *Bridge the Distance* (1985, for LCDT), relationships come and go and seem to be layered with a subtext of exchange of human emotions.

TASK SIXTEEN – *Birds-of-a-feather, part 2*

KEY SKILLS Problem solving
Communication
Working with others

 20 to 30 minutes

FLOCKING. This task uses movement on the spot in the style of Merce Cunningham's *Beach Birds.* This could include slow, soft flexible torso and arm gestures, downward weighted jumps or other ideas that do not travel.

In groups of four, make a diamond formation. A leader is chosen and faces outside of the diamond. The others face the leader and shadow the leader's movement. The leader decides when to change the leaders by saying the next person's name. Everyone turns to face that dancer and the new leader faces outside the diamond. Each dancer improvises when it is their turn to lead. You could also set this to memory and choose a movement cue to signal the change of leader.

> Eventually this flocking could be set so that it fits into Task Four from Chapter Two. You could use the same music for both tasks. Movement from this task connects with Tasks Five and Twenty from this chapter.

Spaces between the dancers

If the dancers are placed close together, they will create a very different set of feelings in the audience than they will if they are placed far apart. Decentralising the space, by positioning and use of different facings of dancers, is a characteristic of Cunningham work and a similar aspect of the work of Sir Frederick Ashton was noted in the following critique:

> . . . his use of space, especially in his purest dance works, *Symphonic Variations* and *Scènes de Ballet* and *Monotones*, was as unconventional as Merce Cunningham. Of *Scènes de Ballet* he said, 'I . . . wanted to do a ballet that could be seen from any angle – anywhere could be the front, so to speak.'
>
> (David Vaughan in *Dance Now*, Summer 1995)

This is more of an unexpected use of the stage space in the context of classical ballet, which is usually designed for the proscenium stage.

Care must be taken, however, not to allow the dancers to be so far apart that the audience is unable to see the whole group. The most common fault of all is placing one dancer on one side of the stage and the other so far over to the other side that the audience is left looking at a hole in the centre, or moving their heads from side to side as if watching a tennis match without a ball!

The use of contrasting levels, and of the spaces that are created between these levels, is often an effective device. Similarly, if the body shapes of the dancers overlap, the spaces in between can be of as much interest as the overlapping shapes themselves. Using the space between dancers to create dramatic tension or simply to connect one dancer to another is also a possibility worth exploring. This can serve to isolate, to put the dancers in conflict with each other, or it can bring about feelings of harmony or uniformity between the dancers.

Relationships between dancers in time

Unison

Dancers moving in unison may do one of the following:

- the same movement at the same time – total unison;
- similar or complementary movements at the same time – complementary unison;
- contrasting movements at the same time – contrasting unison.

An ultimate form of unison was found in the Busby Berkeley chorus numbers such as the revolving fountain in *Footlight Parade* (1933, Warner Brothers). Berkeley was not a trained choreographer and his talent for unison had grown during his years of teaching military drill in the army. He organised a marching routine, with dancers playing drums and waving flags, in *Gold Diggers of 1937* and a unsion with giant bananas as props in *The Gang's All Here* (1943).

Richard Alston uses unison to visually enrich his dances. In *Java* (1983 for Second Stride and 1985 for Rambert Dance Company), he played with images that are associated with the popular music by 'The Ink Spots', such as from social dance and a backing group in a band. The 12 dancers perform the same movement but in a complementary unison, by each having different facings on the stage.

Merce Cunningham's unisons are often contrasting. This is especially noticeable in the opening of *Beach Birds for Camera*, as is the use of many different facings of the dancers. The dancers must have a very strong and accurate sense of phrasing and timing in order to know their cues if they are unable to see each other.

Canon

The device of canon involves two or more dancers dancing one or more motifs at different times. This places demands on dancers' skill at dancing in groups because it requires sensitive timing with, and an awareness of, others. This may give rise to expressive relationships between dancers, such as leading and following; question and answer; co-operation and confrontation. Thus, the dancers' relationships become organised in time.

There are different types of canons:

- A simple canon will be in strict order. Each dancer dances an entire motif, then keeps still while another dancer takes over. This is the simplest type of canon, and it may be made more interesting by allowing the dancer's timings to overlap so that the dancers are always a few counts behind each other.
- A simultaneous canon involves dancers doing the same motif at the same time but starting from different points in the phrase. So, Dancer 1 may do counts 1 to 8; Dancer 2 may start at count 6, dancing 6-7-8-1-2-3-4-5, and another dancer may start at 4, dancing 4-5-6-7-8-1-2-3; and so on. This creates a dense, coherent and interesting look.
- A cumulative canon is just what it says: it accumulates. Each dancer joins in with the lead dancer at various stages during the dancing of a motif, and they all finish at the same time. This gives a look of an increase in force or power, through an increase in emphasis on the movement.
- Loose canons offer more opportunity for the manipulation of a motif. There may be a use of different levels, facings or placements in the stage space. Adding stillnesses is also effective, as may be varying the dynamic or rhythmic elements.

You may now like to try Task Seventeen.

TASK SEVENTEEN – *Fireworks*

KEY SKILLS Problem solving
Communication
Working with others

 20 to 30 minutes

For this task use either a short phrase you know well from technique class or, when workshopping your own group dance for examination, play with a phrase of your own movement. In threes or fours, try the various canons in the list above. Be as accurate as you can throughout, and use your 'radar' (sense of timing and spacing) with the others sensitively. You could also try to vary the facings to add visual interest, or add exits and entrances. See if you can create a sensational firework display of your movements.

Non-contact and contact – other relationship possibilities

Any of the following have a range of expressive potential for your compositions and are worthy of exploration:

- meeting and parting;
- action/reaction;
- different facings;
- matching/mirroring;
- passing;
- side-by-side;
- alone, together;
- back-to-back (experiment with different facings too);
- conversation;
- lead, follow;
- one behind the other;
- over, under, around and through each other;
- near to and far away from others;
- co-operation, isolation and confrontation.

Using this list to guide you, try Task Eighteen.

When you watch choreography you can see such relationships in a continual shift throughout any one dance. A couple of examples will give you a clearer idea of how they can work.

The closeness of ballroom dancing was exploited to the full in the romantic Hollywood films of the 1940s. It was cleverly developed by Fred Astaire in a number where he admires his leading lady, Joan Leslie (*The Sky's the Limit*, 1943, RKO Radio Pictures). Set in wartime, this was a comedy with a darker undercurrent. The song *My Shining Hour*, eventually a hit number, plays on the

idea of the sorrow of departure to war. Astaire, playing an airman on leave, used the contrast of near and far to express his dilemma of leaving. Leslie and Astaire embrace, but he also distances himself from her as he admires her and contemplates his possible fate.

Robert North's *Troy Game* was an all-male dance and full of athletic movement. Jumps and cartwheels were used as dancers went under and over each other in mini-combat moves as they went through their military training.

Figure 3.15 *Troy Game*. **Photographer:** Anthony Crickmay

TASK EIGHTEEN – *Hello!*

KEY SKILLS Problem solving
Communication
Working with others

45 minutes to an hour

MEET AND GREET – A DUET. You can try out some of the relationships listed above in this fun duet and usually some witty dances can result. Memorise the movement as you go through the process. Read and do one part at a time, gradually building up the composition as you go. This step-by-step process can work when you are composing your own dances too, with your own movement ideas.

- Start facing your partner 10 to 15 steps apart. Walk towards your partner and meet in the middle. On meeting make an everyday greeting gesture, do not tell your partner what your gesture will be, so the gestures may not necessarily match. One of you may wave and the other use the Indian namaste. Walk backwards back to your original place.

■ Repeat the whole again with different gestures. After the gestures, go over and under each other – BE IMAGINATIVE! Walk forwards, back to the other side of the space (swop places).

■ Repeat the whole one last time with different gestures. After the gestures dozy-do around each other. And walk back to your original starting place.

Repeat all three sections until you have memorised the whole. Then:

■ Vary how you travel each time – try different steps, jumps, slides, rolls, travel on hands, vary the direction of the travelling. Change where you go - use all the General Space not just one straight line. Vary the pathway – use zigzags, curves and so forth.

■ Add other actions to the gestures – jumps, other gestures with hips, shoulders, legs, turns, falls, stillnesses. Mix and match each others' gestures. Have some fun with this.!

■ Vary the gestures; timing with your partner, mixing of unison with action/reaction; body part e.g. try waving with your leg as well as the hand; vary your body position – wave while your upsidedown.

■ When you meet you could try and add some simple contact with your partner. Perhaps some social dance too.

Vary anything else that you might like to add. The only constant is the basic three meeting and parting structure.

Practise until it is memorised and share with another couple. After you have watched the other couple, name the relationships that you saw in the dance; comment on what you enjoyed and why you thought certain parts were successful.

Music suggestions: Te Vaka *Alamagoto;* Oi-Va-Oi *Seven Brothers;* Chieftains *Changing Your Demeanour.*

The interest of group shapes, placements and timings is enhanced by using contact between the dancers. There are special skills involved here, as well as a need to build trust between the dancers. A whole technique was created around this concept by Steve Paxton in the 1960s as part of the Judson Church post-modern dance group in New York. Paxton was a gymnast who later studied dance and who combined his experiences to produce a style based on giving and taking weight. Trust between partners, if you decide to fall or lean on them, was the priority. Paxton tried to create a Western type of martial art that did not contain any combat. There was an emphasis on equality of partners, between genders, races and abilities. His technique is now used by many dancers all over the world.

It is worth experimenting in duets and larger groups with simple handholds and counterbalances, feeling exactly how much or how little energy is appropriate to maintain a counterbalance and to lose it. Similarly, other contact

back. . . . Let this movement enlarge until you begin to roll around each other . . . feel the circular movement. . . . As you move, find a couple of stillnesses which are resting points. They are comfortable for both of you. Pause in them before continuing the movement. Try to share supporting and being supported equally.'

2 Dancer No. 1: go on all fours, holding a strong flat back. Dancer No. 2: hang over. . . . Ensure that your centre of gravity is over the supports'. . . . Relax as you hang . . . feel balanced. Breathe, melt down to the floor softly and roll off your partner.'

3 'Stand close to your partner. . . . Slowly melt down to the floor, giving way together in contact all the way. . . . Roll apart and return to standing easily.'

4 'Take a walk together, not allowing your partner to fall. . . . Support your partner all the way down, going down to the floor yourself if it is necessary. . . . Speed this up so that the falls are followed by rapid rebounds, and so that the recoveries are seamless with the falling and walking. When you are more confident, add jumps.'

5 See photos (a), (b), (c) and (d) below for the illustrations to this task. Practise making the five shapes shown in the photographs. Connect them, in any order of your choice, with suitable movement which emphasises contact and loss of the same. Try to make the whole phrase as fluid as possible, but with some clear changes of tempo. Make sure that you share roles equally.

a

Figure 3.17 Brighton and Hove Youth Dance

b

c

d

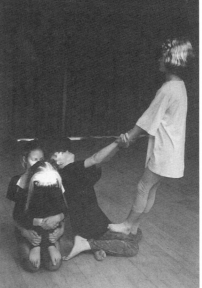

The next three tasks give you a chance to put into action what you have learned in this chapter.

Table 3.2 Characteristic movement features of Merce Cunningham, in *Beach Birds for Camera*

Dancers / Relationship	Action / Body	Spacing	Time / Dynamics
	Overlapping gently moving arms, swaying torsos. Occasional tiny hand gesture	Near to each other – overlapping personal spaces	Sustained/light Gentle/ undulate Occasional flick/dab of hand
• 11 dancers	• Stillness – standing in small parallel	• Varied facings, scattered around the space	
• Soloist 1(F)	• Flexible torso sways to side and bends forward from hips. Arm gestures	• U. St. / centre. Facing windows	
• Soloist 2(F)	• Turns out: Flexible torso tilts to side; one elbow flexed and high to side, other arm straight on a downward diagonal to the side of the body Steps to second position – turn	• D. St. R.	• Sudden
• Others join in gradually	• Steps sideways Torso curling forward. 1 flexed 1 extended arm – sideways torso tilted Flexible torso bends forward from hips and sways to side.		
• Soloist 3(F)	• 2 steps forward, low circular leg gesture, 2 steps forward, close, shoulder flexes forward, torso and shoulder rotate. Repeats a similar phrase but with a turn added	• Travel on diagonal	• Light, successive energy through body parts. Soloist 3(F) 2:2 jump is softer and higher than her partner's
• In background – duet (M) gradually develops (M)	5 one foot to other jumps on spot, legs lifting to back in the air – arms moving back and forth. A second female joins in	• U. St. R.	

Dancers / Relationship	Action / Body	Spacing	Time / Dynamics
	with one 2:2 jump • Steps for men + rib isolations + turns + plié and relevé into turning jumps	• Focus down	
• Trio begins – others perform	• Stepping turn		
• Soloist 3(F)'s jump Soloist 3(F) duet	• Torso curves + stepping turns	• St. L. (F)	• Sustained
• Duet (M)	• Duet into long stillness facing each other Travelling + hops in parallel arabesque, arms by sides	• Focus away from each other D. St. L. • St. R. (M)	• Heavier / increase tempo
• Duets & Trio in contact • 3 dancers (1M / 2F)	• Lifts & supported turns leading to 'rests'/stillnesses • Man shifts ribs side-side in contact with woman – she repeats forward/ backward leg gesture **'Nesting'**– man lowers to knees and ribs shift back/forward, arms bent close to body		• Heavier / increase tempo • Gentle
• All dancers finish in duos or trios	Women in open 4th position lower slowly, torso rotating and shifting side-side Man continues into duet, repeated leg gestures, turns and stillness in relevé with contact of arms	• Finish St. Rt.	
• **9 mins**	• All use cont.act, some counterbalance/stilllness • Trio 3 x 2 foot. to 2 foot jumps, travel diagonal D.St	• Heavy	

Now it's your turn: Complete the following for the next section of the dance:

1 A solo male dancer enters running (stage right) and t _ _ _ _ _ s on the diagonal through the other dancers. He uses three, two foot to t _ _ f _ _ _ j _ _ _s as he does quarter turns and his t_ _ _ _ extends upward and c _ _v_ _ forward. He steps twice, closes and performs a series of ge _ _ _ _ _ _ : a head circle, a shoulder r _ _ _ _ _ _ _, an arm extends to the side, a bent leg lifts forward, upper torso contracts su _ _ _ _ _ y, the torso slowly rotates left. He repeats this p _ _ _ _ _. His solo also repeats the gestures faster and adds on quick steps setting the other dancers off into a trembling leg gesture phrase. But one male dancer dances solo, using bent arms ('folded wings') that ex_ _ _ _ like unfolding wings. He has a jumping phrase using, two to one footed jumps, h _ _ _ and l _ _ _ _ as a duet develops. Other dancers travel, jump and turn. He ends kneeling on a low l _ _ _ _ near the camera, his torso curved forward and arms in a wide curved second. One female dancer raises a leg forwards and gestures with a vi _ _ _ t _ _ _ quality. The trio in the background are holding a prolonged s _ _ _ _ _ _ _ _. The female dancers introduce an arm gesture that makes a curving air p _ _ _ _ _ _ across their bodies, as they walk. The other females join in with the quivering leg gesture. They surround a male soloist. He is in a low level lunge and all the other dancers take the same facing - unison of the trembling leg gesture.

2 A canon breaks the unison. The phrase is:
- sudden arm gestures – in directions f_ _ _ _ _ _ _ _, s _ _ _ _ _ _ _, b_ _ _ _ _ _ _ _
- drop to lunge and lift to wide fourth on diagonal (sudden) – pause
- arm gestures (describe)_____
- upper torso rotates and drop in wide fourth to (describe) _
- 'folded wings' dropped and in standing, upper torso rotates
- upper torso curves forward (in *relevé*) to low *arabesque* – back leg gesture quivers
- 2 steps forward, 2 direct arm gestures to second position – low *arabesque*

3 The dancers perform a contrasting u _ _ _ _ _ mixing several motifs seen earlier. Men travel with steps and hops and direct sudden arm gestures (describe) ....
- Women echo this, but with a s_ _ _ _ _ dynamic, and in a smaller s_ _ _ _. The travelling takes four males to the back, and they use heavy dropping leaps. They help the male soloist up to his feet and then travel to make an inward facing circle f _ _ _ _ _ _ _ _ - curving torsos and arms that overlap to make contact on a m _ _ _ _ _ to low level. Two female dancers take turns to run into the circle; they use a flexible torso to go under and o _ _ _ the men's arms, before leaving the circle. One female travels in a backwards direction and the other forwards to leave the circle. The males dance in unison a phrase that consists of:

- arms...(complete)
- step hops .... (complete)
- hop backwards, leg gesture through to back, drop.

A male duet repeats this phrase, whilst the other two hold stillness. All four men dance heavy, dropping leaps, travelling until the women (in stillness) surround the men. Women repeat the. .... Men – circular leg gesture, rise with upper torso curved forward, full *plié* on *demi pointe*, then with skittering steps, drops and turns they travel on the diagonal towards the camera and exit, downstage.

Relationships between dancers have many possibilities for choreographers to choose from. Another range of expressive possibilities arises when considering the relationships of dancers to set, costumes and props. These will be explored in the next chapter.

Movement components – conclusion

The tasks in this chapter have given ample opportunities to use a variety of stimuli as starting points for improvisation, composition and analysis. These ideas can be carried over into your own work – just adapt them to suit and use them as part of your creative work.

TASK TWENTY-ONE

KEY SKILLS Improving own learning and performance

You could do this task at the start of every term as part of an ongoing self-improvement programme.

- From the list on page 162, choose three areas that you need to improve on. You may need to consult your teacher to identify them.

Always try to describe your strategy for improvements and the progress in anatomical detail. Again you may need to consult your teacher or a friend to help you monitor changes. You should evaluate how effective your programme is.

Area targeted for improvement	Strategy	Needs improvement	Working towards	Achieved
Example: Control of falling	– Ask teacher to help me find a programme of falling which will help me improve my confidence and skill level.	✓ 2nd Sept. I am very unsure of myself when I fall. I know that there are skills to work on. My teacher suggests that I try to build from falling in a half-sit position and gradually build up to standing. I think I'll use a mat at first!	✓ Sept 9 After class I have been spending 15 mins experimenting with loss of balance sideways from a half sit. Now I feel able to transfer weight smoothly, safely and sequentially to lying on my side.	✓ 2nd Oct. I can do a controlled fall (pretty good one actually!) and from one leg on the ball my foot. Like this:
Copy this table into your own portfolio. Select and enter three target areas.				
Travelling – target/name different steps and combinations . . .				
Jumping – safe practice . . .				
Control of stillness . . .			✓ Sept. 16. I can now all safely and confidently from a high kneel sideways. No mat!	Now I'm going to set a new target of falling backwards and forwards which seem to be more difficult in co-ordinating the various body parts
Co-ordination of gestures?.			✓ Sept. 23. Today I experimented with feeling loss of balance from standing. I can feel my centre of gravity shifting ideways and the point when gravity takes over. If I use a stretch away from the pull I find that I can control a smooth fall to lying on my side.	
Control of turning . . . Spatial clarity . . .				
Dynamic range . . .				
Control of time/tempo . . .				
Phrasing . . .				

References and resources

Books and articles

Brown, C., *Chance and Circumstance: Twenty Years with Cage and Cunningham*, New York: Alfred A. Knopf, 2007

Copeland, R., *The Modernising of Modern Dance*, New York: Routledge, 2004

Hayes C. in *New Dance*, no. 42. October 1987

Humphrey, D., *The Art of Making Dances*, New Jersey: Princeton Book Co., 1959

Jordan S., *Striding Out*, London: Dance Books, 1992

Klosty, J. (ed.), *Merce Cunningham*, Clarke, USA: Irwin & Co. Ltd, 1975

Mackrell, J., 'Cholmondeleyism', in *Dance Theatre Journal*, vol. 4, no. 2, 1986

Morgenroth, J., *Speaking of Dance: Twelve Contemporary Choreographers on their Craft*, New York: Routledge, 2004

Nugent A., *The Stage*, 30 November 1989

Reynolds, D., *Rhythmic Subjects: Uses of Energy in the Dances of Mary Wigman, Martha Graham and Merce Cunningham*, Hants: Dance Books, 2007

Robertson, A. and Hutera, D., *The Dance Handbook*, Harlow: Longman, 1988

Roseman, J.L., *Dance Masters: Interviews with Legends of Dance*, New York: Routledge, 2001

Siegel, M., *The Shapes of Change: images of American Dance*, Berkley, University of California, 1985

Video, DVD, CD-Rom

From www.dancebooks.co.uk

Bourne, M., *Swan Lake*

DV8 Physical Theatre, *Strange Fish* and *Dead Dreams of Monochrome Men*,

Merce Cunningham Dance Company, *Beach Birds for Camera*, *Changing Steps* and *Deli Commedia*.

Merce Cunningham: Fifty Years forward 'from Ocean to Ocean', David Vaughan, 2005. CD-ROM

From National Resource Centre for Dance, www.surrey.ac.uk

Alston, R ., *Soda Lake*, 1981

Rushes, Siobhan Davies, 1982. Presenter. Stephanie Jordan

Motionhouse, *Different Dancers, Similar Motion*, 1989, and *The House of Bones*, 1991

From www.kulturvideo.com

Dancing: Volume 3, Sex and Social Dance. Producer Rhoda Grauer. Thirteen/WNET in association with RM Arts and BBC-TV

Websites

■ Companies

Adventures in Motion Pictures www.amp.uk.com

DV8 www.dv8.co.uk

www.thecholmondeleys.org

Wim Vandekeybus www.ultimavez.com

■ General information

www.ballet.co.uk

At the time of going to print several clips of Pina Bausch, Merce Cunningham's works, including *Beach Birds for Camera*, and *Shakalaka Baby* from *Bombay Dreams*, featured on Youtube.

Music

The following have lots of tracks between 2 and 3 minutes long and others suitable for workshopping ideas:

Arnold, M., *English and Irish Dances*, Polygram 425 661 2LM, 1990 – Task Four

Awards for World Music, BBC Radio 3, MANTDCD215, 2003 – Tasks Three, Four, Six & Eighteen

The Chieftains, *The Chieftains Special Guest Collection*, BMG 74321 717402, 1999 – Tasks Four, Eighteen

Cosma, V., *Diva* (film soundtrack), DRG Discovery Label, CD950622 – Task Fourteen

DANCE! – UCA recording, UCA45-2, 2003 available from www.ucamusic. com – Task Twenty. This Cd has 14 tracks highly suited to student composition and improvisation.

Duskis, R., *Arabian Travels,* Six Degrees records, 657036 1957 2, 2001 –Task Three

Easton, M. *Orchestral Works*, Naxos, 8.554368, 1997 – Task Six

Goldenhorse, *Reporter,* Siren EMI 5102382 CDSRN9003 – Task Three

House of Pain, Tommy Boy Music Inc, 16998110562, 1992 – Task Five

Kronos Quartet, *White Man Sleeps,* Elektra, Nonesuch 7559 79163 2, 1987 – Task Three

Kronos Quartet *Released* (as for Chapter 2) – Task Five

Martin, D. *Forever Cool,* EMI, 509995 03452 2 9, 2007 – Task Three

Oldfield, T., *Spirit of the Rainforest*, New World, NWC 195 – Task Twenty

Penguin Café Orchestra, *Broadcasting From Home*, EGEDC38, 1984 – Task Seven

Tomita, I., *Pictures at an Exhibition*, by Moussorgsky (electronic version), RCA ARL1-0838, 1975 – Task Seven

Serra E., *The Big Blue*, soundtrack to the film The Big Blue, Gaumont/Virgin CDV 2541, 1988 – Task Twelve

Superfunk, the funkiest album in the world ever!, Virgin VTDCD30/ 724384000028, 1994 – Task Five

The Best Duets Album in the World . . . Ever! EMI 50999 5143462 5, 2007 – Task Four

The Traveling Wilburys, Warner, Rhino 8122799824 – Task Three

THE CONSTITUENT FEATURES OF DANCE: THE PHYSICAL SETTING

The movement is a main consideration, but of course the complete picture also includes the choices of:

- the performing space or venue;
- the set;
- lighting;
- costume;
- props.

These will be the focus of this chapter.

The performing space

The type of space that a dance is performed in will affect the design of the choreography. The dancers themselves will also need to relate to the environment in which they are dancing. With both the dance and the dancers actively relating to the performing space, the audience should have a clear view of the performance in all its aspects. The following quotation makes this clear.

My first piece *Tank Dive*, was made for a small room . . . that is actually a little auditorium . . . and the whole piece is predicated for that space; I mean one of the walls was curved, so a lot of patterns had to do with that. It has very much to do with site lines.

(Twyla Tharp in *The Dance Makers*, 1980)

Dance has been performed in different countries and in many different types of venues over the years – Indian temples, morris dance on village greens, African dance in village meeting places, tango in Argentinian streets, American Street dance battles – all dancing for different purposes. Nowadays, Western audiences usually expect to see dance on a stage, such as the musical theatre performances in the London's West End or in New York's Broadway theatres, but choreographers work in many different types of venue. Dances can even be seen in enormous spaces, such as in Lea Anderson's *Sportorama* (1999). The site for this dance was the huge arena at Crystal Palace, with both her companies The

Cholmondeleys and The Featherstonehaughs plus 160 other performers. The audience sat along one long side of the hall and watched epic size scenes. A variety of group formations portrayed different sports. On occasion, the performers moved among the audience. In the post-modern era, dancing in airports, tunnels, art galleries, museums and gymnasiums, rooftops and beaches, have all been considered to be suitable for performance.

The proscenium stage

When you go to the theatre, the picture-frame proscenium stage is the traditional set-up. This is the one most often used for classical ballet, and it offers rich possibilities for showing things clearly if it is used correctly.

The historical context

In the fifteenth century, Italians staged lavish indoor spectacles. Theatres dating back to 1580 can be found in Italy. These were fairly open so that the performers, often courtiers, could move easily from the auditorium to the stage. Sometimes, the audience would perform too.

The placement of dancers

Placing and moving dancers around on such stages must take into consideration the fact that different areas have differing degrees of power. Dancers placed upstage will appear distant (in space and time) for the audience, whereas downstage has a feel of more intimacy, and can be used for comic effect. The stage is divided into four named areas as shown in Figure 4.1.

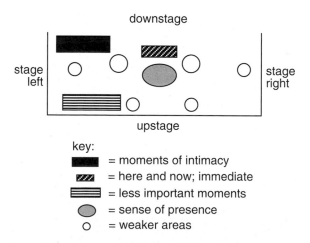

Figure 4.1 To show stage areas and their possible uses

As a dancer, it is helpful if you know and use these terms when working on theatre stages. Also, the presence of the wings of a stage is a rich part of choreography – entrances and exits. Dancers must ensure that they dance with full energy whenever the audience can see them and avoid loitering within the audience sight lines. On proscenium stages, where the side curtains or flats

(scenery) are not in use, dancers waiting in the wings need to be specially sensitive to being quiet and calm so as not to distract the audience. Concentrating on the dancing on stage as you wait, helps to direct the audience's attention onto the important action and away from you.

Matthew Bourne uses the up and downstage areas to great dramatic effect in *Swan Lake* (1995). The Prince, after writing his suicide note, makes his way upstage and contemplates the lake from the very back centre of the stage. It is as if he is about to become a part of the past. In contrast, comic moments, like the walking of the Royal Corgi dog and the hilarious perfumed ballet interlude, are all performed at the very front of the stage.

At the start of Richard Alston's *Java* (1983), the stage placement of two lines, each with three female dancers, enriches the unsion. The lines are positioned on an up/down stage line and dancers' movements mirror a partner in the other line. However, the mirroring relationship is not easy to see at first, because the pairs are not simply opposite each other in the line. Dancer One at the front of the stage left line, mirrors the dancer at the back of the stage right line and so on for the others in the line. The final effect of the unison is that they seemed *not* to be dancing the same movements, and so this clever combination of placement of dancers and relationship avoids a usual predictable unsion look. A choreographic surprise can be most rewarding and enjoyable for the audience. As with Alston, if you know the craft of the stage space and understand how to manipulate movement you can apply the theory in making dance compositions of your own and delight your audiences with surprises.

Figure 4.2 To show a stage from Florence

The movement of dancers on pathways in the stage space

Similarly, the diagonals on the stage are very powerful. According to Doris Humphrey, if a figure walks down from upstage right to downstage left, this action:

> . . . will clothe this figure with heroic strength, all made merely by the use of architecture of stage space.
>
> (Doris Humphrey in *The Art of Making Dances*, 1959)

On this pathway, the dancer will pass through weaker and more powerful points of the stage space – not least of which is centre-stage, where the presence will be at its strongest. Approaching downstage, the dancer will then become more human, someone we care about. This device is used in *Giselle* (1841, Coralli, Perrot) when Hilarion is being thrown into the lake by the wilis. Starting downstage left, bottom corner, Myrtha, Queen of the wilis, seals his fate by ordering him to his watery grave, the lake. He is propelled along the line of the corps de ballet stretching the whole length of the diagonal to the far upstage right corner. The other dancers seem almost invisible, their fine arm gestures, so effortless, stirring the air as he is blown along. Then, he finally exits. Gone from the human world, he is now forever in the distance of time and space, in the immortal world.

There are always exceptions to the rules, however, and choreographer Merce Cunningham, although acknowledging the stage space as such, chooses to ignore the above considerations. He makes it the responsibility of the audience to decide what to select to watch in dances that scatter over the space like leaves blown by the wind. There is no central focus of power. This is particularly noticeable in his dance *Tread* (1970). The electric fans, designed by Bruce Nauman, are regularly spaced across the front of downstage, causing not only an interruption in the audience's sight lines but also a breeze in the first few rows. This puts the viewer in a situation where, as in real life on the street, you must make choices as to what to watch and when. You could focus on the entire stage, or on just one small area between two fans, or on Cunningham's interrupted journey across the stage. It is almost as though the picture frame has gone and the stage is filled with dancers in any number of places, all of equal importance. Cunningham's attitude to space is similar to that of American modern painters of the 1960s and 1970s, like Jackson Pollock whose technique of dripping paint randomly onto canvas gave the effect of a continuous flow through the space.

> Cunningham inherited a stage space . . . a formula of perspective unchanged since the Renaissance. As a result, stage space implied a class society in which centre stage was regal. . . . The sides, the back and corners? Strictly plebeian, home of the brave corps. . . . There is no best

spot on a Cunningham stage. . . . The stage is not merely decentralised, it is demagnetised.

(James Klosty in *Merce Cunningham*, 1975)

When working in venues with an audience on two, three or four sides, Cunningham would give different dancers different fronts. This would create more of a three-dimensional look – one well suited to the next physical setting which we are looking at.

Figure 4.3 *Ocean*, Merce Cunningham Dance Company, 2006
Photographer: Hugo Glendenning

In-the-round: the circular stage

The 'in-the-round' physical setting, which dates back to the ancient Greek chorus set-up, and to circles in ritual dances, alters our whole attitude to – and concept of – design, and even nowadays it is difficult for some to make the adjustment to the circular setting. Consideration must be given to spatial design in the choreography, particularly in the placing and facings of the dancers. This, as just mentioned, would pose little problem for a Cunningham choreography – unlike for most ballet and modern dance works, which may have been framed for the proscenium stage.

Obviously, circle patterns and circular group shapes will work well, and this makes for many possibilities: to face the centre and give a feel of a magical magnetic centre; to spiral around to and from the centre, like the Snail formation in a mediaeval *Carole* (line dance); to place the dancers' backs to the centre and acknowledge the outside space; to proceed around the edge of the circle in a ritualistic manner; to crisscross the circle with other geometric

formations like triangles, squares, lines or less formal clusters of dancers. Acknowledging the power of the circle can lead to much choreographic interest. Using it in an uninformed way, however, may lead to a drab design which does not allow the audience 'in', either because it comes over as two-dimensional or because too much use is made of inward/centre facings. (It is interesting to observe how young children's or beginners' first attempts at choreography often involve working in an inwards-facing circle. All that the audience can then see are their backs, obscuring any interesting movement which may be happening.)

In Robert North's *Troy Game* (1974), the circle is used to emphasise the amusing atmosphere of sparring and competition between soldiers. The group travel around the circle in a motif which allows them to acknowledge the audience, the centre of the circle and each other. It has an alive, three-dimensional quality. By manipulating the turns and the timing, they rotate and try to catch each other out by a sweeping leg gesture, rather like a football tackle to the opponent's lower leg. Each soldier jumps over this tackle just in time. Thus, the circle continues to 'hypnotise' and to amuse the audience simultaneously.

TASK ONE – *Round-a-bout*

KEY SKILLS Problem solving
Working with others

🕐 10 to 20 minutes or several hours

In groups of six or eight, work together to compose a dance entitled 'Black holes, shooting stars, the planets and their spinning moons'. Choreograph it with a view to performing it in-the-round. (Suggested music: *Space to Dream*, Radha Sahar from DANCE!)

Other stages

As well as the performing settings mentioned above, there are others which also require consideration about the placings and spacings of dancers in choreography. Although similar to the proscenium stage or in-the-round, they each have their own individual characteristics:

- end stage: there is no frame or arch, and the stage and the auditorium continue into each other;
- apron stage: part of the stage projects into the audience.

In any of these settings, where the audience is seated – in terms of above or below the stage – will affect what they see. If they are lower than the stage, then the front vertical lines will be emphasised. Meanwhile, the movement in the horizontal plane, the floor pattern and the formation will be stressed if the audience is seated above the stage.

The site-specific performance space

We may think that dance performances out-of-doors are something quite avant-garde and post-modern, but before the courts of Europe introduced the proscenium stage they held spectacles of quite a different type: the wealthy Italian aristocracy of the High Renaissance held spectacular pageants out of doors as well as inside the palaces. Centuries later in the 1960s, dancers and choreographers returned to outside settings as an alternative to the theatres. They also looked for alternative indoor venues in which to present dances which used their environment as a rich source of stimulus for the imagination. And nowadays, dances are performed anywhere and everywhere.

In North America in the 1960s, many artists experimented with these more informal settings, both indoors and out. One such artist was Anna Halprin. Halprin was a member of the Judson Group, New York (started 1962), where dancers worked as a cooperative. This influenced UK dancers later in 1976 when X6 was set up in London.

We don't accept the theatre as a conventional place where the audience is here and you're there, but it is a place. . . . You don't have to be on the stage separating here from there. . . . Everything we do is dance somehow. . .

(Anna Halprin in *The Vision of Modern Dance*, 1980)

A radical approach to choice of physical setting from the early American post-modern dance movement, was *Walking on the Wall* (1971) by Trisha Brown. Dancers in harnesses walked down the walls of buildings. The audience stood below looking up at the wall, but the illusion was that they seemed to be looking down of the tops of the heads of the performers. The performance was a simple act of defying gravity, and all the rigging was in clear view making up, along with the buildings, the set for the dance.

This approach was extreme, but effective in arranging the spatial relationship not only of dancer to dancer, but also of dance to physical setting (i.e. the walls of the Whitney Museum), and of audience to dance. As Sally Banes describes it, the whole orientation of the audience was turned upside down, sideways, every which way:

. . . one has the distinct sensation that one is on a tall building, watching people walking back and forth on the sidewalk below. When they turn the corner on the walls, suddenly one feels as though one were positioned sideways, sticking one's head out of a window, perhaps, and seeing a sideways image of an upright person below.

(Sally Banes, in *Terpsichore in Sneakers*, 1980)

The British choreographers Lea Anderson and Rosemary Butcher typify the attitude of choosing unconventional performing spaces. Butcher had trained in

both Graham and Humphrey techniques, but became involved with post-modern dance as one of, if not the, earliest British dancer to study dance in New York in 1970. By this time post-modern dance had been developing in the USA for nearly ten years and dance was regularly using site-specific performance spaces both indoors and out.

These more informal environments pose very different problems for choreographers. As Rosemary Butcher became aware, in her out-of-doors work, the dance can tend to get lost in the surrounding architecture, or amongst passers-by. For this reason, she later used the perspectives and distances of specific sites to her advantage. In *Passage North East* (1976), Butcher first placed the dancers in the distance: on the far side of the harbour to the Arnolfini Gallery, Bristol. Then, they crossed by boat to end up dancing to the audience in front of the gallery.

Such informal indoor and outdoor settings offer different ways for the audience to relate to the choreography. X6, the dance collective offered dancers a chance to work with 'alternative' post-modern dance ideas. Choreographers like Madée Duprés experimented with how she could build a relationship with the audience in these settings. Breaking down the boundaries between the audience and the performers Duprés invited the onlookers to comment or even to take part sometimes. In *Choice and Presence* (1977), they were invited to make noises of their own choice when she raised a foot. Thus, the audience was involved not just visually, but also audibly and sometimes physically. They would also raise and lower blinds as she improvised the dance. Clearly, this way of choreographing is not concerned with the rules and sight lines of the picture-frame proscenium stage!

In 1996, the Dance Umbrella Festival staged its first site-specific work. Set in the Natural History Museum main hall, *Genesis Canyon* by Stephan Koplowitz used 38 dancers and three singers. It emphasised the Festival director's belief about site-specific work:

. . . it offers the possibility of erasing the belief that dance is for a selected few who have been educated to understand it.

(Val Bourne in *Barefoot in Jurassic Park* by Allen Robertson, *The Times*, 25 September 1996)

Sometimes the audience are inadvertently involved, as in Lea Anderson's *Out on the Windy Beach* (1998).

Perhaps the man who ambled drunkenly up to the raised stage at Brighton's Hove Lawns thought he was suffering from a particularly bad bout of delirium tremens when he saw six fluorescent creatures . . . Staff diverted him away, but for a few brief moments he had shown signs of adding welcome spark to Lea Anderson's new alfresco show.

(Nadine Meisner in *The Sunday Times*, 31 May 1998)

Figure 4.4 Site-specific dance in the Natural History Museum, London, Dance Umbrella 1996 Stephan Koplowitz's 'Genesis Canyon'
Photographer Chris Nash

Figure 4.5 To show outdoor spectacles of the Renaissance, Alcina's Island, 1664, in the grounds of the Palace of Versailles. It uses the lake as part of the set. The island in the centre back was burnt in a huge firework display. The wings are supported by guy ropes.

Architect Mark Foley, who has collaborated with choreographers in designing dance venues, thinks that dance is a unique way for architects to experience space. More and more choreographers are relating their work to architecture. Shobana Jeyasingh thinks that dance and architecture both 'sculpt space'. Her classical South Indian dance vocabulary can be seen as fluid geometry. Task Two gives you a site-specific dance experience.

TASK TWO – *Site-specific*

KEY SKILLS Problem solving

🕐 10 to 20 minutes or several hours

The photos show how an outdoor setting can stimulate ideas for dance.

Figure 4.6
Ashmead school pupil in Greenwich foot tunnel.
Dance Captures: an East London Dance and Laban project.
Photo: Hugo Glendinning.

Find a local site that interests you or walk around your campus and find a place you feel that you could dance in. Spend some time there, and discover what parts of it draw your attention – a space between the buildings, a tree, a staircase, a bench . . . Watch, and listen. What type of people use this space? Do they leave certain energies behind them that may add atmosphere to your dance?

Gradually add things to this place – in movement, or in objects, costume etc. – that make clearer the special qualities of the place. They might echo the buildings, shapes, light, sound, memories evoked. Develop movements which draw attention to your

Figure 4.7 Children on skate ramps
Dance Captures: an East London Dance and Laban project. **Photo:**Hugo Glendinning.

Figure 4.8 Children jumping in front of pylons. Latham School for *East London Dance*
Dance Captures: an East London Dance and Laban project. **Photo:**Hugo Glendinning.

discoveries about this place. What is special about it? Is it dangerous? Is it fun? Is it busy or calm? It is a place for travelling or waiting? What makes it different?

Any basic physical setting may be transformed by whatever a choreographer may choose to place in it. This will be the next aspect of the physical setting to be considered.

The set

In the outdoor environment, of course, 'set' is often already present and the choreographer may choose merely to add to it. On the stage, however, the choice of set is individual to each dance and to each choreographer, and involves anything from leaving the stage plain and bare to covering it with plastic carnations or dead leaves as Pina Bausch did in *Carnations* (1982) and *Bluebeard* (1977). (The trampling of the flowers under the dancers' feet is Bausch's way of telling us that people often crush each other in their relationships; and the dead leaves similarly remind us of a couple whose romance is gradually fading.)

The history of ballet shows how sets gradually evolved alongside the development of technique and choreography.

The historical context

By the sixteenth century, the set began to become important. The theories of Roman architect Vitruvius were revived, and three types of stage set emerged:

1 scena tragica, showing objects suited to monarchs;
2 scena comica, showing ordinary houses;
3 scena satyrica, showing pastoral scenes.

These would underline the messages which the entertainments contained. This is particularly clear to us when we notice the use of complex machinery to make gods and heroes appear from the heavens. Note that at the time of the Renaissance, amazing the audience was the stamp of authority of the ruling families. It would function to enforce their power over others. It was also an acceptance of Aristotle's belief that theatre existed to release the emotions. As the sixteenth century progressed, backdrops became interchangeable through a variety of ingenious devices. The use of perspective to add to the illusion gave events like *Le Ballet Comique de la Reine* (1581) a focal point in the auditorium – which is where the royals would sit, centre front row. This has influenced the design of proscenium stages in theatres ever since.

By the seventeenth century, wings had also been invented. The proscenium became properly established, and a splendour of machinery, colour, light and dance exploded into action.

In the eighteenth century, luxurious Italian and French spectacles were set against meticulously painted backdrops of staggering architectural realism. These larger-than-life sets marked the pinnacle of neoclassical theatre dance in the late eighteenth century and early nineteenth centuries. Respect for order, antiquity, heroism and nobility were the characteristics of theatre design, particularly in Italy. People like Sanquirico designed sets with perspectives painted with mathematical precision, giving an ordered appearance. The French Rococo design was particularly outstanding at this time, and there was also a growing taste for the exoticism of China and the East – as seen in *Les Fêtes Chinoises* (1754) by Jean-Georges Noverre in Paris. This fashion was combined with a move away from seventeenth-century formality in favour of a more natural look. This was in the context of a growing curiosity about freedom of expression both in society and in the other arts generally.

The rebellion against the cold logic of neoclassicism, which itself was a reaction against the more frivolous Rococo style, finally resulted in the great era of romanticism in society and all the arts. Revolution in *society* was a main influence here. The French Revolution was about to explode, and with it the ordinary people were to become leading lights in society, replacing the European aristocracy in the bid for power. As such, they became part of the romantic backdrop from which writers, musicians and painters could choose elements when telling stories.

Ballet was a late arrival to the romantic movement. The writings of Victor Hugo and others began to influence ballet. The breakthrough came with *La Sylphide* (1832). With Marie Taglioni in the lead role and designs by Ciceri, an atmosphere of magical moonlit forest glades and floating sylphs was created. In the nineteenth century, the painted backdrop of the romantic ballet – with its realistic trees and even *real* plants, and its mirrors placed to look like lakes, as in the original *Giselle* (1841) – became the new fashion.

The decline of this burst of freedom of expression, in the middle and the end of the nineteenth century, affected the design of sets as well as the standard of dancing and choreography. Set designs now became largely mindless and decorative, with little meaning or originality. One outstanding exception to this was the Shishkov design for Petipa's *The Sleeping Beauty* (The Imperial Ballet, 1890). He used a theme of the grand reign of Louis XIV as a clear homage to the theatre's patron, the Russian Tsar. The design enhanced the brilliance of the ballet itself. It contrasted two historical styles: an architectural backdrop with vistas of sixteenth-century, Versailles-type magnificence (Act 1), and the eighteenth-century, Baroque-style triple arch (Act 2), where Petipa placed the god Apollo, in Louis XIV-style costume. Only in Russia were standards upheld, and even there tradition was becoming stale. However, it was from here that ballet was to be reborn in glittering glory, like the phoenix rising from the flames, when a rich Russian patron of the arts, Sava Mamontov, commissioned painters to design sets for his private operas. From this, Sergei E. Diaghilev (1827–1929) was inspired by the painters Bakst and Benois and he found the Ballets Russes in 1909, which became a hot bed of innovation. The closeness of designer, composer and choreographer, insisted on by Diaghilev, led to explorations into creative new ideas and ideals for all aspects of the ballet. Diaghilev employed names like Picasso (*Parade*, 1917) and Tchelitchev (*Ode*, 1928) – the avant garde of European painters. Thus, ballet began to look forward once more.

During World War One Europe was in turmoil and in this context the Ballets Russes took on the break with the past, as did cubism in painting and

discord in the new music of such composers as Stravinsky and Satie. It was a meeting point and a melting pot for ideas which struck out in new directions. Consequently, stage design took on many different functions and identities: the humorous novelty of moving skyscrapers in the cubist *Parade* (Massine), where costumes became so extreme that it was difficult not to see them as sets rather than as dancers' clothes. In Massine's *Ode*, the revolutionary use of phosphorescent costumes, neon lighting, puppets and film to tell the story of eighteenth-century Russian court spectacles and revels was astonishing to audiences of that time. The Ballets Russes, from its Monte Carlo theatre, was reaching new heights of innovation. Diaghilev brought in the new wave of French artists such as artist Jean Cocteau and designer Coco Chanel. In Russia the new politics of communism interested Diaghilev. Along with this went artistic developments like constructivism. This movement was influenced by cubism, but focused on making constructions which explored space and form for their own sake. The famous constructivist Gabo designed the set for *La Chatte* (1927, Balanchine). The transparent mica sculptures on a black floor and backdrop were uniquely original in that time. Bakst's design for Fokine's *La Spectre de la Rose* (1911) provided a Grecian setting and included an open window which provided the exit point for dancer Nijinsky. With one last leap he left the stage – in the audience's last view of him, he was still in the air.

Figure 4.9 ca. 1954, USA. American dancer Martha Graham performs with her company in *Appalachian Spring*.

Simplicity and paring things down to their very basics was one of the innovations of the hard-hitting modern dance works of Martha Graham in the 1920s and 1930s. Talking about the difference between traditional painted backdrops and modern dance decors, she says:

... basically a painting enlarged for the stage ... at best can only be an accent for the dance. ... Dance decor can ... serve as a means of enhancing movement and gesture to the point of revelation of its content.
(Martha Graham in *The Vision of Modern Dance*, 1980)

Critic Nicholas Dromgoole described Graham's sets as marvellously economical and how they were as important to the choreography as the dancers. In her collaborations with the Japanese sculptor Isamu Noguchi, in dances such as *Frontier* (1935), the set became integrated into the choreography and served to enhance the meanings in the movements. In *Frontier*, a six-minute solo, Graham appears as a young woman living in the wild western lands of the USA. The set is a section of a fence, from which two large ropes fly out and upwards like the railway track disappearing into the vast open spaces which surround her home. The dance is about the North American pioneering spirit on one level, but it also touches on how the space makes the woman feel. She marks out a square pattern on the floor – almost like the fence bordering a ranch – using tiny steps.

In the American film industry, wartime and the Depression were fuelling quite a different look for dance. Hollywood filmmakers were producing luxury sets. Designer Irene Scharaff used a mix of black and white and colour to produce a visually stunning set for 'Coffee Time' in the film *Yolande and the Thief* (1945, MGM). The floor's black and white wavy pattern set off the brightly coloured costumes of a spinning chorus of dancers, to produce a fantasy with an edgy surreal quality. Films of this era were shot on the 'lot' with specially built sets. It was producer Arthur Freed who first filmed on outdoor location for the film *On the Town* (1949). Filmed in New York City, the film starred Gene Kelly.

The present day

World War Two ended in 1945. It had restricted dance and theatre greatly. Once over, companies such as The Royal Ballet were back in business and the traditional classics were restaged, often retaining the traditional grand style. The reopening of The Royal Opera House, Covent Garden in 1946 was marked by a new production of *The Sleeping Beauty*. Olive Messel's set designs for the Sergeyev version showed off the elegance of the Petipa ballet. They were the essence of fairy tale enchantment, and much needed in the depressed times. Still highly regarded today, the set design may be seen to have influenced later versions.

Stage and costume design by Jean-Denis Maclés for Ashton's *Cinderella* (1948), retained this romantic look with the palace as the perfect ballroom setting. Ashton's later collaboration with designer, Lila de Nobili, for *Ondine* (1958) had more of a sense of realism, in that they set out to evoke the motion of the sea. This is especially dramatic in the second act when a harbour setting

is moved off stage and replaced by a seascape, in order to give the illusion of a ship setting out to sea. Later in the ballet, the scenery was moved up and down and green silks used to depict waves breaking against the ship's hull. The shipwreck scene used the set most dramatically, and was unusual for ballet at that time in England, the ship's masts came crashing down on stage to put the boat in peril.

From this point onwards, a rich variety of set designs opened up. The Ballet Rambert, with new director Norman Norrice, started to include contemporary dance in their classical ballet repertoire. The first American choreographer to work with them was Glen Tetley. He collaborated with Rouben Ter-Arutunian for *Pierrot Lunaire* (1967, first produced in New York 1962) and together they devised an abstract, minimal set to meet Tetley's portrayal of a sad, vulnerable pierrot. The idea for a scaffolding tower became the set for the whole dance. The lead figure, a moonstruck clown and romantic dreamer, danced by Christopher Bruce, was imprisoned by his own pathos and his treacherous fellow commedia dell'arte characters, Columbine and Bighella. The scaffolding captured Pierrot's containment, representing his home and his gallows. The tower also provided the dance with opportunities to climb, hang and use different levels. As Pierrot stretches out for the moon on top of the scaffolding, a particularly sad moment reveals that he will never reach it.

Nadine Baylis designed free moving steel cage-like structures and film projections for the set of Tetley's *Ziggurat*, (1967, for Ballet Rambert). This impelling portrayal of ritual, worship and fallen idols was described by Norman Morrice as, their 'first new-wave ballet' that changed the company's approach to set and light.

Figure 4.10 *Pierrot Lunaire*
Pierrot Lunaire, Ballet Rambert, 1967.
Photographer: Anthony Crickmay

Tetley also took to the sea with his version of *The Tempest* (1979). In the two-act, full-length work, Tetley collaborated with designer Nadine Baylis, and unlike the Ashton, de Nobili set for *Ondine*, this became a very minimal, abstract affair. However, Tetley's sea also used billowing silk waves, but this ocean covered the entire stage, and allowed the dancers, as sea creatures and mermaids, to 'enter' the stage from below. In this way, the set can enrich the possibilities of a conventional proscenium stage space. At the end of the dance, the silks were used as wings for the spirit Ariel and so the set became the costume. The abstract set did not try to depict a mythical story, so much as portray Prospero's inner turmoil- he 'is' the storm. Here Tetley describes a conversation with Baylis, set in an hotel by the port of Copenhagen:

. . . it was the perfect atmosphere for *The Tempest:* the wild sea outside, the clouds scudding by, and all the noises in the masts of the ships. We both felt then that it was not going to be an historical recreation of the play but that it exists in all time and no time; it can be a great contemporary work.

(Glen Tetley in *Ballet Rambert: 50 years and on*)

Christopher Bruce used a painted backcloth depicting the sea as a representational style of set for *Sergeant Early's Dream*. The scene emphasises the dancers' memories of their homeland, offering the wide and distant horizon as a point of focus during the dance.

In a different watery scene, Robert Cohan took the water away completely to create a set with many possibilities for use of levels in *Waterless Method of Swimming Instruction* (1974). The set (Ian Murray-Clarke) is a section cut through a swimming pool on an ocean liner. It was described as 'handsome' by critic John Percival in 1978. The lack of water means that the dancers have to create the illusion of swimming and diving in their dynamic emphasis. The use of floating and sustainment create the illusions of gliding smoothly through the non-existent water. Other sections, like the pool-side swimming lesson, an Esther Williams synchronised swimming spoof and the all-male antics with the lifebelts, take advantage of the different levels of the set and add balance to the more serene sections.

Another set that provided levels was the two-tiered sloping wall that Norberto Chiesa designed for Cohan's *Nymphéas* (1976). The dancers could form friezes leaning against the wall and this was very suggestive of the floating waterlilies in Monet's impressionist style painting. The plain surfaces also gave John B. Read's lighting ample surfaces to play with changes of dappled colours, intensity and mood.

There have been many famous twentieth-century collaborations of choreographers and set designers following in the Diaghilev tradition. Perhaps Merce Cunningham's collaborations with famous avant-garde painters have produced some of the most intense and remarkable moments of choreography. In *RainForest* (1968), the dancers moved among helium-filled silver pillows

Figure 4.11 Two-tiered sloping set by Norberto Chiesa for Robert Cohan's *Nymphéas* in 1976. London Contemporary Dance.

designed by Andy Warhol. This is typical of the unpredictable element in Cunningham's work. The design, music and dance are all independently created, coming together only in performance. This is designed not only to surprise the audience but also to add to the environment in which the dancers are performing. The dancers in *RainForest* moved around and between the pillows with ease and with little concern. The dance and the pillows may be connected or not: the decision lies with each dancer and with each member of the audience. This is a very different attitude from that of Martha Graham whose sets supported the symbolism and emotional meanings of the choreography.

Richard Alston in such work as *Soda Lake* (1981) features sculpture by Nigel Hall. Alston's background in visual art often shows in such collaborations. *Wildlife* (1984) is another example of his more formal style of which he says;

. . . it would be silly for them (the 'kites') to just sit there and say 'Look here's an artwork and we're underneath it . . .' They had to be involved in some way and he (designer Richard Smith) invented motors which were able to turn them and also flew them up and down. So they get right into the space.

(From Rambert Dance Company video, *Different Steps*, 1985)

These are abstract works, intellectually cool, exploring form and space, and show influences of the Cunningham style.

Figure 4.12 Merce Cunningham and Meg Harper in *RainForest* (1968). Music by David Tudor; décor by Andy Warhol; photograph by James Klosty; courtesy of the Archives of the Merce Cunningham Dance Company.

In Britain's New Dance movement, post-modern choreographers were exploring the set as a part of their overhaul of the values and strategies of dance. They presented dance as simply as possible and so no set was often the choice. We should remember that the choice of a bare stage is a 'something'.

Miss Wigman owes curiously little of her success to externals. She has no scenery at all beyond curtains.

(Herman Ould in *The Dancing Times*, 1926)

The choreographers of New Dance chose to focus more on the movement for its own sake. Site specific work was experimented with at this time. The plain stage was a choice for many of these works, but where set, props or costume were used they often carried political meaning or were used in surprising, unconventional ways. The plethora of props and set in Fergus Early's *Naples* (1978) were used to exaggerate the spoof of Bournonville's 1842 *Napoli*. The original romantic fishing village becomes a twentieth-century Naples with a cast of comic caricatures of Italian life on lambrettas, with football fixations and eating Italian spaghetti and ice cream.By the later part of the twentieth century, there was a return to theatricality and the dramatic in set design. Matthew Bourne's use of set design by Lez Brotherston is bright, energetic, pantomime-like in wit and colour. In *Highland Fling – a romantic wee ballet* (1994), characters disappear up the chimney and the whole is suitably set for Bourne's parody and comic narrative. Later in Bourne's version of *Cinderella* (1997), set

in the World War Two blitz of London, the drama of a collapsing set, similar to that of Ashton's *Ondine*, is taken to the full when during a midnight air raid the ballroom is bombed to smithereens. The flashing light, smoke and earsplitting sound effects was a package that made the audience jump out of their seats.

Lloyd Newson has used a great deal of split-level set design. In *Strange Fish* (1992), various entrance and exit points through side doors, windows and hatches are combined with a tank of water to create a world where dancers are isolated and immersed in their subconscious. The set by Peter J. Davidson is active. It falls apart and its architectural structure required dancers to have lengthy rehearsal with it so that set and movement were integrated.

TASK FOUR – *Boxed in*

KEY SKILLS Problem solving
Working with others

45 minutes to an hour (extra time is also needed to collect the boxes)

In a large group, collect as many different-sized cardboard boxes as possible. Mix them with blocks, chairs, ladders, benches and any other structural objects to hand, and arrange these in unexpected angles to create an environment. Explore ways of moving under, over, around and through the structure.

Compose movement around ideas selected from the following:

■ restriction;
■ shape;
■ escape;
■ change;
■ hide and seek;
■ city life.

The use of film as set is popular nowadays. Siobhan Davies has been collaborating with film makers since 1986. Catherine Quinn in 'Dancer's log' described how the designer David Buckland watches rehearsals of *Wild Airs* (1999, Siobhan Davies Dance Company) to decide which sections to film and where he wanted stillnesses projected so as not to detract from the live action.

Set in films can be open to a huge range of imaginative possibilities and perhaps some of the most novel, for their time, were settings such as huge ice rinks for the skating of Norwegian Olympic figure skater, Sonja Henie (*Sun Valley Serenade*, 1941, Twentieth Century Fox). Henje worked with a choreographer and long time Fred Astaire associate, Hermes Pan, on this film. In a similar fantastic style, synchronised swimming scenes featuring Esther Williams (*Bathing Beauty*, 1944 and *Neptune's Daughter*, 1949, MGM) and chorus performed in sets of water.

A set may enhance choreography by reinforcing the images which are being used, or by acting as a complementary dimension in time and space. Or, it may act simply to accompany the movement as an independent element on the stage. Whatever its function within the dance, the set may itself also be changed and transformed by the use of different lighting effects. This other aspect of physical setting is the next one which we will look at.

Lighting

From minute to minute in our everyday lives, we respond to changes in the light around us. This is a natural reaction exploited to the full in the theatre. From the earliest days of classical ballet, through the discovery of the use of ether for stage lighting, to the spectacular possibilities of today's lasers and other forms of technology, the use of changes in light has served to influence the audiences' reactions massively.

Jack Thompson's work as lighting designer is crucial in creating strong atmosphere and highlighting meaning within scenes.
(Lloyd Newson in interview with Mary Luckhurst, from the programme note for *Bound to Please*, 1997)

A change in light triggers an automatic response in us. It attracts our attention and it defines space. Atmospheres of warmth, danger, isolation and fear are here all possible. Boundaries between areas can be established. The use of projected slides, film and video can add to the technical effects.

The historical context

During the Renaissance and up until the middle of the seventeenth century, candles and daylight would have been the only source of lighting for any performances. With the invention of oil lamps and candelabra, however, more elaborate lighting effects became possible. These were then added to by the use of reflection in mirrors, and simple projection was also introduced. Fireworks displays further became common. But it was the invention of gas lighting in the 1830s which was to make a real difference. The romantic ballet could now be danced in a convincing moonlight. The gas itself, ether, became a source of fantasy for writers and poets of the day. Its effect on the mind was to produce hallucinations of mystery, and the word 'ethereal', meaning 'beyond the real, in the supernatural', was born. The ethereal included anything weird and wonderful. Spirits roaming in the dark, deepest forests, not unlike vampires, ghosts or ghouls – anything strange and exotic was the fashion.

In 1822, a designer named Ciceri staged a fairy opera *Aladin ou Lampe Merveilleuse* and first used gas lights. In 1831 he staged *Robert the Devil* at the Paris Opera. The moonlit cloisters, where white-veiled nuns emerged from their stone tombs, marked the beginning of many such scenes in the romantic ballets which followed. The famous Act Two of *Giselle* (1841) must have been

a revelation for the audiences. Ciceri's forest glade was both dark and light but with a ghostly supernatural moonlight, and here the spirits of maidens who were abandoned on their wedding night roamed, vengefully seeking out victims, without pity for any man who may wander their way. In the gaslight, the wilis – as they were called – must have seemed to have been floating off the ground.

The present day

Before going on to look at the modern-day use of light in dance, it is first of all worth considering a few technical aspects about lighting.

Different sorts of lights consist of the following:

- *floods*: these give a general wash;
- *battens*: these are rows of lights;
- *spots*: there are two kinds: one gives a softer look – a fresnel – while a focus gives a harder edge – i.e. a sharply defined beam. Both of these can have attachments which restrict the size of the circle of light: an iris diaphragm, and barn doors which reduce the spillage of light into unwanted areas;
- *gels*: these can be slid into frames and fitted onto the front of the lights to give colour. Warm pinks and ambers, cooler light blues and steel or intense greens and deep reds and blues are all possible. Mixing gels will give other tints, like yellow (red 1 green) or purple (red 1 blue), but this will dim the brightness of the light.

When using lighting, the colour of the costumes must be considered. Costumes will usually look better if lit by a mix of pale, sympathetic tints. The choice of light colour can change the mood, create images and add a symbolic meaning to enhance the dance.

The *direction* from which the light shines is another important consideration. In dance, a side light at torso level works well because it gives depth and moulds the flexible body of the dancer.

Lighting for dance differs from other theatre lighting. Bodies are sculpted as they move in and out of the beams. Side light at low level 'lifts' the dancers whereas at a high level it creates shadows pulling the dancers forward. At a high level it also shines over the dancers' heads so it cannot be blocked by the moving bodies. So the most appropriate plots for dance use side and overhead light with pools, and any dark areas filled with front light.

It is always advisable to *cross-light*, that is, light an area from more than one direction. Large amounts of light from front-of-house above will give a stagey look, whilst light shone from a low level only can create eerie shadows.

The *intensity* of light can also vary to give effects like – at the end of a dance – a slow fade-down or a snap blackout. Similarly, at the start of a dance, the scene may gradually become visible, or figures may first appear just as silhouettes or as lit figures in general darkness. A *cross-fade*, where some lights fade up as others fade down, may be used to change from one scene to another – changing the atmosphere from, say, cool to hot.

The *cyc* is a light-coloured backdrop suspended from a batton. Light is thrown onto it so that a wash covers the back. It is lit by striplights in front and above it. It can be lit from the floor behind but this may put the dancers' feet in the dark. A black backdrop is often used but it is less flexible for lighting than a cyc.

Effects such as *gobos* (cut-out patterns placed in front of a light) can create patterns for dancers to move through – such as a forest glade. This can also be done by the projection of cut-out designs, a device which can distort the bodies of the dancers. Flashing lights, in turn, can give a lively, disco feel, and strobes and colour wheels can be useful too.

The work of Alwin Nikolais is renowned for its stunning and elaborate blend of light, slides and effects. Nikolais transforms the human shape of his dancers, makes them disappear and then makes them reappear in kaleidoscope patterns of colour. His *Somniloquy* (1967) made use of a slide projection onto a gauze curtain, in a setting like the mouth of a cave. Dancers appeared behind this curtain, their faces lit by hand-held torches. When they shone the torches onto the gauze, they made patterns on it. The projections changed colour many times: blue, green, red, purple, silver. Finally, a projection of many white dots placed the dancers in a snowstorm. Nikolais' concerns in his choreography are with the environment that we all live in. It changes, and we too change in a constant battle for survival.

In almost total contrast, the dance *Soda Lake* (Richard Alston, 1981) is daring in its simple use of plain white light. This post-modern solo is danced in simple black costume, accompanied by silence and by minimalist sculpture for the set.

Plain white light (lighting design, John B. Read) was also used in Cohan's *Waterless Method of Swimming Instruction* to enhance the luxury-cruise liner's poolside setting against a sky-blue lit cyclorama. However, colours were added to some sections to suggest different moods and characters, blue for the sunbather and warm amber for the bathers. During a livelier section for the lifeguards and swimmers, the music takes on a beat for the first time and the lighting shifted to alternating and flashing colours blue/pink, amber/green. An underwater section used dappled shadows in blue and the whole finished on a deep blue with a tinge of pink sunset, as the day drew to an end.

Simple use of spot lights can increase intensity and carry the meaning of the dance. This is particularly expressive in *Swansong* (Bruce, 1987 for London Festival Ballet). An overhead spot on the chair is suggestive of the prisoner's interrogation and torture. At the end a final 'window' light (high diagonal stage left) evokes the feeling that the victim's only escape is for his spirit to fly up and out towards the light. Shin level lights are used during the piece and produce eerie, threatening shadows on the backdrop.

The use of shadows, in a rather more playful manner, is found in Ashton's *Ondine* (1958). In the 'Shadow Dance', the sea sprite Ondine, originally danced by Margot Fonteyn, discovers her own shadow. Childlike, she engages in shadow-play made possible by the angle of light.

Figure 4.13 Waterless Method of Swimming Instruction, London Contemporary Dance, by Robert Cohan.
Photographer: Anthony Crickmay. Colour photography, London, England, ca. 1973.

We may think that projection is a relatively recent idea, but in 1933 it was used in Balanchine's *L'Errante: A Choreographic Fantasy*, when the designer, Pavel Tchelitchev, arranged the ballet to be performed with a background of transparent white screens. According to ballet photographer and expert Cecil Beaton in his 1951 book 'Ballet!', the startling effect of the dancers' shadows in the dance 'was to have the greatest influence on stage decors for many years to come'. One of the shadows showed the dancer Tilly Losch's famous backbend as having similarities of line with the Graham style.

The lack of a leading ballet company in Europe allowed smaller companies to develop and Balanchine worked in England and France in 1933 with 'Les Ballets 1933', before going to America. Edward James funded the company, in the one year of its existence, to give 20 performances and allowed Balanchine to work on his own choreographic style. Losch and James were married and when they divorced the company disbanded.

Siobhan Davies' *The Glass Blew In* (1994) explored the differences between human qualities and those that have to do with shape and texture. The lighting was designed by Peter Mumford and the original programme note says it all:

The piece is a sensuous, poetic interplay of colour, pattern, dynamic and sound

. . . Mumford has marked out the stage with a rectangle whose floor is at different times, a wash of green violet or magenta. . . . It gives full rein to

Davies' fascination with borders. She presents her dancers not only inside the rectangle, but also on or outside its demarcation.

(From the original programme for *The Glass Blew In* by Siobhan Davies, 1994)

The closeness of the dance and its lighting design is seen at its most intense here. Not only does the light support the mood, it also defines the actual space environment in which the dancers move. This characteristic use of light to define areas of the stage space has long been a feature of Davies' work. In *New Galileo* (1984, for LCDT), Mumford lit the stage with two overhead strips of light running up and down the stage. As the small movements of the choreography gradually increase in size the lighting also expands until a state of brilliant light covers the whole stage. The backdrop (David Buckland) depicted large images of the moons of Jupiter and the whole design seems to enhance the notion of the opening up of dark to light in an awakening universe – maybe Galileo's own awakening when he first saw the moons, as described in his book *The Starry Messenger* (1610).

In Lea Anderson's *Go Las Vegas* (1995, lighting by Simon Corder for the Featherstonehaughs), the audience itself contributed to the lighting. On entering the theatre, they were provided with small torches and instructions were given in the programme, and verbally by one of the dancers, on exactly when and how these were to be used. At a signal, the torches are shone onto the dancer's phosphorescent silver suits, so that these light up whilst the dancers' faces and hands remain in blackness. The suits thus dance as if they have a life of their own. It is a fitting finale to a dance which has shredded the glitz and glamour of faceless showbiz – another direct hit at an aspect of our society which Anderson scrutinises.

TASK FIVE – *Lighting plan*

KEY SKILLS Problem solving.

45 minutes to an hour

From the list of dance titles below, choose one and describe how you would light it. Make clear how it would start and end. Describe any changes which occur during the dance. Keep it simple.

Be sure to include notes on colour, direction, intensity and special effects.

- 'The corridors of power'
- 'Water scene'
- 'Silent movies'
- 'What goes around comes around'.

You may not have access to lights, but when next at the theatre or watching dance on video, be sure to keep an eye out for how the lighting is used to enhance the dance.

191

Costume

Any costume can be worn in relation to a dance. One can make the most of its restrictions or one can use it to enhance both the general visual design and the particular ideas/concerns of the dance. In this sense, it is like choosing the right sort of lighting: it should be appropriate to, and should enhance, the overall purpose and expressivity of the dance. The following are the most basic considerations in the choice of costume:

- shape;
- colour;
- material.

The historical context

In the spectacles of the late sixteenth and early seventeenth centuries, costumes were highly theatrical. Rich fabrics and fantastic designs were often used to enhance character. Some designs were grotesque and evil, others were harmonious, and the animal world was represented by the decoration of animal skins, the use of parrots and so on. Mortals and immortals mixed together in a world of magic and illusion.

Figure 4.14 To show Berain design Ballet Costume (w/c on paper) by Berain, Jean II (the Younger) (1674–1726)

By the middle of the seventeenth century, the world of fashion and very expensive clothes were a priority for the courts of Europe. The professional dancers of the court ballets had to dress elegantly and stylishly. The costumes were decorated symbolically so that the story was clear to the monarch and the

court. After all, the ballets were usually about them, and so court dress with some decoration suited the occasion. According to the etiquette of the court, a dancer representing the monarch would be presented on stage for the monarch himself to admire! The way a man bowed or received bows told everything about him, and the audience too understood the symbolism of the costumes and choreography. The court life was thus presented in dance and everything was done to support the power of the monarchy. Often the ruler would be shown in the finale as the god Apollo or as the Sun, the supreme being within his domain. It must have been a fine line between who was just a performer and who was part of the real court, and hence the entertainments could make both political and imaginative statements at the same time.

The male dancers' costumes allowed freedom of movement, but the females' skirts had to reach the ground. Masks were popular to show stylised characters such as sweet nymphs or hideous demons.

Gradually the court ownership over the theatres of Vienna, Milan and Paris weakened, and a more independent, professional dance tradition emerged. At the Paris Opera in the early eighteenth century, ballet found independence as a performing art. The success of *Les Fêtes Chinoises* (1754, Jean-Georges Noverre) revealed a new interest in the foreign and exotic. The rigid rules of costuming according to prescribed characters were less important, and as the need to move took priority, skirts shortened. In the 1730s, Camargo shortened her skirts from floor level to a few centimetres above the ankle. This enabled her renowned *entrechats* – the crossing or beating together of the feet during a leap in ballet – to be seen by the audience. In the writings of Noverre in the early eighteenth century, the major changes that were happening in ballet were clearly stated in his comments on costume.

Obstinacy in adhering to outworn traditions is the same in every part of the opera; it is monarch of all it surveys. Greek, Roman, shepherd, hunter, warrior, faun . . . all these characters are cut to the same pattern and ostentatious display rather than good taste has caused them to be spattered at caprice. Tinsel glitters everywhere. . . . I would banish all uniformity of costume. . . . I should prefer light and simple draperies of contrasting colours worn in such a manner as to reveal the dancer's figure. . . . I would reduce by three-quarters the ridiculous paniers of our danseuses, they are equally opposed to the liberty, speed, prompt and lively action of the dance.

(Jean-Georges Noverre, *Letters on Dancing*, 1760, translated by Cyril Beaumont, 1930)

Noverre was against warriors who were dressed in their Sunday best, and he rejected masks as artificial. He was then moving towards greater natural design.

Around the corner lay the French Revolution and the new romanticism. Adoration of the exotic, peasant life and local colour, mystery and the supernatural was seen in Taglioni's *La Sylphide* (Paris Opera, 1832). The design,

by Ciceri, included romantic, moonlit forest glades into which the white tulle tutu, fitted bodice, flowery crown and pink tights fitted perfectly. The invention of the pointe shoe allowed ballerinas to float over the earth, spirit-like. Costumes now also conveyed national identities from far-flung places – Scotland, Bulgaria, India.

The sumptuousness of the costumes towards the end of the nineteenth century is typified by the Russian Petipa's *Sleeping Beauty*. Some of the 1890 original costumes can be seen in The State Theatre Museum in St Petersburg. They drip in gold and pearls and by today's standards would be very restricting on a dancer's movement. Also the tutus are longer than the style of modern ones. In the 2000 Kirov reconstruction of the original version, the costumes were redesigned to allow for greater freedom of movement, but in an effort to make the production authentic the costumes were still heavier than those we are used to seeing.

The influences of the artists Leon Bakst and Alexandre Benois produced a revolution of design and colour during the rebirth of ballet in the Diaghilev era at the start of the twentieth century. In the costumes for *Schéhérazade* (Fokine, 1910), there was a startling new use of intense, sensuous and powerful colours. The whole look was daring, vibrant and fantastic.

Figure 4.15 Costumes for Great Eunuch, Shah's aide-de-camp and Zobeide the Favourite, 1910, for ballet Schéhérazade by Nicolai Rimsky-Korsakov, 1844–1908, Russian composer, illustration from French publication *Comoedia Illustré*, artist BAKST, Leon (Lev Rosenborg): 1844–1924.

This taste for the shocking and avant-garde reached its height in 1917 with Picasso's humorous, absurd and modern designs in *Parade*. The movement of the Managers – the characters who ran the travelling show – was impeded under the heavy wooden frames of their skyscraper costumes. The dancers themselves became a secondary consideration to the design.

Figure 4.16(a) Bakst costume designs for *The Firebird* by Igor Stravinsky (1910).

Figure 4.16(b) Illustration for the 7th season of the Russian Ballets. Léon Bakst's watercolour of Nijinsky, in *L'Aprés-midi d'une Faune*, 1912.

(a)

(b)

The present day

Shape

Costumes can often make life difficult for dancers (as in *Parade*). Dancers usually rehearse in their most comfortable clothes and when suddenly dressed in an unfamiliar costume, their whole sense of the movement may change. Costumes should move with the dancer, so that the dancer feels able to move with all the fullness required. Frederick Ashton had a favourite designer in Sophie Federovitch. He said of her:

She believed firmly that nothing must hide the dancing or impede the dancers, and that the background should not distract.

(Sir Frederick Ashton in *Making a Ballet*, 1974)

Costumes for ballet tend to be more traditional in style than those for modern dance companies, and they usually flatter and enhance the dancer's classical lines. Merce Cunningham's trademark, the all-in-one unitard, reveals every line in the dancer's body and is especially effective in showing the mobile and incessantly moving torso, arms and feet. The figure-hugging costume shape was widely used throughout the 1960s to the 1990s by many western modern dance choreographers, but in perhaps one of its first appearances in 1912 was worn by the legend of ballet Vaslav Nijinsky in *L'Aprés-midi d'u Faune* (1912). Bakst designed a costume that seemed like a second skin on Nijinsky – the skin of an animal.

There are shades of similar design in Nadine Baylis's open-mesh unitards for the men in Glen Tetley's *Ziggurat* (1967, for Ballet Rambert), the irregular holes revealing skin underneath. Baylis constructed the costumes from pieces of crochet that the dancers had been given to do using millinery elastic. As the dancers were beginners at crochet, the irregular look of the final costume expressed the suitably wild mood of the dance. Later costume designs, such as for Christopher Bruce's depiction of a flock of birds in *Wings* (1970) and the impelling *Black Angels* (Bruce, Baylis 1976), which explored the myth of the fallen angel, continued to explore the exposure of skin in the unitard. *Black Angels* added fluid moving fabric, also slashed through, to give the impression of wings in a world of dark and light, good and evil.

Figure 4.17 Nijinsky as the faun in *L'Aprés-midi d'un Faune* (1912)

The shaping of the zebra costume in David Bintley's *Still Life at the Penguin Café* (1988, The Royal Ballet, costume: Hayden Griffiths) is effective in extending the lines and dynamics of the movement. A unitard with zebra stripes combines with face paint and head-dress which is like a mane running down the spine to the tail. Tassels are fixed to the arms connecting the dancer to the earth and emphasising the line of movement beyond the hands. The zebra skin is echoed in the women's dresses but they are frilly and manmade, posing the threat that an animal's fate may be to walk the catwalk next season.

Animals played a part in Ashton's *La Fille Mal Gardée* (1960), in a humorous opening to the ballet. A cockerel and attendant hens appear pecking around in the farmyard. The cockerel costume was made of sateen fabric that gave the gloss of feathers, over lightweight foam and topped off with a mask and

Figure 4.18
Ziggurat.
(1967) Glen
Tetley, Ballet
Rambert.
Photographer:
Anthony
Crickmay

headdress. Osbert Lancaster designed the wings to be lightweight and secured them to dancer's arms so as not to restrict the movement.

A costume may be chosen deliberately to distort the lines and shape of the body. Alwin Nikolais combined this idea with his extraordinary lighting effects:

In this piece a faceless trio, entirely covered by sacks, comes to life through various patterns of body pulsations. . . . They remind me of a collection of potato sacks pulled up over a mound of bubbling rubber.

(Elinor Rogosin in *Dance Makers*, 1980)

Nikolais is concerned with imposing limitations on the dancers and with the way that this reflects the problems that humans have in managing their own environment. He rejects the Graham interest in Freudian psychodrama, heroines and national pride in favour of the relationships between human and nature. The question of the role of technology and a 'green' focus moves him to create, on stage, other worlds for our contemplation.

Colour and materials

After the 1920s, there was a reaction against the opulence and excesses of the Diaghilev era. Designers restricted their use of colours to a more austere range, and shape too became pared down. There was still fine traditional design for the world of ballet, but now also forward-looking designers for the new choreographers who formed the rebellious movement in modern dance.

Figure 4.19 *Five Brahms' Waltzes in the manner of Isadora Duncan*, by Frederick Ashton
Photographer Catherine Ashmore, Dancer Lucy Burge, costume by David Dean

Isadora Duncan was the first to make a real impact, choosing to wear flimsy fabrics in the style of a Greek tunic – shocking to many at that time. This was beautifully reproduced in the tribute work *Five Brahm's Waltzes in the Manner of Isadora Duncan*. Danced by Lynn Seymour and choreographed by Frederick Ashton in 1975 (and later revived for Lucy Burge by Ballet Rambert in 1984), it too used the free, floaty fabric that had made Duncan famous. The material enhanced the freedom of the movement and its energetic patterns through the air.

The choice of soft light fabrics, plus the many frills and lace trims, for the dresses of Ginger Rogers in Hollywood films, such as *Swing Time* (1936), were ideal for the romantic and elegant mood. The hems of the dresses were weighted so that they added to the swirling movement. Such dresses were the perfect complement to the formal suits of the male leads. Astaire was known to choose his own clothes, and always on the leading edge of male fashion, with an air of nonchalant style. In the song 'Isn't it a Lovely Day (to be caught in the rain)' from *Top Hat* (1935), Ginger Rogers' masculine riding clothes and Astaire's tweed sports jacket, soft-cut flannel trouser, suede shoes and stylish accessories make the perfect complementary statement, not only in fashion and elegance but also in the gender equality of the dancing in this number.

Figure 4.20 Fred Astaire and Ginger Rogers – 1935 'Step by Step'
Ginger Rogers (1911–1935) and Fred Astaire (1899–1987) as Dale Tremont and Jerry Travers respectively, in a dance routine from the RKO film, *Top Hat*. The film was directed by Mark Sandrich with costumes by Bernard Newman and choreography by Fred Astaire and Hermes Pan.

Alternatively, the texture of a plastic mac adds colour, texture and fun to dancing in the rain:

Figure 4.21 Gene Kelly and Debbie Reynolds – 1952 'Singin' in the Rain'

Such partnerships as Merce Cunningham and Robert Rauschenberg pared down costume and rejected decoration. Simple, all-in one, tight-fitting leotards, often in plain pastel shades of colour or – as in *Summerspace* (1958) – painted to match the background with tiny dots or soft sprays (design Rauschenberg), were used. These costumes would make the dancers appear not as if they were in space, but as if they themselves were space.

The dance of Martha Graham was for austere times and to be taken in a serious mood. Graham often designed the costumes herself and they were frequently inspired by the movement itself. Take Martha Graham's solo *Lamentation* (1930), where the intense repetitive rocking and sorrow was moulded into the tight-fitting sheath. New fabrics like stretch jersey were now used for the first time. This use of costume enhanced the main idea of the dance.

The post-modernists of the 1960s onwards produced an enormous range of ideas on costuming dance. At first, they rejected all the achievements of their forerunners in modern dance.

No to spectacle no to virtuosity no to transformations and magic and make believe no to glamour . . . no to style no to camp.

These are the words of iconoclast of the 1960s Yvonne Rainer, and natural everyday movements and simple street clothes were the final product. The dancers of New York, and later the UK, were working on shoestring budgets, and this factor had a significant influence on the look and values of dance.

From a choice of the dullest, most insignificant rehearsal clothes, we move to the imaginative designs of present-day French choreographers, Regine Chopinot and Philippe Decouflé. In Chopinot's *KOK* (1990), the costumes were designed by Jean-Paul Gaultier, the king of French avant-garde fashion. The final result is stunning and chic, with rich colour and pattern, as well as upfront sexuality.

In Britain, costume design takes many and diverse forms – from the cool, simple cut of the Siobhan Davies company, as seen in the jeans and denim shirts of *Wyoming* (1988), to the leather jackets of the Cholmondeleys in *Metalcholia* (1994) or the long silver dresses made in the new Liquid Jersey in *Flesh and Blood* (1989/1993). Lea Anderson's choice of the metal, fluid, reflective fabric similarly reminds us of the chainmail of St Joan. Depending on the light, this latter fabric would change colour and texture during the various sections of the dance. This effect was also seen in Robert Cohan's work *Nymphéas* for the London Contemporary Dance Theatre. Sections of Monet's impressionist painting of waterlilies were painted onto all-in-one leotards. The colour of the paint changed with the lighting, so that typical impressionistic changes in light and weather were reproduced on stage – from a calm, blue summer's day to the sudden dark of a passing storm, the deep brown and greens soaking into the costumes.

In Richard Alston's *Wildlife*, the sharp zig-zags of Richard Smith's set of moving kites are echoed in the strident designs and vibrant colours of the painted leotards. The dancers are in some imaginary deep forest and their sharp, angular movements, enhanced by the costume and set design, convey moments of animal instinct and their struggle for survival. There is an image of the broken lines of camouflage of animals in the undergrowth.

Figure 4.22 *Wildlife* by Richard Alston, design by Richard Smith
Photographer: Catherine Ashmore

Masks and body or face paint offer other possibilities. Masks were particularly well used in the film *Shall We Dance* (1937, RKO Radio Pictures) in the song of the same name. As Astaire dances solo, the all-female chorus wear Ginger Roger's masks. Near the end of the number Rogers, also masked, enters and Astaire unmasks her and they dance together.

In *Ghost Dances*, by Christopher Bruce for the then-named Ballet Rambert, the ghosts of South American myth appeared ghoulish and sinister in body paint which emphasised their skeletons, and in white eerie masks which hid any signs of mortality or human feelings.

Body paint is used to great effect on the swans in Bourne's *Swan Lake* (1995). The skin is whitish-grey and looks quite haunting. Combined with the black stripes on the head and face, the wild swan look is complete. The heavy 'feathered' trousers are the finishing touch.

We can say here, in summary, that costume may enhance the intentions of a dance by doing one of a number of things:

- emphasising the mood by choice of colour, shape, fabric, texture;
- enhancing the formal properties of movement through certain lines and shapes;
- clarifying character and story.

TASK SIX – *Lucky dip!*

KEY SKILLS Problem Solving
Working with others.

🕐 20 to 30 minutes

Fill a box with as many items of clothing and fabrics of different texture as possible. Place it in the centre of the room and let dancers take turns at 'Lucky Dips'. Whatever is pulled out of the box gives rise to movement ideas which everyone copies. The dancer passes on the item to another dancer who continues to improvise with it before abandoning it and dipping in for another. This idea can be further developed by making deliberate choices instead and then working in small groups to form short dances using the clothing chosen as a main source of movement ideas.

Props may also be added to the box if desired.

Props

As with set and costumes, props are an integral part of a dance. When used thoughtfully, they will not only serve as decoration but will also enhance the intentions of the dance and add to the audience's appreciation.

Props may:

- enhance a character;
- have symbolic meaning;
- add to the movement itself;
- in the case of very large props, become almost the set itself as well.

When using props it is important to include them as much as possible in the dance, as if they were another dancer. You should use a prop in as many ways as are relevant to the dance – be imaginative. Looking at a few examples will help you to understand the power of props.

Props which have symbolic meaning/enhance character

A wide range of props has long been associated with the world of classical ballet. Magic wands, flowers, swords, garland hoops, a variety of weapons have all played a part over the years in defining characters and telling the story. One of Ashton's humorous dances in *Cinderella*, uses props to add to the sense of ridiculous in the characters of the Ugly Sisters. They dance with oranges. Ashton's inspiration for this came from an Astaire Rogers step from the 1924 musical *Lady, Be Good!* The famous 'Oompah step' was a favourite of Astele and Fred Astaire which involved a 'runaround', side-by-side as if on a bicycle in large circular pathways. Ashton and Helpmann performed it with accompanying

nodding heads and ostrich feather headdresses, whilst balancing oranges in their hands. Equally funny is the exaggerated use of over-the-top use of facepowder using enormous powder puffs, as the Sisters prepared for the ball. Cinderella's solo with the broom is full of gentle playfulness and humour as she dances with the broomstick and imitates her sisters' clumsy attempts to do the gavotte.

Fred Astaire was renowned for the use of a cane as a prop. He not only used it to add extra beats to his tapping but also, as in *Top Hat*, to enrich the meaning. In the number 'Top Hat, White Tie and Tails' (Irving Berlin), which the romance story was built around, Astaire uses the cane as a handgun, a rifle, a machine gun and a bow and arrow to dispatch with the mysteriously threatening chorus.

Martha Graham is once again not to be overlooked, in her collaboration with sculptor Isamu Noguchi and the innovations which it produced. For them, sculpture coming to life on stage is part of the whole ritual, and it enhances both the meaning of the movement and the audience's emotional response. In *Night Journey* (1947), a rope binds together Jocasta and her son Oedipus. The rope is a symbol both of the umbilical cord and of sexual love. This Greek myth of doom and destruction is powerfully told from the women's point of view.

George Balanchine, originally of Ballets Russes, also worked with Noguchi. The design for Balanchine's *Orfeus* (1948, for Ballet Society, New York) included a variety of costumes, masks sculptures and props, such as a lyre, a singing harp, played by Orfeus to persuade Pluto, god of the underworld, to release Eurydice.

Following in the Graham style, work like that of Robert Cohan for the London Contemporary Dance Theatre in the 1970s and 1980s produced some delights, like *Waterless Method of Swimming Instruction*. In one section, for the men only, huge rubber rings take on lives of their own, providing boats for the dancers to row and, when piled up on top of one dancer, completely entrap him. Cohan trained and danced with Graham, but developed his own style of work that included a broader emotional range, including humour.

In Christopher Bruce's *Sergeant Early's Dream* the section entitled 'Geordie' uses the lyrics of a song which tells of a woman's lament for her hanged husband. Her scarf becomes the symbol of the hangman's noose in the final image of the dance, reinforcing the characters and the narrative of the song and dance. A chair, red noses and canes are used as props in Bruce's *Swansong*. They are manipulated by the guards and the prisoner to represent a wide range of images associated with interrogation. The canes double as accessories for tap dance and as weapons of torture; the red noses humiliate and panic the victim and the chair is a weapon, a shield, a comfort and prison bars.

The prop-set

Sometimes, like costumes, the set too can double as a prop. In 1928, the Russian artist Tchelitchev combined an innovative range of elements in his stage design for the Ballet Russes' *Ode*. This presented a modern view of the

festivities of the Russian court of the eighteenth century. The dancers were covered entirely so that they became anonymous figures. They held cords which wove a web over the stage and were connected to lines of dolls at the back of the stage. Such were the interconnections here that it seemed difficult to know where the costumes ended and the props or set began. This kind of distortion also features in the later work of Alwin Nikolais, where again props are simultaneously costumes, and it can be difficult to know whether or not they are also part of the set.

Similarly, Georges Balanchine, in his design for *Orfeus* (1948, for 'Ballet Society'), chose a white silk curtain to fall in a dramatic swirl like lightning, and a rope which, although a part of the costume of the Dark Angel, also became an integral part of the movement. Balanchine had been working in America for 15 years at this point, after the death of Diaghilev in 1929 and the collapse of the Ballets Russes. It is of note that in his ballet *L'Errante – A Choreographic Fantasy* (1933, for 'Les Ballets' 1933) another tale of myth and lost love, the designer Tchelitchev incorporated a curtain of fine white silk that falls on Errante beneath, as her lost spirit-lover ascends a rope ladder into the sky. The wealthy Lincoln Kirstein, brought Balanchine to America and they co-founded of many joint projects including the company 'Ballet Society'. Notes in Kirstein's diaries show his presence at rehearsals for *L'Errante*, in Paris.

An early work of Robert Cohan, *Hunter of Angels* (1967), used a huge ladder which was both set and prop at the same time. Based on the Bible story of the twins Jacob and Esau in the *Book of Genesis*, the dance depicts their rivalry and struggle as symbolic of a variety of factions: between good and evil; confrontation between nations; between men; the inner turmoil of one man. The ladder was moved around with great skill (considering its size and weight) to become the wings of an angel, a womb, a labyrinth and Jacob's ladder to heaven. In this way, at different times, it was both an extension of the dancers' bodies and a set to be explored in countless ways for movement possibilities. The story goes that the ladder just happened to be in the studio and that Cohan was inspired by this chance happening. Cohan, as had Martha Graham, used biblical themes in other dances such as *Songs, Lamentations and Praises* (1979) and *Stabat Mater* (1975).

Task Seven gives you an opportunity to find out more about Cohan's choreographic style and it is linked to a practical task in the next chapter. Glen Tetley, another American choreographer from the Graham legacy who came to Britain in the 1960s, used dance vocabulary, flexed feet and flexible torsos, and mythical themes similar to Cohan. However, Tetley included more classical balletic technique. They also share a similar use of set-props. Study the photograph of The Tempest . . . notice how one dancer, as the character spirit Ariel, is trapped inside the set-prop. This is reminiscent of Graham, when in *Cave of the Heart* (1945) she played Medea in the blood thirsty Greek myth. In the dance she is entwined in one of Noguchi's prop-sets of slender bent steel rods.

Figure 4.23 A prop-set in Glen Tetley's *The Tempest* (1979), design by Nadine Baylis

TASK SEVEN – *View Robert Cohan's dance style*

KEY SKILLS Problem solving

🕐 45 minutes to an hour

This task involves some research at first that will help you when you view and respond to video footage of Robert Cohan's *Hunter of Angels* (1959 and 1967 for London Contemporary Dance Theatre).

1 Find Chapter 25, verses 21–25, Chapter 8, verse 12 and Chapter 32, verses 24, 26–28 in the *Book of Genesis, The Holy Bible*. In your own words give an outline of the story about twins Jacob and Esau. Why were they in conflict? Why was Jacob's confrontation with the angel important and what difference did it make to his future?

2 Watch *Hunter of Angels* (14 minutes) and make notes on:
- the three different characters that appear in the dance;
- the significance of the red and blue costumes;
- the different uses (especially levels) and images portrayed by the different uses of the ladder as prop-set.

Now answer the following questions:

1 What dance vocabulary can you see that is influenced by Graham technique?

205

Tennis racquets are used to enhance the movement and meaning in Matthew Bourne's *Late Flowering Lust* (1994, for BBC TV). The racquets enhance the illusion that dancers are making contact with the ball. But the larger theme of a group of small beautiful young things enjoying their weekend house party in pre-war England has a darker side. They seem oblivious to the despair of one of the friends, played by actor Nigel Hawthorne.

Choreography using sporting motifs goes back to Moliére's comedy of manners, *Les Facheux* (*The Bores*, 1661). Sports such as bowls and shuttlecock were featured as a platform for a satire on manners and social privilege, similar to *Late Flowering Lust* some three centuries later. Valsav Nijinsky also choreographed using tennis as a metaphor for modern manners in the 1913 ballet *Jeux*. *Jeux*, for Ballets Russes, is now thought of as the first to use a modern theme, and it used a tennis racquet and ball as props. At the time Digahilev consulted social commentary and painter Blanche to find a suitable theme. After much consideration and discussion it was decided that sport would suit, because of the 1912 revival of the Olympic Games and the rising popular image of an amateur sporting elite. This has many similarities with the glamour of sportsmen such as David Beckham today, and it is interesting to note that Bakst's costume design first showed Nijinsky as a soccer player. The dance began with the ball bouncing on stage. A triangular tennis and love-match evolved into *Jeux* and was rooted in the reality of Nijinsky's complicated love life at the time. A version of *Les Facheux*, by Bronislava Nijinska, was choreographed in 1924.

Figure 4.25 *Late Flowering Lust* (film title). *The Tennis Dance – Adventures in Motion Pictures*, BBC Film, Matthew Bourne choreography, 1994.
Photographer: Gabrielle Crawford

TASK EIGHT – *Props relationships*

Select a number of objects as props, such as:

- a pillow;
- an umbrella;
- a large pole or stick;
- a large hoop;
- a feather;
- a picture frame;
- a balloon;
- a newspaper;
- a doll;
- a cardboard tube;
- a large piece of silk or chiffon.

Experiment with how the object affects the way you move when, for example, you carry it or attach it to you. Let the objects become something other than what they are. For example, if they are heavy, let them become light, or if they have an obvious use, use them for something else totally different. Try different relationships with the prop: struggle, play, chase, hide.

Finally, choose one object and let it lead to a dance; or arrange a few of them around the stage space and create a story or landscape or 'scene' with them. (Suggested music: *Underneath the Bunker* by The Orb.)

The dance production now requires only one other constituent feature to complete the picture: the accompaniment or aural setting. This is an area full of possibilities and choices. What the audience hears also needs to be appropriately chosen to support your movements, sets, lights, costumes and props, so that what is heard and what is seen can be combined into an understandable whole for and by the onlooker.

References and resources

Books

Banes, S., *Terpsichore in Sneakers: Post-modern dance*, Middletown, CN: Wesleyan University Press, 1987

Cohen, S.J. (ed.), *Dance as a Theatre Art: Source Readings In Dance History From 1581 to the Present*, New York: Princeton Book Co., 1992

Crisp, C., Sainsbury, A. and Williams, P., *Ballet Rambert: 50 years On*, London: Scolar Press for Rambert, 1981

Kirstein, L., *Dance: a Short History of Classic Theatre Dancing*, New York: Dance Horizons, 1969

Sorrell, W., *Dance in its Time*, New York: Columbia University Press, 1981

Spencer, C., *Leon Bakst & the Ballets Russes*, UK: Academy Educational, 1995, well illustrated

Videos

■ Available from www.dancebooks.co.uk

Swansong (Bruce), English National Ballet (1995)

Still Life at the Penguin Café, David Bintley for The Royal Ballet (1991)

Ghost Dances and Journey, by Christopher Bruce, the Houston Ballet

■ Available from www.surrey.ac.uk

Body as Site, Rosemary Butcher (1993), performance in Guilford Cathedral

Hunter of Angels, Robert Cohan

Websites

■ Companies

www.merce.org – Merce Cunningham

www.sddc.org.uk – Siobhan Davies Co.

On the history of costume a very wide-ranging site is www.balletdance.about.com

www.nga.gov.au/russia – informative site of costumes of the Ballets Russes, 1909–1933, as exhibited at the National Gallery of Australia, Canberra. Well illustrated

www.artslynx.org/dance – huge range of dance information

Music

DANCE! – UCA recording, UCA45-2, 2003 available from www.ucamusic.com This CD has 14 tracks highly suited to student composition and improvisation. *Underneath the Bunker* by The Orb, Polygram Island label IMCP219, 1996

5 THE CONSTITUENT FEATURES OF DANCE: THE AURAL SETTING

Accompaniments for dance

There are many types of accompaniment (aural setting) to choose from for dance. The most obvious one, music, is often chosen, but it must be stated loudly from the start that it is also worth trying out others. The list of choices includes:

- silence;
- the voice;
- sound (both natural and found sound);
- music.

The final choice must be one selected, like the movements themselves and other constituent features, with great care. In the end, both what the audience receives *visually* and what it receives *audibly* should be compatible in some way, even if this is because these aspects are very different. The differences may create interesting contrasts and clashes.

Silence

The early German expressionist dancers, like Mary Wigman at the start of the twentieth century, often chose silence as the accompaniment to their dances.

Nearly all her most original dances are unaccompanied by music . . . music is secondary, almost superfluous.

(Herman Ould in *Dancing Times*, April 1926)

Without any sounds to hide behind, a dance must be clear and strong in content. It must have its own vibrant internal rhythms and form. Silence is the equivalent of the spaces in visual art or the stillness in dance. The apparently negative aspects of any art form are just as important as the obviously positive ones. They exist woven together.

All kinds of movement and atmospheres are possible in silence. *Water Study* (1928) by Doris Humphrey is an outstanding example of the use of silence.

> . . . the dance without music . . . increases concentration and attention onto movement to an astonishing degree. . . . 'Water Study' . . . was composed for fourteen girls whose bodies rose and fell, rushed and leaped like the various aspects of water, the only sound being the faint thudding of feet in running movements, reminiscent of surf.
>
> (Doris Humphrey in *The Art of Making Dances*, 1959)

The use of silence in Richard Alston's *Soda Lake* (1981) enhances the complex rhythmical changes in the movement. There are sudden changes of speed, from quick allegro footwork to prolonged stillnesses. The enormous empty space of a real desert landscape exists in a vast silence, and in this work the overall bare, minimal look is similarly well balanced by the accompaniment of silence. There is a real atmosphere of quiet openness and solitude where the dancer performs.

Sometimes, a few seconds of silence at the start or end of, or during, a dance can add contrast and avoid predictability. It may also serve to highlight moments of greater importance by allowing the onlooker's ear to rest and focus more on seeing the movement. Siobhan Davies' choreography often continues the movement when the music has stopped. We see this in *White Man Sleeps* (1988). The female solo, at the end of part 3, continues echoing the last phrase of the music and eventually fading into stillness. At a different point in the dance, dancers also hold a stillness shape of the animal head motif while the music plays quietly. Both of these have the effect of maintaining pace and balance and holding the viewer's attention.

Voice

When people move, they often accompany their movements with voice, in song or in words, quite naturally. Other peoples' voices may be used, or the voice could be on tape. The accents and types of sounds could blend smoothly with, or they could act as a contrast to, the movement. The voice may use words, human sounds like giggles, sighs and so on, or song. The speech may also be distorted and it does not have to make sense. For example, it may sound like a rap with a repetitive rhythm (in the original text, the words may not have been repeated and consequently the sounds become like a musical score). *Dutiful Ducks* (1982), a solo for dancer Michael Clark by Richard Alston, used a sound tape (text score by composer Charles Amirkhanian) which repeated a few rhythmical phrases of words, like: 'Dutiful, d-d-d-d dutiful ducks, dutiful ducks . . . in double L.A. Tree tops sway.' The phrasing, rhythm and accents of the movements all matched those of the text score. The sources of voice and text may be found in poetry, stories, diaries, newspapers and magazines.

In the first section of Ian Spink's *New Tactics* (1983), for Second Stride, dancers spoke expressing a range of emotions from the absurd, 'Someone has put all the jelly babies down the loo and fed Rice Krispies to the potplants', to the terse, 'Will you cut that out?' These statements and questions were contentious and sometimes ignored or received with hostility. An overall atmosphere of cold isolation was created and when, in later sections, the dancers seem to be in

relative states of closeness this hinted at the theme of the dance. Dancers shared humour on a stage filled with pillows and seemed less shut off from each other when the sets of chrome bars were raised from the stage. But this is one of those dances that different viewers will 'see' quite differently from each other.

Kenneth MacMillan uses poetry in a Mahler score in his *Song of the Earth* (1965). It does not literally translate the words into dance, as he did in *Images of Love* (1964), which was based on Shakespeare's love sonnets. He said:

> I don't expect the audience to know what the words are about, although I'm pleased when they do . . . the audience can take the ballet on any level . . . I have to pick a poetic image that will go with the words rather than illustrate them.
>
> (In *Making a Ballet*, 1974)

So how was MacMillan treating the words and voice? Perhaps the easiest way to think about it is that he chose images which capture the broad themes of the poems. These were enjoying and saying goodbye to the joys and beauty of the world, and the promise of renewal after death. An example of this is in the first scherzi, 'Of Youth', the dance is full of youthful energy, fun and beauty. As the poem mentions the reflections of the scene in a smooth, quiet pool the soloist is momentarily upside down.

Dancers' own voices are often used by Lloyd Newson. In *Strange Fish* (1992), Nigel Charnock's solo as a misfit at a party is accompanied by his voice. He babbles on, mostly about loneliness, people and being a 'party animal'. His interest, he tells us, is 'collecting people' and his rantings reveal deep down his despair and longing to be one of the 'crowd'. As his banter speeds up it sparks a chain reaction in the other dancers as they try to avoid him. It accompanies them as they run away and dive into each other's arms and he continues to chase them chatting incessantly.

To succeed in the Hollywood musicals of the 1930s and 1940s dancers had to be able to sing as well as they danced. There were several successes, including Fred Astaire, Debbie Reynolds, Gene Kelly, Judy Garland and many others. Garland and Kelly starred together in *For Me and My Gal* (1942) and she featured with Astaire in the famous comedy number from *Easter Parade* (1948). Choreographed by Robert Alton, 'We're a Couple of Swells' depicts a couple of down-at-heel tramps in a comic song and dance routine. *Easter Parade* was produced by one of the biggest names in this Hollywood genre, Arthur Freed. Freed was the first to employ specialist choreographers for his films and he nurtured many talents including Gene Kelly, Michael Kidd and Bob Fosse. In 1939, he produced the timeless *The Wizard of Oz* for which he talent spotted the 14-year-old Garland to play Dorothy. She went on to make other hits with Freed including *For Me and My Gal* (1942, with Gene Kelly), *Meet Me in St Louis* (1944) and *The Pirate* (1948). In Hollywood at this time, children often started young. Anne Miller, another tapping talent, was working in California's nightclubs when she was 11 years old and made her film debut, like Garland, aged 14.

Figure 5.1 *Wizard of Oz* – Judy Garland and Ray Bolger

Figure 5.2 *Easter Parade* – Judy Garland and Fred Astaire; 'We're a Couple of Swells'

Many of the melodies and songs became smash hits in their own right; hardly surprising considering that some of the best songwriters and composers of the time were employed to write the scores. Irving Berlin and Max Steiner (*Top Hat*, 1935 and *Follow the Fleet*, 1936), Artie Shaw (*Second Chorus*, 1940), George and

Ira Gershwin (*Shall We Dance*, 1937) were just some of the notables. The Gershwins' previous hit Broadway shows in New York, 1924, *Lady Be Good!* and 1927, *Funny Face*, were obviously the right pedigree for the cinema. Broadway composer Leonard Bernstein had his show *On the Town* (1944, choreographer Jerome Robbins) adapted for film of the same name in 1949. Gene Kelly starred in and choreographed the film.

Sometimes starting with words can stimulate the movement ideas and the sound or music score. When choreographer Glen Tetley was making his two-act version of *The Tempest* (1979) for Ballet Rambert, he collaborated with composer Arne Nordheim. They shared a fascination with a love of nature and mixing sounds. They worked together on the score for three and a half years, going through Shakespeare's play and finding in the words a musical construction. This partnership was ideal (as pointed out by Tetley) to express the key speech of the monster Caliban: 'The isle is full of noises, and a thousand twangling instruments. . .' For Tetley this was a key element in the dance and musical settings.

TASK ONE – *Once-upon-a-time. . .*

KEY SKILLS Problem solving
Working with others

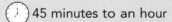

45 minutes to an hour

Choose a short fairy story. Photocopy it and cut it up into separate phrases that make sense. Let each dancer choose at random one or two phrases and improvise them, saying the words at the same time as moving. Show each other the results. Try to mix everyday movement with dance and mime. Use a variety of the Six Dance Actions.

Discuss how the phrases may be put together into a group dance using silences, repetitions of phrases and an understandable narrative. Try to add humour and drama so that the story becomes more than it was in the original version.

Sound

Non-human sounds from nature and the environment can be very appropriate for some dances. The sounds of wind, water, storms, street activity, railway stations, birds, football crowds or telephones are just some of the possibilities. You could sample some yourself by taking a portable tape recorder out and about and making recordings. In Robert Cohan's *Forest* (1977), the sounds of wind, running streams, thunder, rain, bird calls and a wolf howl were mixed with an electronic score to create a forest atmosphere (Brian Hodgson). The dance movement mixed images of the animals who inhabit the forest with their calls which ricocheted around the space.

The sound of a train whistle is used as a link between sections in Alvin Ailey's *Blues Suite* (1958). It works well as a transition device to 'glue' the sections together, but it is more than that. The whistle also emphasises the expression and meaning of the piece, because it suggests other ideas: where these people live, 'the wrong side of the tracks', and their poverty; the fact that the men who visit the cheap saloon are travelling workers. So a sound sets a clear social and expressive context for the dance. The sections of the dance are accompanied by traditional blues music, the lyrics, tradition and atmosphere of which also set the tone. Such choices as the life of black Americans, their struggle and traditional blues music are characteristic of Ailey's work. At the end of the dance, a mournful bell tolls and this sets the dancers into quite a different dynamic and mood. A writhing contraction from the men lying on the floor acts a reminder that their fun in the barrel room is fleeting and that hard work is ever present around the next bend of the railway tracks.

When dancing in an outdoor location, the found sound can become the accompaniment itself. For example, the sound of passing traffic can draw attention to desired issues in a dance that is concerned with environmental pollution. Cunningham and composer John Cage play off this to some extent in the score for *Beach Birds for Camera* (1991). Cage's score *Four3* hints at the tinkling of shells on the sea shore as they are moved in gently lapping ocean waves. On the whole, this creates a peaceful sense of repose, matched by the slowly undulating arms and torsos – or with eyes half closed a flock of Oyster Catchers at low tide.

To John Cage (composer for Merce Cunningham) any sound or noise is music. He gave piano concerts consisting of sitting and not playing for 20 or so minutes, thus forcing the audience to listen to the everyday sounds around them. In his view, this was a way of experiencing the environment. Technological advances also meant that the dancers themselves could create their own aural settings as they moved. In *Variations V* (1965 Cage and Cunningham), the dancers' movements activated antennas on stage which sent signals to the orchestra pit. Triggered by light intensity, the antennas set off tape recorders, radios, and so on, to make electronic sound. In this way, the dance was not at all dependent on the accompaniment – rather, the score depended entirely on the movements.

The sounds the dancers themselves make can often serve as the accompaniment. Stamping, clapping and breath sounds all provide possible aural settings. Tap dance, Indian and flamenco all use the sounds of the feet and hands to enhance the rhythmical experience for the audience. Metal taps on the shoes, bells on the ankles and wooden castanets in the hands all serve to emphasise the aural aspect of the movement.

Tap dances were one of the most eyecatching features of Hollywood musicals and films. Astaire's tap solo 'Slap That Bass' in *Shall We Dance* (1937, RKO Radio Pictures) is set in a rather stylish ship's engine room. In the middle section of the dance, the music drops out and is replaced by rhythmic engine sounds. This scene was unusual for its time, when racism was rife in showbiz, because it

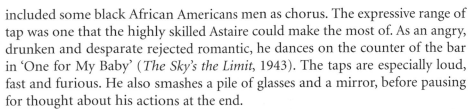

included some black African Americans men as chorus. The expressive range of tap was one that the highly skilled Astaire could make the most of. As an angry, drunken and desparate rejected romantic, he dances on the counter of the bar in 'One for My Baby' (*The Sky's the Limit*, 1943). The taps are especially loud, fast and furious. He also smashes a pile of glasses and a mirror, before pausing for thought about his actions at the end.

In Christopher Bruce's *Swansong* (1987), the idea of the interrogation of a political prisoner in a South American jail is cleverly brought to life. The feet of the interrogators and the prisoner tap out and shuffle question-and-answer conversations. Claps and finger clicks are also used. All of this is mixed into an electronic sound and musical score (Philip Chambon) that heightens the intensity of the plight of the tortured prisoner. They play cat and mouse with him, and in a macabre setting of red noses and music-hall song and dance, we feel that his fate is sealed. Bruce also uses intermittent silences to enhance moments of particular drama, such as at the start creating a sense of imminent danger and again near the end when the music suddenly stops, as if the prisoner's heart has too.

You may be thinking now about the rich possibilities of mixing various types of accompaniment together and this may, or may not, include music.

Music

The most obvious thing to do is to set movements to music, but this may make a dance totally reliant on the aural setting. It is the movement that should be the main concern of the dance. As George Balanchine once remarked, the audience should see the music and hear the dance. The relationship of dance to music is discussed in greater detail later in the book. What we are concerned with here is choosing music that has a positive influence on the dance. The dancer should feel able to be 'inside' the music, as if the air is full of it.

Choosing music

A poor choice of music can ruin a dance. Ideally, the dance and music should support one another. There are a number of things which should be considered when choosing music:

1 *Balance.* A piece of music which has large numbers of instruments or a rich production quality may not be entirely suited to a solo dance. On the other hand, some music is sparse in its style and so may not be ideal for a large group dance.

2 *Avoiding the obvious.* Music from the Top Ten, or old favourites which you enjoy listening to, are not always the best for dance. Similarly, some well-known classical music or hits from West End shows can also prove difficult because people know them so well that they already have their own set ideas about them and this may mean that your choreography will be overpowered by their preconceptions. Often, much of this type of music is the wrong length anyway, and cutting it is not only illegal but also unartistic. After all,

how would you feel if a musician cut off the last minute of your dance because it was too long to fit to the music? This shows a lack of respect for the artistry of the other artist.

Of course, there are always exceptions to the rules. Michael Clark used the well-known song *Shout* by Lulu to great success. This can be seen in Charles Atlas' film about Clark and in Clark's work called *Hail the New Puritan* (1986). Clark followed the simple structure of the song to the note. It was the unorthodox choice of movement style, involving his typical fast classical footwork and flexible torso combined with a sharp, clean execution in the dynamic range, that made for the success. Clark's highly technically accomplished dancers held their own with the music. The contrasts between the visual and aural features served to hold those two aspects in balance. Furthermore, the use of humour or satire in a dance may be enhanced by choosing music which holds within it many known clichés.

It is your responsibility as a choreographer to research the availability of music. These days, there is a massive range of music available. Explore this by visiting your local music library, or go online and try listening to things with names on them that you may have never heard of. There is no excuse for not finding the wildest, whackiest of music for your work.

I think that there's a difference between music that dialogues with dance and music that I might like to listen to at home.

(Shobana Jeyasingh in interview with Christopher Thompson in *The Stage*, 1992)

Perhaps one of the most famous examples of taking risks with new and difficult music was in 1913 when Vaslav Nijinsky (1889–1950) used a score by Stravinsky for his third ballet, *Le Sacre du Printemps* (The Rite of Spring). Nijinsky had already shocked audiences with his barefoot chorus, parallel use of the body, sexual inuendo and animal quality in *L'Aprés-midi d'un Faune* a year earlier, but that was overshadowed by what happened next. The Stravinsky music was difficult, not just for the audience to take but for the dancers to understand too. Diaghilev employed a young student from the Dalcroze School of Eurythmics to help to count the music for the dancers in rehearsals. This assistant was to become Marie Rambert and found Ballet Rambert from the previous Ballet Club in 1935. The rhythmic pulses that drive the dancers counterpoint the score, making for a non-balletic style. Inevitably, Nijinsky added more layers of innovation on top of the discordant music and non-metrical movement, to challenge the audiences of the time. His pagan, prehistoric setting and dark mood for the ballet and, one step further on from the use of a parallel body, the turned-in legs of dancers, plus the heavy down weight of the movement challenged the Parisian audience who near rioted! However, it is widely acknowledged that

Nijinsky's choreography matched up to the demanding music, and it is a pity that the dance was lost – whereas the music lived on because of the score.

3 *Quality*. Whenever possible, it is important to use top-quality recordings. It is best to make a rehearsal tape and not to use the original all the time but to save it instead for performance. Recordings full of scratches and jumps or that are hardly audible, are unacceptable unless that particular effect has been chosen for a special reason. For example, if you wished to create the feel of an old black-and-white film, it may be appropriate to choose such recordings.

4 *Style*. Music set in a particular country or period of history needs careful handling. It is possible to mix and match modern music with, say, that in an Indian style – as Shobana Jeyasingh frequently does. Mixing different styles needs proper editing.

On the whole, the overall styles of the dance and music need to be matched, as is frequently found in the dances of Christopher Bruce when he sets the dance in the place or time that matches the music. Scottish, Spanish, Irish, African, Renaissance, mediaeval, impressionist, romantic, neoclassical and jazz styles are all useful if handled properly. There can be some playful possiblities too. If these labels are unfamiliar to you, then perhaps a little research into music would be helpful.

5 *Live music*. Ideally, live music should be used whenever possible, but of course access to this can be difficult. You may know other students who study music and who may be willing to play for you. It may help to make a recording of their playing for you for rehearsals. There may even be someone who can compose and this could be very exciting. Improvising together can be great fun, and very productive. Using percussion instruments for dancers to accompany each other in improvisation can be surprisingly effective. In the final choreography, the musicians may play an equal part in the performing.

Live music is played in Siobhian Davies' *White Man Sleeps* (1988, score Kevin Volans) The musicians of the string quartet are on stage, but only partly visible through the muslin screens of the set.

Ian Spink's choreography of the 1970s and 1980s had a highly personal style, noticeably different in movement style and structure from many other choreographers of the time. His work was more abrupt, absurd and used an almost disjointed structure that brought with it surprise and interest for the viewer. His dance *De Gas* (1981, music Jane Wells) started from the Degas paintings of female nudes going about their ablutions – washing and combing hair and such. Spink chose male dancers for his work and a range of props including jugs, water, bowls, mirrors and towels. At one point an oboe player enters to play seated with his feet soaking in a bowl.

If you are lucky enough to have someone compose music for you, then you will be part of a long tradition. Diaghilev, the driving force and entrepeneur behind Ballets Russes, commissioned many scores for the ballets. He first commissioned the young composer Igor Stravinsky in 1910 for Fokine's

choreography of *The Firebird* and *Petrushka*. Stravinsky worked closely with Fokine and designer Benois to blend dance, design and music into a seamless whole. Diaghilev went on to commission music from many of the great modern composers including Debussy for Nijinsky's *Prélude a L'Apres-midi d'un Faune* (1912) and *Jeux* (1913), and Satie for Massine's *Parade* (1917). Satie and designer Cocteau worked closely with Massine on *Parade*, but Diaghilev still had a say in production and he refused to allow Cocteau's request to use the spoken voice in the dance. However, megaphones were allowed, as were sounds of ship's horns and typewriters. *Parade* was highly innovatory and combining talents such as Picasso, Satie and Massine created cutting-edge theatre – and fun. This was a popular ballet with audiences of the time. Throughout World War I, Ballets Russes struggled on with their policy for innovation with great difficulty.

TASK TWO – Percussion moves

KEY SKILLS Problem solving
Working with others

20 to 30 minutes

This activity is great fun and gives you a chance to try your hand at playing percussion combined with moving and words. It's an association game and uses an action–reaction relationship with a partner. It can just be a simple improvisation, but it can also lead to new ideas that may work for your own choreography as an alternative to the usual recorded music.

In pairs, select a variety of percussion instruments (bells, cymbals, shakers, glockenspiels, tambourines, triangles, castanets, indian bells etc.). Follow the sequence below, doing each stage as many times as you wish – the more you repeat, the more interesting the results:

- One plays a percussion instrument, partner moves at the same time.
- One plays – stops – partner moves.
- One plays – stops – partner gives a word as a response.
- One gives a word – stops – partner plays.
- One gives a word – stops – partner gives a movement.
- One gives a single movement – stops – partner gives a word.
- One gives a movement sequence- stops – partner plays percussion.
- One moves and partner plays at the same time.

Once you have found a few ideas that you like, put them into a short combination as a dance, using movement, words and percussion. Be inventive with how you work the percussion into the dance and try to make picking up or putting down the instruments part of the dance. You could even keep them on your person somehow if you're really imaginative.

Using music

There are a number of ways that a dance may be formed with music:

- dance and music composed together;
- dance created first, then music composed for it;
- compose music first, then dance to it (most common);
- a dance sketched in, then either music composed for it or suitable music is found;
- music and dance composed separately, only coming together in performance.

When a piece of music is chosen first, you need to do a number of things to prepare for the creation of the dance:

- Listen to it over and over again, carefully.
- Improvise to it.
- Develop an understanding of its feel, form, meter, tempo, instrumentation and so on (use written notes to help your memory).

Remember, music and the dance do not have to match exactly. The dance needs a rhythmical life of its own which is not dictated by the music.

Abstract dancing is analogous to abstract music. The same three elements are there – the tone, rhythm, melody and harmony, with the addition of the kinesthetic appeal only possible in the dance. This means that to a sensitive onlooker there is a constant stream of primitive excitement going on inside . . .

(Doris Humphrey in *The Art of Making Dances*, 1959)

Robert Cohan's choice of *Serenata 2* (Bruno Maderna, 1957) for *Hunter of Angels* was appropriate because both the music and the movement were in an abstract style. Also the sections of the music supported the shifts of emotion in the story of the dance. Task Three gives you the chance to work on ideas from this chapter and Chapter Four to develop some dance in the style of Robert Cohan.

Sometimes in rehearsal it is fun to try lots of different types of music for a dance. The results can be surprisingly successful!

TASK THREE – A biblical beginning

KEY SKILLS Problem solving
Working with others

 Several hours

This Task links to Task Seven in Chapter Four.
Individually, or with a partner, compose some movement phrases in a style similar to that used in Cohan's *Hunter of Angels*. Choose

ONE suitable prop to enhance the expression of your dance (this can also be a costume or a prop-set). One dancer can play two different roles. You could try to use a combination of accompaniments, such as voice, silence, natural sounds, percussion and music, if possible. Or you could try: Arvo Part's *Como cierva sedentia*, verse IV (3m 27s); Garbareck, J. *Procedentem Sponsum* (2m 50s), or *De spineto nata rosa* (2m 30s). These tracks have many rich changes of mood, as there was in the Maderna score used by Cohan. Use the changes in the music to develop movement and meanings for your dance.

Possible starting points for you to choose from are based on themes that were used in the 1970s by London Contemporary Dance Theatre:

- *Stabat Mater* (Cohan, 1975) – worked with images of Mary in sorrow at the foot of the Crucifixion of Jesus. Cohan used his usual vocabulary but also incorporated 'active stillness'.
- *The Annunciation* (Robert North, 1979) – worked with images of the dialogue between Mary and the Angel Gabriel on the news of the oncoming birth of Jesus.
- *David and Goliath* (Robert North) – a giant is taken on by a boy, with only a stone sling as a weapon.

For all of these themes you should research the verses in the Bible. Images from paintings for themes (1) and (2) may help too: 13th century, Giotto *Virgin annunciate, Denunciation*: Martini, *Annunciation*; 14th century, Angelico, *Annunciation*; 15th century, Botticelli, *Pieta*; Van der Weyden *Pieta, Deposition*; Avignon School, *Pieta*; 16th century, Leonardo da Vinci, *Annunciation*; Bartolommeo, *Pieta*; del Piombo, *Pieta*.

The tasks below allow you to try new approaches to accompaniment and music that you may not have considered before.

TASK FOUR – *Pick 'n' mix*

KEY SKILLS Problem solving
Working with others

These tasks can be helpful when you are working towards your examination pieces as a way to shape new dance compositions. Just apply them as appropriate!

1 Several hours

Find a copy of 'The Jabberwocky' by Lewis Carroll. Select certain key words and phrases which may be spoken by a narrator or by the dancers themselves. Decide on an overall format for a group of five or six dancers which is not too literal but may use certain atmospheres, moods, moments and meanings. The monster might be made up of many individuals and not just one. Also, the fighting scene could involve all the dancers fighting an invisible Jabberwocky. Notice here too the form of the poem itself, in that the first and last verses are the same. Find some music or sound effects which the text can be easily woven in and out of. It may be music that creates a general atmosphere of fear and mystery without a particularly strong beat. (Suggested music: the soundtrack of the film *Diva*.) Using text, music and silence, compose the group dance.

2 🕐 45 minutes to one hour

Using percussion instruments for accompaniment, make three dance phrases of 5-5-8 counts. Dance them whilst accompanied by the group playing 6 measures of 3/4 in a steady tempo, accenting count 1 of each bar. Take it in turns to dance and play.

3 🕐 45 minutes to one hour

Use K.D. Lang's song 'Big love'. Listen to it carefully, then write down the number of beats and measures in the verses and chorus. Make movement phrases which have irregular counts that are not the same as the music but that add up to the same total at the end of each verse or chorus. Practise until the two fit together. Start or finish with a silent section of movement.

Leaving a final word to a well-known and highly respected choreographer:

I listen to a lot of music and I love it, but I don't often work with it. Or rather I work with it 'in private' in that I get many ideas about time, rhythm and time structures from music. . . . I found at one time if I used music that I really liked I ended up creating something that was very enjoyable to do, but the movement tended to be banal and very simple, getting into nothing but steps, running around on the beat. . . . I began working with ideas because body rhythms are different from musical rhythms.

(Richard Alston in *Making a Ballet*, 1974)

The different possible relationships between music and dance movement are explored in the next chapter.

References and resources

Video, DVD, CD-Rom
From www.dancebooks.co.uk
The Kirov Celebrates Nijinsky – Scheherazade, Le Spectre de la Rose, Polovtsian Dances, The Firebird. Published: 2004

Les Noces; The Firebird. The Royal Ballet. Published: 2002

Return of the Firebird – The Firebird, Petrushka and Scheherazade. Published: 2002. Three Fokine ballets recreated in the famous Mosifilm studios in Russia

The Royal Ballet – Ondine, Firebird. Published: 2004. Filmed live on stage at the Royal Opera House in 1960, this DVD includes abridged performances of The Firebird and Ondine, and the second act pas de deux from Swan Lake

Music

Cosma, V., *Diva* (film soundtrack), DRG Discovery Label, CD950622: Task 4

Garbarek, J. and The Hilliard Ensemble, *Officium*, ECM New Series 1994 445369-2: Task 3

K. D. Lang's song 'Big Love' from *Absolute Torch and Twang*, Sire 7599-25877-2, 1989: Task 4

Part, A., *Orient Occident*, ECM New Series 1795 472080-2, 2002: Task 3

6 CHOREOGRAPHY – SKILLS AND IDEAS

Choreography is the art of making dances – forming a blend of the movement components, dancers and physical and aural settings that best expresses a theme or idea.

> The work as a whole must be one of stuff, as an emerald is all emerald – crush it to powder, and each tiny pinch of that powder will still be an emerald.
>
> (Ted Shawn in *The Vision of Modern Dance*, 1980)

It is the overall unity of the dance which the audience sees and hears in performance.

This chapter examines how the movement features are organised so as to produce the final 'look' of the piece and express the ideas that you choose. You will find ideas to help you choreograph your dances for assessment in the tasks in this chapter. Many of the tasks can be used with themes of your choice, or you can enjoy them just as they are.

Form

Form, in its raw state, is all around us in the world we live in. Morning, afternoon, night, the four seasons, birth, life and death are all universal forms which everyone recognises. In making dance, music, poetry, painting or film, we take our sense of order and recreate it in an imaginary world.

> Form is the shape of the content. Form without content becomes form for the sake of form. . . . The form should contain the original impetus out of which it was created.
>
> (Hanya Holm in *The Vision Of Modern Dance*, 1980)

Form should express content, as in the meaning in the dance of Martha Graham, or it can be the message itself. In rehearsal, the choreographer will start by working with some basic ideas for the constituent features. A gradual process of developing and structuring the materials – including, of course, the dancers

themselves – eventually leads to a cohesive dance form which must satisfy the choreographer's own ideas, but also be clear to the dancers, and to the audience.

Richard Alston's choreographic style is formalist. For example, in *Rumours, Visions* (1994) he forms the dance around the music's structure. Alston reflected the crisp, staccato music in the dynamics and phrasing of the dance. Jumps, leg gestures, sudden drops to the floor and step rhythms reflect Benjamin Britten's music. However, often the content of Alston's work also uses other imagery and Britten's music evokes images of the sea that are reflected in the dance movement, so that the audience see and hear imagery such as choppy ocean waves, light bouncing off the water's surface and flocks of seagulls swirling through the sky.

The ways in which the movement is manipulated, and how the various constituent features interrelate throughout the dance, make each dance unique. As well as using intuition during the creative process, the choreographer needs knowledge about certain possible procedures. As in music composition, there are certain useful traditional devices and structures in choreography which comprise the skills of the craft, the tools of the trade. Like the physical skills involved in the training of a dancer, these technical skills will increase the choreographer's own range of expression. And again, as with the dancer's training, it is the physical participation in the solving of choreographic problems, improvisations and compositional exercises, that will develop your choreographic skills. Playing with movement is not only fun, but is the best way to learn about choreography.

Once experience and understanding are increased, these 'rules' will add both depth and a wider range of choice to your choreography, and, of course, they may be broken where justifiable. Without a knowledge of such choices, the choreographer may be stuck only with what they already know, plus what they have learnt through trial and error, and this situation may well narrow the individual's range of expression rather than enhancing it. Practical experiences in the following categories are necessary:

- compositional devices;
- compositional structures;
- the relationship of the dance to the accompaniment.

The final finished dance should have a natural, organic feel. Each part of it should grow naturally, almost inevitably, into the next just as a seed grows into a flower.

Compositional devices

Motifs are a single movement or a short phrase of movement which embody the style and content of the dance. They are repeated, varied and developed by manipulating the movement. These manipulations usually involve some change in the movement components of action, space, time dynamics or relationships (see Chapter Three).

Repetition is the simplest way of using a motif and this is commonly used in unison chorus routines in musical theatre such as seen in *Born to Dance*

(MGM, 1936). Starring Eleanor Powell, this film, typical of blockbusters of the day, included one big musical number. Dancing on the decks of a large navy battleship bedecked with sparkling canons to Cole Porter's *Swinging the Jinx Away*, Powell was accompanied by a mass chorus of dancers and a corps of singing sailors.

In many dances the repetition of motifs is irregular – motifs appear and disappear on and off throughout a dance. This repetition helps to glue the dance together and express the content, ideas, images and themes of the dance to the audience. A good example of the use of motif repetition and variation can be seen in *White Man Sleeps* (Siobhan Davies, 1988). The motif, described as the 'framing face', has a quiet, calm feel and is first seen in the second part of section 1 when one dancer traces hands around another's face. Then later in section 2 it is accented through repetition in a solo. It is also varied in section 3, when its dynamic softens, and again in section 4. This motif's small, gentle movement, performed in close relationships between the dancers, clearly expresses the content of the dance – intimacy between people in real life relationships.

Varying a motif is a real test of compositional skill. Unlike developing a motif, varying it involves keeping the original order of the movements the same, so the original motif must be sufficiently interesting to keep the attention of the audience. The variations then take the form of subtle adjustments in the movement such as in the dynamics, space, style, mood and tempo. Below is a list of ways in which motifs can be varied.

- change the size;
- change the level;
- use different parts of the body;
- alter the focus;
- change the direction, dimension or plane;
- alter the air or floor pattern;
- increase or decrease the tempo – augment or diminish, i.e. make slower/faster;
- vary the pattern of the beats of the rhythm;
- change the accents;
- change the facing;
- change an aspect of the relationships between dancers;
- change the dynamic or quality.

The variation of the motif of a hopscotch stepping pattern in *Four Scenes* (Christopher Bruce, 1998) is a link throughout the dance. It reappears with variations of dynamics and spacing and glues the dance together. In *Okho* (1996), Richard Alston used variation effectively in a male duet. The dancers perform a motif with unison timing, but in a mirror relationship placed on a diagonal on the stage. As the dancers perform the movement on opposite sides of the body to each other, a simple but eye-catching effect is created.

The musical structure 'theme and variation' takes a motif and repeats it slightly differently each time. Task Six gives you a chance to test your compositional skill in this structure.

Motif Development uses more drastic changes in the movement than variation. Below is a list of ways in which motifs can be developed:

- Alter the basic body posture, say from standing to lying, sitting, upside-down or twisted.
- Embellish the motif by adding a new feature such as another action.
- Retrograde it – reverse the order of the movements.
- Fragment the motif – use only one part repeatedly or some parts only, or change the order of the parts.
- Alter any of the aspects of the physical setting.
- Mix bits from different motifs together.

Motif variation and development are ways of producing a lot from a little, while also avoiding too much repetition – which may be boring for the audience. Motifs organically provide logical development, contrasts and eventually unity. We all know those awful moments when inspiration is not happening! Once, after much practice, you are able to do it spontaneously, motif development will help you to avoid drying up. Task One gives you a chance to try a formalist style of motif development. You can use the movement suggested, or try this with a simple movement from one of your own compositions.

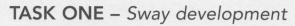

TASK ONE – *Sway development*

KEY SKILLS Problem solving
Improving own learning and performance

45 minutes to an hour

Develop a simple sway right – left, standing in second position arms by sides motif as follows:

1 Repeat it.
2 Add an arm gesture as you sway.
3 Add another action on so that you now have three parts: the sway + 1 arm gesture + 1 another action (turn, travel, jump, fall or stillness).
4 Repeat just the sway.
5 Reverse the order of the three parts – i.e. retrograde.
6 Fragment the three parts by changing the order.
7 Dance all three parts, but add a new detail – i.e. embellish it.
8 Repeat one part three times.

Practise this whole sequence 1 to 8 until it is memorised.
Suggested music: *Telek,* by Abebe (2m 50s).
When variation and developments are used in different canons and unison relationships between dancers, the visual effect can be stunning.

Contrast

Contrast introduces new material which is noticeably different from anything so far seen in the dance. This can be introduced suddenly or gradually. For example, a light, slow motif can be contrasted with large fast jumps, and this can be done by gradually increasing the tempo and strength, or by switching from one to the other in an instant. Dynamic contrast is cleverly used by Alvin Ailey in *Revelations* (1960). Dancers move with heavy earthiness in the opening section, their legs and torsos deeply bent and heads bowed. Then the mood brightens with the lights, as dancers celebrate a baptism. A procession of dancers, dressed in dazzling white, travel exuberantly to the song 'Take me to the Water'. Immediately, the mood swings again as a male soloist dances in anguished repentance with sudden contractions of the torso. Finally, in the last section a celebratory mood returns and energy bursts into a joyous finale. This is one of Ailey's best-loved dances that celebrates the faith and strength of African Americans to win over racist oppression and poverty.

Figure 6.1 Revelations. Alvin Ailey's American Dance Theater.
Photographer: Anthony Crickmay

The bright and dark characters in ballets such as *The Nutcracker* and *Sleeping Beauty* create dramatic tension in their conflicts. In a contemporary *Swan Lake* (Bourne, 1995) the whirl of the ballroom and shooting scene are in dramatic contrast to the scene which follows. The Prince is sedated by the team of nurses who perform a motif of minimal arm and hand gestures with frightening surgical precision.

Highlights

Highlights will maintain the interest of the audience and draw attention to particular features or images that the choreographer may wish to emphasise. Usually, a dance has a few moments which the audience remembers the most vividly. These therefore function to make clearer the meaning or content of the dance. Highlights inject pace. As the audience is swept along in the stream of consciousness of the piece, the highlights enable them to maintain a grasp on its overall direction more easily, and this clearly heightens their enjoyment, understanding and appreciation.

There are a variety of ways of creating highlights. One approach – similar to that found in the development of motifs – is to manipulate a movement component. One technique is to make use of rhythmical and dynamic accents. Highlights can be created by using a stronger dynamic, but they can also arise from emphasising a softer, gentler dynamic. A prolonged stillness, in anticipation of something happening, is also effective in creating tension and interest.

Expectancy and the unexpected are both attention-getters, and the skilful uses of each are unbeatable.

(Doris Humphrey in *The Art of Making Dances*, 1959)

For dramatic and narrative structures, the creation of tension and pace is vital, and highlights can be useful to do this. One method used by choreographer Ian Spink in *Further and Further into the Night* (1984) was the repetition of motif. This dance was based on Alfred Hitchcock's classic film thriller *Notorious* (1946), a story of romance and intrigue. Many of the motifs relate to movements from the film, so that everyday movement is used a great deal. At one point, the gestures involved in serving a drink are repeated over and over creating humour and also tension.

Merce Cunningham uses the spacing of dancers to create a peak that marks the ending of the black and white section of *Beach Birds for Camera*. After a long section where the dancers are scattered loosely around the space, four male dancers make contact in an inward facing circle. Even though they are on different levels, the circle is a regularly shaped and solid group formation that contrasts the material earlier in the dance. This makes for a memorable moment and signals a smooth transition that leads into the colour section.

An increase or decrease in the numbers of dancers may draw attention to themes like isolation, rejection or celebration, as used in *Revelations*. Also in *Revelations*, Ailey uses set, props and light to highlight the baptism scene. Two huge silks, one blue, the other white, envelop the procession, as if the river of holy water surrounds them. One female dancer carries an enormous white parasol to protect the two baptism candidates. The use of the physical setting lifts the exuberance of the mood and energy.

In 1988, Siobhan Davies returned to Britain from a study trip in the USA, during which she studied with Merce Cunningham and travelled the country.

Earlier in her career she had also worked with Richard Alston. All three of these influences were clear in *Embarque*, the first dance that she made on her return. The dance idea is based on her travels across America. The feeling of racing along past rushing scenery is strongly expressed in the pace and power of the fast, fluid travelling motifs that cover the stage space with curving and direct floor patterns. Davies's formalist, highly abstract style builds two noticeable highlights by using all eight dancers, and these sections feel like the intense travelling times between important arrival points.

Ghost Dances (Bruce, 1981) has highlights built into each section. Towards the end of each section the ghosts infiltrate the ordinary people. Their presence is ominous and threatening and they catch our eye, smoothly leading into the highlight of a section when they 'strike' and another person is killed or 'disappeared'.

Climax

There may be several highlights in a dance, but there is only one main high point: the climax. The dance should be organised to gradually build towards this, making it seem inevitable, organically right. This again involves a crucial pacing of the constituent features.

Pacing is a balancing act which requires a delicate and subtle treatment of all the interconnected layers of the dance. It follows the logical progression and direction of the piece, whilst also continually providing enough interest and even diversion, so that the climax happens at just the right moment. When the final climax happens, it should confirm what the audience has expected and yet also provide a certain element of surprise so that it is not too obvious. It should sum up everything that has happened before it. The climax might be a fast and furious outburst of energy and action, or it could fade away to a gentle quiet place, or may be marked by the end of a particular story. Or, it may well be that the climax does not come at the end of the dance.

The actual ending of the dance is, however, the last thing that the audience will see, and they will remember it the best, and so it must be memorable – it must not disappoint or puzzle, or leave the audience uncomfortably up in the air not knowing whether or not to applaud. It is noticeable that the endings of Lea Anderson's works are often glitzy and fast. We see this, for example, in the shiny phosphorescent suits of *Go Las Vegas* (1995), and in the ending of *Precious* (1993), which depicts the process of alchemy turning base metals into gold. The dancers realise their dreams by changing their perspectives. Finally, they achieve the golden state of equilibrium, and the movement's pace increases to a furious tempo. In contrast, Siobhan Davies's dances often end 'quietly'. *White Man Sleeps* (1988) ends with the dancers in turn gradually coming to stillness. A motif of a low hovering arabesque is the final lingering image. *Embarque* is an exception to this. As you just read, this dance has two highlighted sections when all eight dancers fill the stage with fast travelling motifs. One of these section closes the dance and builds faster than the previous highlight section. The actual end of the dance is brought to a fitting climax by Davies's use of a sudden,

unexpected stillness from a remaining duo. This marks the end of the rush of the journey and perhaps hints at the expression of how Davies arrived at the idea of making *Embarque*.

TASK TWO – *Surprise!*

KEY SKILLS Problem solving
Working with others
Communication

Several hours

'Surprise me!' Ensuring that you use contrast, highlights and climax, compose a duet which has a surprise for the audience. (This was set as a choreographic task by Robert Cohan in 1986 at the London School of Contemporary Dance. It proved to be very testing for all the choreographers present.)

Balance

The proportions of the sections of the dance need to be appropriate to the individual movement phrases and how they relate to each other. As phrases develop and lengthen, they become whole sections, and each must be an appropriate length for its movement to be appreciated fully. Similarly, if there is a meaning in the movement, enough time is needed for this meaning to be put across to the audience.

In rehearsal, the choreographer will be making spontaneous and intuitive choices about how single movements grow into phrases, and about how long those phrases are, and how long the sections are that are the sum of those phrases. These are delicate decisions which will give the dance its final pace and overall form. Throughout the creative process, as movement is developed, the process of giving the dance a balanced structure is occurring simultaneously. Sometimes, the order and length of motifs, longer phrases and whole sections is obvious early on in rehearsal, but at other times it may require some experimentation. Finally, the choreographer decides what is, for them, a sensible and appropriate ordering and length for all the parts. This will amount to the final balance and proportion of the dance.

Forest (1977) by Robert Cohan provides a good example. The dance is based on three simple motifs:

1 the 'calling' motif;
2 the 'prowling' motif;
3 the 'pairing' motif.

Through repetition, variation and development, the motifs combine in numerous ways to create the balance and form of the dance. Several sections become obvious to the audience. Many short sections overlap by means of

frequent entrances and exits, making their beginnings and ends clear. The dance has nine sections which fall into four main parts (ABCD) during which different moods are expressed: romantic; the darker menace of a pack of prowling predators; calmness; tense nervousness.

There are interesting similarities in balance and structure between *White Man Sleeps* (Davies, 1988) and *Forest* in that the sections are linked by dancers' exits and entrances. Also the balance of content within the sections, solos and intimate duets mixing with faster groups travelling in canons are similar. Even the devices of motif repetition, development and variations bear some resemblances. Davies would have danced in many Cohan pieces as a dancer with London Contemporary Dance Theatre in the 1970s. Although, her work is more abstract and uses different movement vocabulary from Cohan's expressionist, dramatic Graham style there are some formal aspects of structure that their dances share.

Inevitably choreographers of the same day and age may inspire each other. In 1964, when Merce Cunningham Dance Company came to London for the first time, they performed *Nocturnes*, to music by Erik Satie. Dancers wore all-white unitards and the structure bore Cunningham's trademark scattered, fluid style. In 1965, Sir Frederick Ashton's modern ballet *Monotones* was premiered and may well have been inspired by seeing *Nocturnes*. *Monotones*, costumed in white all-in-one leotards and skull caps, captured a combination of classical balletic elegance and abstract formality to Satie's 'Gymnopédies. Motifs of arabesques and attitudes provided the basic building blocks from which repetitions and variations of tempo, direction and relationship were used to scaffold other material. The calm fluidity is shared with the music and the lack of a climax in the dance was well-suited to the timeless mood. Balance is further emphasised by the ending itself which, again like the music, is sudden, but suggests that the dance may continue on and on, after the lights go down.

Transition

Transitions are the links between movements, phrases and sections of the dance, and as such they are an integral part of the dance. As one movement or phrase grows into the next, the organic and logical progression should also flow.

Transitions can differ in:

- length – gradual or abrupt;
- complexity – as simple as a plié for a jump, or involving a whole phrase of movement.

Transitions usually correspond to what they are linking, so that a transition between whole sections may be more complex than that which connects two simple actions. In *Septet* (1953) by Merce Cunningham, the dancers' exits and entrances at the end of each section use everyday movements like hand shakes, nods and waves. This drew attention to the gaps between the sections, making the transitions as important as the dance itself. Bourne's use of transition in his *Swan Lake* is often quite traditional, reminding us of a conventional ballet in

that the front curtain may close between acts. This allows for complex scene changes and adds a sense of theatre. Other transitions include the use of set, for example, when the Prince's oversized bed is turned around so that it becomes the palace balcony from which the royal family wave to the public below.

Four Scenes (Christopher Bruce, 1998) uses a simple transition to link the sections. A soloist, usually in silence, dances briefly to link the theme of the four stages of life. Each solo provides a thematic link in its choice of motif, often echoing the previous section and/or hinting the next.

Logical sequence and proportion

Sequencing a dance logically involves organising the natural progression from start to finish. Part of this process includes consideration of the individual proportions of the beginning, middle and end sections. The final chosen order and length of the sections and their constituent features must give the appearance of a unified whole and be the most expressive sequence and proportion for the corresponding content.

The proportion of the beginning, middle and end, not only of the whole dance but also of each individual section is vital to correct pacing and the expression of the content. For instance, a long, gradually building opening section leading to a shorter middle section and an abrupt end may well be suited to some dances. In other instances, a dance may be more suited to a fast short opening section, a long middle section of some complexity, and a gradually winding-down ending. Task Three gives you a chance to work on these ideas.

TASK THREE – *Proportion*

KEY SKILLS Problem solving
Working with others
Communication

🕐 20 to 30 minutes

1 Look at the titles below and choose appropriate proportions for their beginning, middle and end sections. Write these out in table form. Give brief descriptions of the length of sections and the general motifs and images used.
- 'The rebellion goes up in smoke.'
- 'The river from source to sea.'
- 'Obstacle race.'

🕐 45 minutes to an hour

2 In groups of four or five, choose one of the themes above and improvise around the chosen sections. (Suggested music: Side 2 of the Penguin Café Orchestra's *Broadcasting from Home*.) As you work, select the most appropriate track for your needs.

Unity

No matter how complex the form of a dance is, it must still work as a whole unit. Too many unrelated components or ideas will be confusing for an audience to comprehend. The flow of the piece, its peaks, troughs and conclusion, is what gives the piece its unity or overall form. The central concern of a dance helps to maintain the flow, giving it coherence. This may involve either a particular meaning or a concern with the movement for its own sake. The central theme is selected, then the process of manipulating and selecting appropriate constituent features follows in rehearsal.

Consider Petipa's formula for making a ballet, as stated by Joan Lawson in *A History of Ballet and its Makers*, 1964. He examined each step of the classic vocabulary, assessing its merit and quality as it were, and allotting it to one of the seven categories of movement so that it could:

1 Be a preparation or provide a link between one movement and the next.
2 Add lightness, height, depth and breadth to the dance.
3 Add brilliance and sparkle, even wit.
4 Lend continuity to the flow of the line. . . and complete the total pattern of steps.
5 Add speed and excitement.
6 Become the highlight or finishing point of an enchaînment or dance.
7 Lend the finishing touch to the total picture.

It is well known that Ashton admired and studied Petipa's choreography as an inspiration for his own and the above list could be analysed to reveal much information about the devices of transition, highlight, contrast, phrasing, climax and balance in Ashton's ballets.

Contrast and variety are a part of the overall unity, and they too must be selected in a way appropriate to the central concern of the dance. Sometimes, even the most unlikely and incongruous ideas can work if these fall within the main purpose of the dance. Then, by their very differences they enhance the central idea and help the onlooker to grasp the main mood or meaning of the dance.

The structure of a ballet might be tight, compact, like the structure of a building; good ballets move in measured space and time, like the planets.

(George Balanchine in *Complete Stories of the Ballets*, 1954)

Richard Alston may well agree with this statement and his formalist style is influenced by his interest in and knowledge about structure in architecture, visual art and music. Alston's *Brisk Singing* (1997) is a good example of this. Watching its complex canons and changes of direction can feel like looking at constellations of stars twinkling and shooting across the night sky. The

structure of the dance is spatially complex, but rhythmically dazzling and clear.

Alternatively, choreographers may look to structures which are pre-set and are often derived from music or art or literature. In the next section, these structures will be examined in detail.

TASK FOUR – *Your planet*

KEY SKILLS Problem solving
Improving own learning and performance
Working with others
Communication

Allow at least three one-hour sessions for this task

This process could also be used with your own motifs for assessment pieces.

- Look at the pictures below. Use them as a score for a dance.
- Improvise and select short phrases/motifs for each.
- Memorise these and teach them to three or four dancers.
- Randomly choose which order they appear in, asking the dancers to perform them so that you can observe. Continue to do this until you are able to select one or two of the orders as the most successful. Note that this will involve making transitions if there are sticking points.
- Gradually, by careful observation:
    develop and extend the motifs so as to make sections;
    decide on the length of the beginning, middle and end sections;
    give consideration occasionally as to the climax and the end;
    consider if there is enough suitable contrast and variety;
- At any point, you may like to consider trying out different accompaniments as you work, until you find one which is most appropriate.
- Give the finished dance a title.

The above task should produce a dance which could, after rehearsal, be performed, and it should have overall form and unity, the content is based on the photographs. The organic structure of the dance will have grown through the gradual manipulation and selection of movement and the use of choreographic devices.

(a)

(b)

Figure 6.2 *Task 4*

Compositional structures

Compositional structures are traditional frameworks which have set patterns. These frameworks are often found in music, literature or art, and fit into one of the following three categories:

1 sequential;
2 contrapuntal;
3 episodic.

Sequential structures

These contain themes which progress in a definite order. Letters of the alphabet are used to label each theme or section. The simplest sequential structure is AB. Choosing the structure which best expresses the dance idea is essential. Unity is still necessary between the themes A, B, C etc. – again, they have to have something in common, even if it is through contrast. The themes also have to be linked with appropriate transitions. In songs, a transition is often called a bridge and it is usually an instrumental section.

Sequential structures may contain movement which has been developed using choreographic devices like motif development. These structures are set, but may be applied creatively to become organic wholes – for example, to become the framework for one section or for the entire dance. A dance may

even involve a mixture of different choreographic structures and these arrangements are freer in style, such as AABCDAD. This is a more intuitive way of working, and is probably the one which you will use most. Trying new approaches and structures like the ones listed below may be difficult at first, but they will help you build greater skill in your choreography.

The AB structure – binary (two-part)

This is the simplest form, like a verse and a chorus of a song. It is typical of many folk dances and songs. A and B may repeat many times and in any order: ABBAB, ABAB, AABA, ABAAB etc.

The ABA structure – ternary (three-part)

This is a form which is very comfortable to watch because of its feeling of completeness. A is the unifying theme and the centre of interest, then B gives contrast. The original A returns either as an exact repetition or in an easily recognisable variation or development. It is important that A and B be linked by transitions, and these may become important in their own right as they mix together features from both A and B. This allows B to grow out of A and then to flow easily back into A. The sections are still independent, but also connected. This gives balance and unity.

Many popular songs use this structure: the chorus A, a verse B, and a repetition of the chorus which is often augmented or elaborated in some way to emphasise the idea of the song.

TASK FIVE – A, B, C, Easy as 1, 2, 3

KEY SKILLS Problem solving
Improving own learning and performance

 Several hours

Listen to *Just a Girl,* by No Doubt. Analyse the music using A, B, C, etc. When you are satisfied with your analysis, compose motifs which fit with the music structure and counts. The movement may, however, be of a contrasting and unexpected style – e.g. balletic vocabulary with a strong, fast, dynamic quality.

ABACADA structure – rondo

The basic theme A returns after each contrasting theme. A must appear at least three times, but it can be varied. Indeed, the variations of A will maintain interest in the theme. The other sections should be individual and different, but should also be linked with appropriate transitions to provide continuity for the audience.

The rondo structure was popular in Europe in the eighteenth and nineteenth centuries as a lively round dance. A would be danced by everyone, and the B, C and D sections by individual soloists.

The Martha Graham solo *Frontier* (1935) is in rondo form. In a series of scenes from life on the frontier of the Wild West, Graham is first seen against the fence looking out across the vast plains. After each exploration away from the homestead, she returns to the fence in a clear rondo.

TASK SIX – *Theme & variations*

KEY SKILLS Improving own learning and performance
Communication
Problem solving
Working with others
Application of number

Several hours

Listen carefully to *Theme & Variations* by Fernando Sor and distinguish the four variations on the opening theme. The fourth variation is preceded by a bridge in the music and at the end runs into a call/response form. Or use *Tarantella* by the Lounge Lizards – there are some fun parts where the instrumentation gives variation changes of mood and some witty use of different tempi and dynamics. Using the idea of 'A Garden Party', compose a dance with five others to show the various garden inhabitants: birds; insects and spiders; reptiles; humans and their interactions.

Tasks Six, Twelve, Thirteen and Fifteen require you to listen carefully to the music so that you have a good understanding of it before you start to choreograph. This is a procedure that Richard Alston would follow.

Contrapuntal structures

The above structures give forms which are sequential, but there are also structures in which the main theme appears throughout. Again, these are musical forms also. The main theme is seen/heard against itself, or against one or more other themes. This leads to a weaving of material, through which the main theme must be clear and strong enough to stand out from the complex structure. These structures are called contrapuntal, and in music, they create polyphony, that is a playing of two or more independent melodies heard together. The final effect is more complex and richer than the sequential forms. There are three different kinds of contrapuntal structure:

1 ground bass;
2 round (or canon);
3 fugue.

In *The Nutcracker* (Petipa, Ivanov, 1892), the Tchaikovsky music was written to the requirements of Petipa's scenario so the episodes are well ordered. One example is the start of the ballet. Petipa wrote:

The President and his wife and guests decorate the tree
(delicate, mysterious music 64 bars) . . .

The fir tree is burning brightly, as if it were magic (modulated music 8 bars)

The door is thrown open (noisy happy music for the children's entrance 24 bars)

The children stop, full of amazement and delight
(a few bars for the children Tremolo)

(As translated by Joan Lawson, 1960)

The music for this ballet blends the story, magic and its darker elements into a fluid connected series of episodes which move along and reveal the narrative and its characters to the audience.

Any fan of *EastEnders* or *Coronation Street* will recognise the addictive nature of this structure, and in Bourne's story ballets the dancers play real people whose movements carry the plot.

In narrative form, the episodes must reveal the story, otherwise they are more of a collage of scenes with a unifying theme. This latter type of structure is seen in Christopher Bruce's *Sergeant Early's Dream* (1984). The different episodes in this work do not tell a story but present different scenes from one community. The scenes are linked via entrances and exits so that each flows easily into the next.

The episodic structure is not only a story-telling tool, it can have a range of subtle meanings. In some dances, where there is no intended story, viewers may make up one of their own. There is a belief that all dances contain some sort of story no matter how minimal. This would make a great issue for debate for your group.

Ashton's ballet *Jazz Calendar* (1968) used an episodic structure and is the basis for Task Fourteen. Ashton used separate episodes to depict a different character for each day of the week from the children's rhyme 'Monday's child is fair of face . . .'. He mixed different size groupings from solos to septets, ending with a full cast finale. The dynamics and moods ranged wide to match the different characters. There was humour, lyrical sadness, sensuality and liveliness. The wide range of characters and images included a self-admiring fashion model (Monday), ideas about transport such as planes, boats, trains (Thursday) and on Saturday four male dancers parodied working hard in the studio.

Siobhan Davies's dances contain human emotions as in *Wanting to Tell Stories* (1993) where she explores how to express feelings that are deep-seated in human movement, e.g. jumping for joy. Often her dances seem to explore people in relationship to each other as well as her own personal movement style. She may not be the teller of stories like Matthew Bourne, or the interrogator of issues and relationships like Lloyd Newson, and she may insist that dance can communicate

on its own terms but perhaps its terms are inevitably, unavoidably human. The form may be intended to be pure dance for its own sake, but gestures often suggest emotions, characters, communities and the associated 'stories'.

Other compositional structures

Natural structures

As mentioned at the start of this chapter, form is all around us in the natural world. The seasons, life cycles and so on offer rich material for organic dance structures. The passing of a day from waking to sleeping is used as a structure along with the four ages of life in *Four Scenes* by Christopher Bruce (1998).

Collage

Sometimes, juxtaposing the unexpected can create a unity of its own. This is an approach used greatly in visual art. In the paintings of surrealists like Dali and Magritte, fantastic and absurd images are created which often result in surprises for an audience. The overall form remains a whole even though the content may be illogical.

Lloyd Newson's *Strange Fish* (1992) has this structure. Almost dreamlike, perhaps more nightmarish, it throws things together that may surprise and shock us. A woman as a Christ figure on the cross is one such image, and Newson's choice of such subjects confronts issues of loneliness, desire and social isolation, but using the absurd and surreal styles of expression

The collage structure is a difficult structure, requiring careful and sensitive handling if it is not to fragment into an unconnected, discordant jumble. Task Sixteen gives you a chance to try it out.

Chance

The pioneers, in the early 1950s, of this type of structure in dance were Merce Cunningham and the composer John Cage. They made detailed charts showing timings, spatial designs, sounds and movements. Then they would toss coins to decide on choices and the order of performance. This was how the dance *Suite by Chance* (1953) was composed. In 1969, different movements were matched to playing cards, and *Canfield* was the result. This method involves a detailed and careful choreography of the dance movements involved, in order that these be secure in the dancers' minds: then, and only then, can they be performed in different orders and spatial placings.

The chance structure was the beginning of a post-modern approach in dance which highlighted an interest in the creative process for its own sake. The idea of the content of a dance having a specific meaning was rejected in favour of movement being important for its own sake. This innovation was taken up in the UK in the early 1970s by choreographers such as Richard Alston. (Up until then, modern dance had been very much based within the technique and expressionist style of Martha Graham.) Cunningham himself visited the UK, as did others who had worked with him – like dancer Viola Farber. They visited

The Place, in London, which offered a staple diet of Graham tuition, but at the same time a great deal of experimental work was happening. In 1972 the new experimental company 'Strider' was founded by Richard Alston. The founder and benefactor of The Place, Robin Howard, encouraged all such experimental work, as did Robert Cohan the artistic director.

Siobhan Davies became acclaimed as one of the UK's foremost choreographers in the 1980s and 1990s. Davies was trained at the London School of Contemporary Dance at The Place, and she went on to dance with the London Contemporary Dance Theatre, under the direction of ex-Graham dancer, Robert Cohan. By the 1980s she was making more independent work. One such work, which developed the chance-type structures, was *Plain Song* (1981). Made up from seven complex phrases for seven dancers, she reshuffled the order of the parts of the motifs, changed their facing on stage, changed the dimension they were performed in, or developed them by adding lifts or falls. In this reordering, new phrases and motifs would also be created. Task Eight is in the style of Davies and gives you a chance to try a chance dance method, based on her dance entitled *Signatures* (1990), when the dancers contributed their own movement ideas. In my own work, I have used this idea for many years with students of all ages. It's great fun and can produce some lovely compositional work.

TASK EIGHT – *Name game!*

KEY SKILLS Improving own learning and performance
Communication
Problem solving
Working with others

Several hours

You can approach this as a solo or work with a group of four dancers that you guide so that they make their own signature motifs. Then you can use the chance process to choreograph the signature motifs together. The random process should give you some visually exciting counterpoint effects as the different motifs vary in relationships between the dancers. Music suggestion: *Bob the Bob*, The Lounge Lizards (2 mins). You could play this softly during the improvisation.

1 Sign your first name (or nickname – at least four letters) using gestures in the air in your Personal Space. Mix upper and lower case letters – you choose.

2 Repeat using a different body parts and areas of your personal space for each letter. So 'Linda' could go L – strong arms infront of body; I – knee up and down followed by a punch from a fist to dot; N – shoulder at side of body and so on. . . Try saying the letters as you dance. Use the space as interestingly as possible and use change of levels – stand kneel, lie, etc.

3 Now draw your second name in the General Space using the rhythm of your name to make a rhythmical travelling phrase. You could make the pattern of the letters on the floor like snail trails, or in the air as you travel. Try adding jumps and changes of level. Again, use your voice as you move to help build a strong rhythm.

4 Make sure both motifs are put together fluidly and have a clear starting and ending stillness. Once both motifs have been combined into one and memorised proceed to work as a group.

5 The group of four dancers learn each others' motifs. Whilst the choreographer prepares a random process as follows. On separate pieces of card write:

- Solo
- Duet – 2 in unison
- Duet – 2 solo motifs
- Trio – 3 in unison
- Trio – 2 in unison + solo
- Trio – 3 solos
- Quartet – 4 in unison
- Quartet – 3 in unison + 1 solo
- Quartet – 2 unison duets
- Quartet – 2 in unison + 2 solos
- Quartet – 4 solos

Once the dancers are ready, draw the cards at random to decide on groupings for one section. Number the dancers 1, 2, 3 and 4. Then from the hat pull out numbers 1–4 to decide who is dancing when and which motif is being used for any non solo sections. For example, if Trio – 2 in unison + solo is drawn , then the next draw may select dancers # 1, 2 and 4 and another draw will decide the soloist (dancing their own motif). A final draw selects which of the other three motifs the duet dance in unison. This continues until the music is finished. Use the motifs for transitions, entrances, exits and stillnesses.

You could have other cards to decide what part of the space your dancers will be in or what relationships they use. It is also fun to work in the dancers' voices calling their names clearly at appropriate points in the dance. This can easily be extended to a quintet if you have time. If you choose the solo option you can make a set of cards to tell you when and how to repeat, vary and develop your motifs.This task can be combined with others or your own choreography to decide the order of appearance of dancers and/or motifs.

It would be fun for you to think up a system of your own that would enable you to create a dance-by-chance. You could use coins, dice, playing cards, or board games. Through the random use of the categories of action, space, dynamics and timing, movement phrases may be composed. Then, the order, place and time of their performance, on your own or in a group, may again be decided by a chance device.

TASK NINE – *Test & try*

KEY SKILLS Problem solving

🕐 10 to 20 minutes

1 Read the following list of dance titles and decide which of the above compositional structures would give it the most supportive form (answers on page 337). Explain briefly why you have chosen that structure.

  (a) A dance to *Chocolate (Spanish dance)*, from The Nutcracker music by Tchaikovsky, 1 minute 9 seconds.

  (b) A dance entitled 'United We Stand, Divided We Fall'.

  (c) A dance entitled 'Mood Swings'.

  (d) A dance based on the story entitled Amazon Sisters which tells of a group of women in the Amazon who fought against a large electricity company building a dam because it would ruin the environment.

  (e) A dance based on a collection of letters and images from a magazine.

  (f) A dance entitled 'The Planets'.

  (g) A dance to *Fishin' Blues* by Taj Mahal from The Collection.

  (h) A dance entitled 'Random Dance'.

2   **KEY SKILLS** Improving own learning and performance
            Communication
            Problem solving
            Working with others

🕐 Several hours

Choose one of the above and if not already stated, find a suitable accompaniment for a composition for three, four or five dancers. Choreograph a group dance.

Compositional structures – a conclusion

Choosing and using these pre-set structures for your dances can be a helpful way to form your ideas into dances. Try to use them in ways that are appropriate to what a particular dance is trying to convey. This may have a dramatic emphasis, or may be more involved with the movement content for its own sake.

The relationship of dance to the accompaniment

When more is meant than meets the ear.

(John Milton, *L'Allegro and Il Penseroso*, circa 1632)

In the preceding sections of this chapter, the devices and structures which give a dance its overall form were examined, and by now you should have tried out many new ideas from which to start your choreography, or new ways to organise your ideas. You may have also read earlier about choosing from a variety of possibilities for accompaniments for your dances, and you now realise the wide variety of choices available to you. The most commonly chosen accompaniment (aural setting) is that of music, and so this next section of the book is going to look in some depth at this aspect. As well as an enormous range of choices for the style of music itself, there are also choices to be made about how the movement will interrelate with the sound. An understanding of these choices will help to make choreography interrelate with the music in more appropriate, varied and skilled ways.

Dancers and choreographers need an awareness of the structural elements in music. As we saw in the previous section, musical structure is rich and varied. This is similarly so for the elements which go to make up these structures. In dance, we manipulate the elements of action, space, time, dynamics and relationships. In music, composers are faced with similar factors.

This section will focus on:

- musical terms;
- different possible relationships between music and dance.

Musical terms

In the Schöenberg score there aren't any long phrases. He states his theme concisely. He uses little repetition, but there are extremes of sudden, fast tempos, and there are slow tempos that happen quickly, and then that rhythm's broken too. Another score like 'Voluntaries' . . . one of Poulenc's best . . . takes me to the opposite extreme. That's an inward score with a beautiful . . . lyricism and a deep religious feeling.

(Glen Tetley in *The Dance Makers*, 1980)

Could you be so specific in describing a piece of music? The description above shows a real understanding of music and its terms. Before you can consider how dance and music interrelate, you need an understanding of various musical terms that will help in your dance compositions:

Rhythm

Rhythm is the basic pattern of sound and silence. It can be a steady pulse or beat, or it can be made up of regular repeated groupings.

All Musick, Feasts, Delights and Pleasures, Games, Dancing, Arts, consist in govern'd measures.

(Thomas Traherne, 1657)

During the classic and romantic ballet periods, most music was written in even rhythms: in 2, 4 and 8, or the steady metre of the waltz in 3. Rhythms can, however, be both even and uneven. An example of an even rhythm is 4/4 because there are always 4 units in one bar (or measure):

= 2 bars of 4/4, containing crotchets (or quarter notes)

After about 500 years of even rhythm in music, modern Western composers, such as Chopin, began to write in uneven rhythms – 5/4 or 7/4, for example. They also began to vary rhythms within one piece of music. This trend reflected the social context of the twentieth century, and of course affected choreographers such as Vaslav Nijinsky and Martha Graham. Life in society was no longer so predictable or balanced. The pulse of society was reflected in the phrasing of sound and actions.

An uneven rhythm combines notes of different values in one bar:

(a)   (b)

= 2 bars of 4/4 containing (a) – crotchets + 1 minim (or half note), and (b)
    2 quavers (or eighth notes) + 1 crotchet + 2 quavers + 1 crotchet

Accumulative rhythm is where each new bar adds one extra count:

| 1 | 1 2 | 1 2 3 | 1 2 3 4 ‖

Subtractive rhythm is where one count is lost from each new bar:

| 1 2 3 4 | 1 2 3 | 1 2 | 1 ‖

Musical notation – the time value of the notes

As you saw above, musical notes have different time values. In the score example shown:

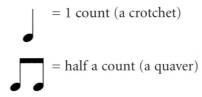

        = 4 counts (a semibreve or whole note)

        = 2 counts (a minim)

The time value of 8 quavers is the same as the time value of one semibreve.

        = 1 count (a crotchet)

        = half a count (a quaver)

It is possible to divide a single note into three. So, one crotchet is equal to a triplet.

Accent

An accent is an increase in the stress on a beat, and is shown here by the sign '>'. A less heavy accent is shown by '/'. This is seen in the score example shown. Shifting the accent away from the first beat in a bar creates a more irregular feeling in the rhythm. When this shift is set in a regular measured rhythm, it produces syncopation. Syncopated movement can be very exciting to watch because the accents fall in unexpected places and give an element of surprise.

Both jazz and tap dance use syncopation. In tap, 'Cuttin' were street corner challenges, popular in USA in the early 1900s. Standing in a circle dancers would battle to see who had the trickiest rhythmical taps and moves, similar to battles in street dance and capoeira. Originally the circle formation and challenge relationship emerged from African spiritual *Ring Shout,* as used by the slaves to disguise the praising of *their* gods from the slaves' owners who would have thought that the prayer was to the christian god. In tap dance, the tappers would step into the circle, dance their challenge then invite someone to change places. Entering the circle would involve cheeky step patterns to impress the others, before the main solo where improvisation created new steps. 'Cuttin' soon became so popular that it grew into organised competitions on Broadway.

In 1928, one competition discovered talents such as Bill Bojangles Robinson and Fred Astaire. Bojangles (1878–1949) became one of the greats in tap, famous for his light precision and viewed as the technician who brought tap onto the toes. His signature dance was performed on a flight of stairs. He performed in vaudeville and in Broadway musicals such as *Blackbirds of 1933* and *Hot Mikado* (1939). His film appearances included several with child star Shirley Temple in *The Little Colonel* (1935) and *Rebecca of Sunneybrook Farm* (1938). In 1943 he performed in the film *Stormy Weather* (20th Century Fox, director Andrew Stone), one of only two Hollywood films of the era to have an all-black cast. This film was based on his life story. It also starred the Nicholas Brothers, Cab Calloway and modern dancer Katherine Dunham.

Here are some examples of syncopation.

(a) The accent is usually on beat 1, but now is on beat 3.

(b) Missing beat 1 shifts the accent to count 2

(c) Usually

becomes

(d) This is a progressive accent.

TASK TEN – *Steps in sync*

KEY SKILLS Improving own learning and performance
Problem solving

🕐 10 to 20 minutes

1 Syncopation can be easily felt by walking in regular 3/4, 2/4 and 4/4 rhythms and then changing the accent to any of the above variations. As you move, feel where the up-beats (the weaker beats) and where the down-beats (the stronger beats) are.

2 Take any travelling technique phrase that you know well, or one from your own choreography, and alter the accents so that it becomes syncopated. Now play with interpretation so that you can increase or decrease the speed differently in each or 3 or 4 repetitions. Find your own body rhythm. These changes are called *rubato* and this is how musicians would interpret modern classical music such as that of Satie and Chopin.

Dancers do not have to stress the same beats as those stressed in the music. Indeed, the choreography can be richer and more interesting if the dancer's movement uses the offbeat. In this way, a feeling of increase in speed results, and this is called double time. Clap this repeatedly.

Time signature

The time signature is a number that tells you the number of beats which make up a repeated group (i.e. a bar or measure). It is always shown at the start of every piece of music. The time is divided up by a regular accent or emphasis and this gives the metre.

The number of beats in a bar (measure) gives the time signature. For example:

The top number shows how many beats are in one bar; the lower number shows what kind of note receives one count.

There are many common time signatures in music: 2/2, 2/4, 4/4, 3/4, 5/4, 7/4, 3/8, 6/8, 12/8. Each one has its own distinctive feel. For example, 2/2 can feel military and march-like, where 6/8 has a lively steppy feel. 3/4, in turn, is more lyrical and swing-like. The asymmetrical rhythms – like 5/4 – favoured by modern composers and choreographers, may feel distorted and unstable for an audience. Actors using an uneven walk to enter into a scene know that the audience will respond by feeling an emotional disruption. Clearly, emotional responses of the dancer, the choreographer and the audience can all be influenced by the use of different rhythms.

When two metres of unequal length and accent are combined, a resultant rhythm is produced. Combining 2/4 and 3/4 makes 6/4, 3/4 and 4/4 combined result in 12/4 as in the example shown.

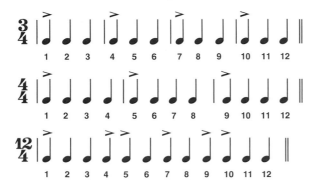

A *mixed metre* is the result of mixing two time signatures which have different underlying beats. This results in bars with different time values – for example, combining 3/8 with 2/4 , or – as shown below – 2/4 and 3/4:

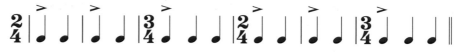

Or, combining 4/4, 1/4 and 2/4:

Some metres mix more satisfactorily than others.

TASK ELEVEN – *Clap, walk, compose*

KEY SKILLS   Improving own learning and performance
Communication
Problem solving
Working with others
Application of number

🕐 20 to 30 minutes

1 Clap the 12/4 resultant rhythms in the example shown. Then, walk the rhythm clearly, showing the accents by stamping. Then, walk the rhythm and use other movements to show the accent – e.g. a jump, arm gestures, clapping or a change of level.

2 In trios, let one person move to the 3/4, another person to the 4/4, and the third person to the resultant 12/4, simultaneously. This will create counterpoint between the dancers. Each dancer is aware of different rhythms of the other without joining them. Counterpoint is also developed in Task Eight.

Tempo

The tempo is the speed of the beat. This may speed up or slow down. The tempo is usually shown at the start of the music score. Doing triplets, travelling with clear changes of tempo is an easy way to experience how an increased tempo changes the mood from lyrical to a sense of urgency and directness. The Italian terms that music uses to describe tempo are (from fast to slow): presto, vivace, allegro, moderato, andante, adagio, lento, largo. 'Allegro' means briskly and brightly, whereas 'largo' means very slow. The speed is measured by a metronome, so:

- Presto = approximately 180 beats per minute.
- Adagio = approximately 100 beats per minute.

If a tempo gradually increases, it is acceleration, and if it is gradually slowed down, it is deceleration. The intensity of the music can also change if the force with which it is played alters. If the volume and force of the playing increase, the music will rise to a crescendo. By decreasing the same, a diminuendo results, as the dynamics softens.

Ostinato

An ostinato is a musical idea (phrase) which repeats itself throughout a piece or a section of a piece. A melody is a succession of notes, of differing pitch and with a rhythm, that results in a recognisable and repeated tune.

As in dance motifs, musical motifs can be varied and developed. They may be:

- played faster;
- played at a higher pitch – i.e. transposed;
- inverted – i.e. played upside down;
- played backwards – i.e. retrograde;
- played with longer notes – augmented – or shorter notes – diminished;
- or any combination of these.

Polyphony

Polyphony is music consisting of two or more independent melodic lines which sound together and which counterpoint each other. This technique was first used in fourteenth-century Europe. Counterpoint is produced when two phrases, or themes, are played against one another. This can look effective if used in choreography.

Harmony

Harmony results when a succession of chords is played. Chords are three or more notes that are played at the same time. In the romantic period, harmonies, like rhythm, were evened out so as always to be pleasing to the ear. This approach was challenged by modern composers, and the richness of dissonance gave music a new raw edge. Impressionist composers like Debussy and Satie worked in this way, as did Stravinsky to an even more extreme extent. Painters of the time like the impressionists Monet and Seurat experimented in similar ways in their use of paint: they broke up the colour rather than mixing it in the palette, and the viewer now had to make the mix for themselves.

So too in modern dance:

. . . the modern dancer has infused movement with that vibrant restless texture and that inner concentration typical of our psychologically oriented age.

(In *Modern Dance Forms*, by Louis Horst and Carroll Russell, 1961)

The inward searchings of the works of Martha Graham into the new psychologies of Freud and Jung represented the dissonance and discord of the modern dance world.

Different possible relationships between music and dance

Different choreographers use music very differently. Some stay very close to the score, while others may not even hear the music until the première. These are clear extremes of approach, but both of them have one thing in common: the dance is the most important element, and it is not a servant to the music.

The new ballet, refusing to be the slave either of music or of scenic decoration, and recognising the alliance of the arts only on the condition of complete equality, allows perfect freedom to scenic artist and to the musician.

(Michel Fokine in his letter to *The Times*, 6 July 1914)

This could have been a quote from Merce Cunningham!

The perfect relationship is one where dance and music support and enhance each other, whether through their similarities or through their differences. The relationship can involve any one of the following:

- direct correlation
- music visualisation
- mutual co-existence
- call and response
- disassociation
- showing or emphasising of character and narrative

Direct correlation

In direct correlation dance and music work together, so that, for example, in quieter moments in the music, the dance also uses a softer dynamic. This may be the result of dance and music having been composed together. Marius Petipa, the ballet master of St Petersburg, Russia, worked with the composer Tchaikovsky on *The Sleeping Beauty*, 1890. This was a fine score, and it won over audiences. Petipa gave very clear instructions to Tchaikovsky in the form of a libretto (a text written for and set to music in an opera etc.). In this scenario, the full story is told and broken down in fine detail showing when each section requires musical changes. The final result was music which directly correlated with the action, mime and movement – as, for example, in the celebration waltz for the birthday party. The opening prologue serves wonderfully to introduce the characters. It involves variations for each of the fairies at Aurora's christening.

In my choreographic creations I have always been dependent on the music. I feel a choreographer can't invent rhythms, he only reflects them in movement.

(George Balanchine in *Dance From Magic to Art*, 1976)

The way of composing dance that Balanchine describes here results in dance and music appearing as one statement. Balanchine and Stravinsky once described their way of working as being able to hear the dance and see the music. Balanchine once wrote that everything the composer Stravinsky wrote could be choreographed, 'every note of it'. The final result is movement which has a life of its own and yet which relates closely to the musical structure. Balanchine's earliest ballet *Apollo* (1928) is a fine example of this. The music tells how the god Apollo gives each of the muses poetry, mime and dance their creative energy, before returning to the heavens. In a series of solos, duets, trios and quartets, the movement is syncopated with the music by shifting the accents into unexpected places. The typical clean, sharp lines of Balanchine's movement style were distinctive of his neoclassical style and mixed with Art Deco sculptural shapes and percussive hip isolations of jazz, fashionable at the time. Together, they illustrate and visualise the music sensitively.

In the genre of modern dance, Martha Graham, assisted by composer Lois Horst, would usually commission the music for her choreography. Graham would supply the scenario of action, mood and timings of each section. She and the composer would then collaborate during the writing of the score, and the composer would be free to add detail. Once the music was written, she would start to choreograph working on the dramatic idea, and so she did not then need to interpret the music because this already correlated directly with her choreography. In *Primitive Mysteries* (1931), the rhythms, cadences and silences in the music are used to great effect. All the processions take place during the silences, conveying the ritualistic, spiritual feel of the religious event. At one point, a 5-count melody which had captured the dancers in a repeated back and forth motion changes to a 6, and the now even rhythm releases them into a jumping section. Their energy rises up towards heaven. Often the cadences draw attention to the main figure of the virgin, as when a soloist rises as the other dancers sink and fold in, bowing to her. In another, two women fall and the soloist quickly stands up in a crucifix-like pose. The titles of two of the sections, 'Hymn to the Virgin' and 'Crucifixus', show Graham's intent to portray intense religious feeling, probably a result of her encounters with American Native Indians who had been converted to Catholicism. The music seems to drive the spiritual forces at work in the women. As dancers and characters, they seem possessed by the dance idea and the music simultaneously.

It may be worth finding a music student to collaborate with. There are no rules about how to start. It may be your idea or it may be the musician's. You may talk about what the starting point, images, structure, instruments and so on may be, and so arrive at the overall direction together.

Music visualisation

Diaghilev was a catalyst in the close collaborations of choreographers, composers and artists in the work of The Ballets Russes. For the ballet *Petrushka* by Fokine (1911), the mood of Stravinsky's music was visualised scene by scene in the movement. The solos for the sad puppet, who comes to life, are movingly contrasted with the crowd scenes at the fairground, and his failure in love is made to look even sadder by its juxtaposition against the contrasting gaiety of the carnival.

In the genre of modern dance, the work of Robert North is a good example of music visualisation, as seen in his dance *Death and the Maiden* (1980) and his jazz style *Lonely Street, Lonely Town* (1980) The dances fit the music exactly one following the Schubert score of the same name, which tells a story of a confrontation between death and a young woman, whilst the other interprets the lyrics of songs from blues singer Bill Withers. Christopher Bruce also relates the dance to the music in this way, his *Sergeant Early's Dream* (1984) shows the dancers performing movements which illustrate the lyrics almost word for word sometimes.

TASK TWELVE – *Shorts*

KEY SKILLS Improving own learning and performance
Communication
Problem solving
Working with others

Several hours

As a class activity each half of the group should use one piece of music and not have heard the other piece, if possible. Prepare in your own time a solo of 2 minutes or less. Your solo should directly correlate to EITHER *Co Era So* by OK! Ryos OR *Ta P'tite Flamme* by Amélie-Les-Crayons. Use the music from the very beginning of the piece. Once choreographed:

- Perform the dance for a partner in silence.
- As a group discuss the expression, feelings or images that you saw in the dance.
- Repeat the performance to the music for the same partner.
- As a group discuss any changes in the expression that the second performance had.

Repeat the process for the second piece of music.

Showing or emphasising character and narrative

This is commonly used in the genre of ballet. In Adam's score for *Giselle* (1841), the use of leitmotiv identifies the main characters. This approach usually involves a mixture of music visualisation and direct correlation.

In John Lanchbery's score for Frederick Ashton's *La Fille Mal Gardée* (The Unchaperoned Daughter, 1960), the actions of the characters are clearly supported by the music. In the section entitled 'Lisa and Colas', Act 1, scene 1, the two lovers are involved in a flirtation. There is a romantic melody theme in the music which opens the scene over five bars as Colas approaches Lisa. Then, nine bars of butter-churning music play as she ignores him and tries to look busy. The two themes are interwoven as he in turn tries to catch her attention,

giving counterpoint. The music then changes to a polka as they play together. We see a clever use of the music to show a range of character and story in the disco scene of Bourne's *Swan Lake*. The original libretto (1877) is followed closely at the end of Act 1 as the Prince becomes drunk and dances with the 'peasants' who are a range of characters: sailors, strippers, Teddy Boys, gangsters and molls. The story moves quickly as the characters interact in fights and in social dancing.

In the modern genre, Robert Cohan found Maderna's music for *Hunter of Angels* (1967) to be absolutely right for the narrative of the bible story of the twins Jacob and Esau, conveying the conflicts of the twins and the angel's fight with Jacob. The final ascent to heaven in the epilogue was also suitably enhanced by the music.

In some instances, the narrative may not involve something as obvious as story-telling. Siobhan Davies is a case in point here. In her *Something to Tell* (1980, music by Britten: Cello Suite No. 3), the source is a text by Chekhov. A woman, lonely and isolated, is depicted in the various sections of the dance at different stages of her life. These show a number of her troubles and comprise less of a story and more of a description of her personality as she goes through

TASK THIRTEEN – *Dancing the music*

KEY SKILLS Improving own learning and performance
Communication
Problem solving
Working with others
Application of number

Several hours

Use *L'allegro, Il Penseroso ed Il Moderato* by Handel, Part 1: 'Hence vain deluding joys' (53 seconds), 'Haste thee nymph' (solo and chorus, 2 minutes, 26 seconds).

1 Listen very closely several times until the structure and elements of the music become clear. You should have a pencil and paper handy to write down notes on the rhythms, phrasing, motifs/ostinato, repetition, variation and developments, metres, accents and lyrics (it would help to have a copy of the score).

2 Consider the context of the music (consult the sleeve notes or information at the library), particularly how the poetry of Milton contrasts 'cheerful' and 'pensive' attitudes, and how this is reflected in the soprano, tenor and bass voices. There are many images in the poetry which can give ideas for a group dance.

3 Compose such a dance for four, five or six dancers which works either by directly correlating with, or by visualising, the music. You may choose to use the characters as depicted in the poem.

a troubled and unsatisfying relationship. This was one of the pieces where Davies fitted the dance rhythms to the music. At the start of the dance, the music has phrases which alternate between a high and a low pitch, and this gives the dance an opportunity to explore the idea of a conversation in a duet between Davies and Robert North supporting the narrative, in its broadest sense.

TASK FOURTEEN – *In the Ashton mood*

KEY SKILLS Improving own learning and performance
Communication
Problem solving
Working with others

Several hours

This task links to Task Eighteen and tasks in other chapters of the book.

Use an episodic structure for this dance, based on the children's rhyme that Ashton used as a starting point for his ballet *Jazz Calendar*. The jazz music, written by Rodney Bennett, was also based on this rhyme:

Monday's child is fair of face,
Tuesday's child is full of grace,
Wednesday's child is full of woe,
Thursday's child has far to go,
Friday's child is loving and giving,
Saturday's child works hard for a living,
And the child that is born on the Sabbath day
Is bonny and blithe, and good and gay.

Balletic vocabulary would work with the Ashton style for this task, but you could use jazz or contemporary styles. You will have to make transitions between each episode and should try to fragment and mix motifs from sections to make entrances and exits, where the two days meet along the way. As these transitions overlap with the music some effective counterpoint can result.

The suggested music is balletic and would work well because it has lots of very short sections to choose from: Your selections from Elgar's *The Wand of Youth Suites No. 1 Op. 1a & No. 2 Op. 1b*, or *Nursery Suite*.

If time is short, this could be a solo task where different students take different days and then collaborate to choreograph them into one dance. Or a choreographer may take on the whole as a group project mixing solos and different size groups for each day. Chance can be used to decide who dances which day – or you could go by when dancers were born!

Call and response

Indian and African genres often use this relationship between music and dance. The master drummer in African ensembles signals to the dancers when to change steps by calls on the drum. In Indian dance, the musicians watch the dancer and change when the movement does. In *Bharatha Natyam*, the dances tell classical stories, and there are also abstract sequences. The dancer and drummer play off each other in improvisation, rather like in jazz. The dancer wears bells on the ankles, and the stamps weave with the beat of the drum. The final effect looks and sounds exciting. Call and response, as in much African music, can become a complex relationship when different rhythms are played simultaneously. Often we see this device used by Siobhan Davies.

In *White Man Sleeps* (1988) a motif is developed by fragmenting it into smaller parts and sharing it between different dancers. The notes and instruments in the Kevin Volan's score have the same structural relationship.Richard Alston describes his use of music as one involving timing in a 'conversational rhythm' and can be seen in *Strong Language* (1987). The movement often has its own logic and independence, loosely working in response to the music. In the section named 'Strumming', the musical count is in 8, but the movement is counted 3-3-2. The effect is a resultant rhythm of shifting accents and metres which gives a look of music and movement being fresh and complementary. The mixed metre of the dance would also help to give an energised appearance, full of rhythmical delights for the audience. It would further help to avoid predictability, and yet still provide a very strong overall structure.

Task Fifteen gives you a chance to play with musical structure in the style of Richard Alston. In Alston's *Brisk Singing*, he uses a three-dimensional figure-of-eight air pattern for the arms to lead and complement the rest of the body. In the task this is likened to a Möbius Strip. You can make a Möbius strip very easily: Take a paper strip and put a half-twist in it. Stick the ends together and you now have a single continuous curve.

Figure 6.3
Möbius Strip

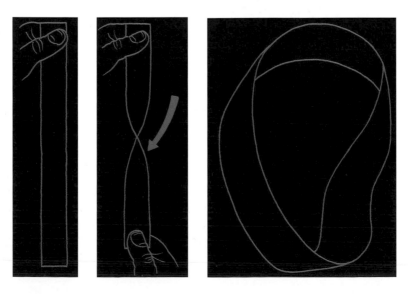

TASK FIFTEEN – *Möbius Alston*

KEY SKILLS Improving own learning and performance
Communication
Problem solving
Working with others
Application of number
Information technology

⏱ Several hours

- Watch Alston's Brisk Singing on the video Essential Alston.
- Research Möbius Strip online. You'll find it has been used in many different ways and your dance might be inspired by some of them.
- Using dance vocabulary in a style similar to Alston, compose a short solo based on the idea of the Möbius Strip. Vocabulary can include:
  - curving back and torso;
  - use of the diagonal for lines, travelling and facings to cover the general space;
  - clear rhythmical relationship with the music, capturing the detail of the sound;
  - triplet phrases with soft suspensions and falls;
  - lively buoyant jumps – sometimes with flexed foot;
  - figure of eight patterns in arms, legs, floor and air patterns;
  - dynamic changes.

In the solo or group dance use the following devices: motif repetition and variation; motif development especially – fragmentation and embellishment.

Music: *Purple Haze* by the Kronos Quartet (3 mins). Listen to this track carefully and note the progression of sections: **A-A1-B-A-A2-C-A+finale.** Listen until you have the counts, accents and musical devices noted. Can you hear embellishment, call and answer and discord?

Mutual co-existence

The innovative choreography of Vaslav Nijinsky for Diaghilev's Ballets Russes was difficult for the audiences of the day who had been used to a direct correlation between dance and music. Nijinsky's ballets such as *L'Apres-midi d'un Faune* (1912) and *Le Sacre du Printemps* (1913) broke many rules. In Faune, the score by Debussy contained clear rhythms, but Nijinsky did not follow these. Instead, he used them almost as a background to give atmosphere, using more of a *rubato* style of interpretation.

Siobhan Davies and Richard Alston often work in this type of relationship with the music, using the device of canon to create cross-rhythms between dancers enriches the interrelation with the music.

Lea Anderson treats the music in a similar way, working closely with the composer on the overall structure. In her collaboration with Steve Blake on *Flesh and Blood* (1989), the tempo of the music rather than the phrases is her main point of focus for the movement. The dance and the music run alongside each other, sharing the interpretation of the mood, but they are not so concerned with sharing devices and structures.

TASK SIXTEEN – *Anderson and the disco*

KEY SKILLS Improving own learning and performance
Communication
Problem solving
Working with others

Several hours

This task uses the movement style of Lea Anderson and could produce some amusing dances. You should use movement that is typical of her style, including some of the following:

- tiny hand, arm and face gestures
- repetition
- exaggerated everyday movement
- unison
- clear rhythm
- parody of disco dance style
- floorwork
- contact work

Using a collage structure, choreograph a trio dance entitled '*Three Sabre-toothed Sharks Head off to the Local Disco, Double Quick*'. Work with the music in the style of Anderson. Music suggestion: *Shark's Can't Sleep* (3m 6s) by the Lounge Lizards.

Disassociation

Allowing both music/sound and dance to develop totally independently of each other was the innovation of Merce Cunningham and John Cage, and many others have since followed this approach. The strategy of bringing dance and accompaniment together for the first time only on the opening night itself gives both of these aspects its own separate value.

> It is hard for many people to accept that dancing has nothing in common with music other than the element of time and the division of time. . .
>
> (Merce Cunningham in *The Vision of Modern Dance*, 1980)

Balanchine and Cunningham are thus almost opposites in this regard. For Cunningham, the only way to make the dance is to scrutinise the phrases of movement. It is from these phrases that the rhythms of the dance emerge. In his performances, the dance and the music live together, but their effects on the audience are disassociated from each other. For Cunningham, time is not beats to the bar. For him, 'dancing is propelled by dancing'.

The early work of Siobhan Davies used commissioned music scores that were also created separately from the dance, with little direct relationship between the two. Often, the music served merely to set the mood or atmosphere – as in *Relay* (1972), where the musician improvised jazz piano. In her later work, Davies developed movement which responded more to the structure of the music in mutual co-existence.

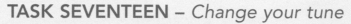

TASK SEVENTEEN – *Change your tune*

KEY SKILLS Improving own learning and performance
Communication
Problem solving
Working with others

⏱ Several hours

1 Use the group dance which you composed to *L'Allegro, Il Penseroso ed Il Moderato*, from Task Thirteen. Dance it to the following pieces of music:
Purple Haze, by the Kronos Quartet, 3 minutes;
Speaking in Tongues II, by Sheila Chandra, 3 minutes 8 seconds.

2 Assess the effects of the mutual-coexistence and disassociation approaches on the look of the dance. Did the contrast of the music with the dance emphasise and enhance features of the choreography? Was the disassociation uncomfortable but of interest for you as the viewer? Are you prepared to allow discord to be both interesting and challenging to the way you see things?

The relationship of music to dance – conclusion

It is a good idea to try to listen to as many different types and styles of music as possible and see if you can hear and analyse what the composer is doing with the sounds.

It is probably clear to you by now that the elements and structures of dance and music have a great deal in common. When the two come together in choreography, a whole Pandora's box of surprises, delights and troubles pops open! The relationship between the two aspects opens up several choices for the choreographer. If appropriate choices are made, and if accurate performances are given, successful choreography should be the result.

TASK EIGHTEEN – *Creating a group dance for performance*

KEY SKILLS Improving own learning and performance
Communication
Problem solving
Working with others

Several hours

(This task can be adapted to suit many tasks in this chapter and the next.)

You should record your progress in this task. Your teacher may assess you on this evidence.

You will work in a group of between three and six, but can be assessed as an individual on:

- working with others – in rehearsal and project management;
- choreography – contribute movement and ideas to the dance.

Working as a group:

1 Choose one of the tasks from this book.
2 Outline the project schedule. Each individual should contribute two or three ideas/suggestions/tasks and should take responsibility for putting them into action.
3 Research the idea to find: accompaniment, movement or equipment as appropriate.
4 Rehearse to produce the dance: each individual is responsible developing movement for the dance.
5 Perform the dance according to the agreed schedule.

You should evaluate your personal work and progress using the grid on pages 264–265. Back up with further records and evidence in your journal, e.g. a record of schedule, research data you found.

On page 103 you will find an evaluation grid to assess your performance skills. This could be used for the group dance.

Self-evaluation grid

DANCE/PROJECT TITLE _____   NAME _____

START DATE _____   FINISH DATE _____

How well did you. . .?	Strategy	Needs improvement	Mostly effectively	Consistently/ imaginatively achieved
1 Work with others Example: Communicate and listen	✓ Ask teacher to help me find a way to improve my listening skills. She has suggested the 10-second rule.	✓ 2nd Sept. Once I start talking I have a habit of going on and not letting others speak. Sometimes I make it worse by dancing about to make my point. My friend has suggested that I should find a way to stop this.	✓ 9th Sept. I am counting to 10 before I speak and find that the others have good ideas. Also my friend has a secret sign which he uses when he thinks I am going on and it's working quite well.	✓ 2nd Oct. We have nearly finished the dance and the group are much friendlier to me now. Also our dance is looking very good and we are ahead of our schedule because we work so well together. When we pool our ideas we end up with better dance. I'm not so anxious about having to listen to others.
Copy this table into your own portfolio. Select and enter three target areas.				
Take direction from others . . . Support others' ideas/ suggestions . . . Contribute two or three ideas . . . Respect the ideas of others . . . Make clear and put your ideas into action* . . . Keep to schedules				

How well did you. . .?	Strategy	Needs improvement	Mostly effectively	Consistently/ imaginatively achieved
Punctuality . . . *See Chapter 6 for more detail on rehearsal strategies				
2 Contribute to choreography Research ideas . . . . Example: Improvise to find movement Keep a written record of your movement . . . Select as appropriate: motifs/devices . . . structure/form/style . . . Use appreciation process in rehearsal to refine ideas* . . . *See Chapter 6 for more detail on rehearsal strategies	✓ I need to organise my time to include experiment with movement for the group dance. One of the things I forget is to book time in the studio.	✓ 2nd Sept. I tend to use the same movements all the time. Usually they are the ones that a teacher has taught me. But they don't express lots of things and so I have to try and think for myself more. In the past I always forget what I improvise, so I'm going to try to write down movements as I find them.	✓ 9th Sept. I booked an hour in the studio to find some motifs for our group dance. I had done research and found some music but it wasn't right so I worked in silence. Funny really but even though I didn't find much I have a couple of phrases which seem very expressive. The rest of the group like them.	✓ 16th Sept. Success is patchy but I wrote down a couple of things that aren't good for this dance but I like them and maybe one day . . . My ideas are now in the dance and we have developed them as they feature a fair amount and help to express the content.

References and resources

Books

Balanchine, G., *Balanchine's Complete Stories of the Great Ballet*, New York: Doubleday & Co., 1954

Caplan, R., *Rhythmic Training for Dancers*, Champaign, IL: Human Kinetics, 2002

Lawson, J., *A History of Ballet and Its Makers*, London: Dance Books, 1964

Pomer, J., *Perpetual Motion*, Champaign, IL: Human Kinetics, 2002

Videos

Available from www.dancebooks.co.uk

Alvin Ailey: An Evening with the Alvin Ailey Dance Theatre, 2004

Alston in Overdrive, 2003

Essential Alston,1998

Music Dances – Balanchine choreographs Stravinsky, 2005

Sleeping Beauty – The Australian Ballet; Petipa choreography reproduced from the Sergeyev notation by Monica Parker, 2000

Sleeping Beauty – The Bolshoi Ballet, Yuri Grigorovich production

Swan Lake, Adventures in Motion Pictures, 1999

The Nutcracker, Adventures in Motion Pictures, 2002

The Nutcracker, Birmingham Royal Ballet, 1994

White Man Sleeps, Wyoming – Siobhan Davies Dance Company, 1989

Music

Chandra, S., *Speaking in Tongues II*, RW24 07777 7 867227. Task Seventeen

Elgar, E., *The Wand of Youth; Nursery Suite*. New Zealand Symphony Orchestra. Naxos, 8.557166, 2004. Task Fourteen

Handel, *L'allegro, Il Penseroso ed Il Moderato*, Soli Monteverdi Choir, English Baroque soloists, Erato, 2292-45377-2, 1980. Task Thirteen

Kronos Quartet, Nonesuch, 75559-79111-2, 1986. Tasks Fifteen, Seventeen

No Doubt, *Tragic Kingdom*, MCA, IND 90003, 1995. Task Five

Penguin Café Orchestra, *Broadcasting from Home*, EGDC 38, 1984. Task Three

Putumayo Presents, *Blues around the World*, P986-SL, 2006. Task Seven

Putumayo Presents, *Music from the Winelands*, P986-SL, 2006. Task Twelve

Putumayo Presents, *South Pacific Islands*, Putumayo World Music, PUT231-2, 2004 (free recipe for chicken in coconut cream!). Tasks One and Twelve

Sor, F., Romantic Guitar, 450 146–2 10, Karussell UK Ltd., 1994. Task Six

Taj Mahal, *The Collection*, Castles Communication, CCSCD180, 1987. Task Nine

Tchaikovsky, *The Nutcracker*, recording by the Royal Opera House Orchestra, Conifer Records, ROH 002 (or similar recording). Task Nine

The Lounge Lizards, *Voice of Chunk*; Lagarto Productions Inc. LAGCD003, 1989. Tasks Six, Eight, Sixteen

7 MAKING AND REHEARSING DANCES

Making dances

This chapter breaks down the process of making and rehearsing dances step by step. As you read the chapter, you may be making a dance for performance or assessment. Use the tasks and log entry sheets in this chapter as a guide to compose your dance. The process that is set out for you can be used with your own ideas, or with tasks set by your teacher, or for an examination, or with many of the tasks in this book. You will see that Task Fourteen from Chapter Six is used as an example in some of the log entry sheets. Adding your own ideas and journal entries will make the process more valuable for you.

One of the most frequently asked questions about dance composition is: 'How long did it take you to make that dance?' There is no single answer to this question, but from start to finish you should allow yourself plenty of time. Table 7.1 gives you a schedule that you could follow. Use it in your choreography journal and log in your own dates. Start with the date of the performance and work backwards on a calendar so that you know when to start. The Table is based on 3–4 sessions per week. Each session in the studio should be around one to one hour 30 minutes. Preparation is everything! Table 7.1 shows the three stages of the making a dance process. They are:

- preparation: research and improvisation;
- rehearsal: shaping, selection, organisation: working with dancers;
- refining and polishing: performance.

This icon shows when you should make a journal entry.

Preparation involves researching ideas and information for the content of the dance, improvising and gathering resources such as accompaniment. If you need help to decide on an idea to start with try Task One. Other tasks throughout the book may also help you to find a stimulus.

Research your idea as thoroughly as possible. The more you know about your idea the easier it will be to find movement for your dance. Give yourself plenty of time to research from books, online, on film. For example, if your idea starts with a painting, research the artist's life and why the painting was important, what it expresses, what technique the artist used, the mood, images and colours. Keep notes about your findings in your journal.

 Table 7.1 A timeline for the process of making a dance

TIMELINE	ACTIVITY	TASKS
Weeks 1–2 (Between 3 & 6 hours each week)	Research dance idea	■ Select starting idea/images for the dance content ■ Research the idea thoroughly ■ Start your process diary/journal ■ List ideas for accompaniment and/or music possibilities ■ Book studio for your rehearsals week 3 to 4
Weeks 3–4	Personal movement exploration in studio`	■ Improvise around your content ideas/images ■ Select suitable movement components ■ Sketch ideas for 2 or 3 motifs ■ Keep your diary/journal up to date ■ Start to think about the overall structure of your dance ■ Decide on number of dancers and who would be best suited to your style/idea ■ Approach dancers to see if they are available – discuss when everyone is available. Agree on regular weekly rehearsal times ■ Book studio for these times.
Weeks 5–8	Rehearsals with dancers in studio Refinement of your dance – ask teacher or other student to watch your dance occasionally for feedback Ongoing check that dance is safe for your dancers and help them to understand the movement and content	■ Keep journal and/or film rehearsals ■ Follow up rehearsals with preparation for next rehearsal – where to next? Record your 'feedforward' ideas ■ Ongoing selection of most suitable movement ideas for your content ■ Gradually build up the overall form and structure of the dance
Weeks 9–10	Refine dance and the dancers' performance and interpretative skills	■ Give an informal show of your dance to a small audience and teacher ■ Keep journal and/or film record to check for improvements
Weeks 11–12	Performance	■ Rehearse in performance space

TASK ONE – *Searching*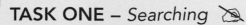

KEY SKILLS Communication
Working with others

⏱ 10 to 20 minutes

Try to do this exercise as quickly as possible.
  In groups of three or four, brainstorm content that would translate into movement. It could include poetry, sculpture, current events in the news, movement itself. Keep the list handy because this task continues in Tasks Two, Three and Six.

Richard Alston often starts with the music. He listens over and over to it and reads the score until he is really familiar with the feel, structure, sections, phrasing and so forth. He also researches when the music was written and the composer's life or what occasion the music would have been played for. For example, in *Light Flooding into Darkened Rooms* (1997) he chose seventeenth-century French lute music (Denis Gaultier) and contemporary mandolin (Jo Kondo) that was inspired by the style of the older music. Alston noted the music's structure of repetition, ornamentation of phrasing and the particular style of playing that broke up and stretched the chords. He used these structural ideas in the motifs' repetitions, variations and embellishments. Alston also researched into Dutch seventeenth century paintings of domestic life and looked at the detail of people engaged in quiet intense activities, such as having music lessons. As you can see all that research and thinking would have taken Alston a long time. From his research, he used the idea that the music painted a picture of people in close contact and from there began to improvise movement.

TASK TWO – *Dear diary . . .*

KEY SKILLS Improving own learning and performance
Communication
Information technology

Begin keeping your own log/diary of all your work. This should be an ongoing activity to which you add daily or weekly.
You could record any of the following:

■ movement (improvised, composed or taught);
■ ideas and thoughts on content/style;
■ deadlines and how you managed your time to meet them;
■ ideas for dances which you might like to make 'one day';
■ notes on music, costume, lights, set props which may interest you;
■ notes on diet, injury and health;

- feedback and comments from other people about your work or comments that you have made about the work of other students and professional work which you have seen.

To keep the diary you could use a mix of:

- your own writing, diagrams, number;
- Labanotation or Benesh;
- magazine/newspaper cuttings;
- photos, sound tapes and if you can access a video camera you could keep footage of your rehearsals;
- information found on the Internet.

Start a working journal or diary so that you can keep a track on progress. Your working diary may include things which you decide to throw away, but you never know when they might be useful so the golden rule is 'Write It All Down!' The tables may help you to keep a track on your ideas, but your journal is a personal document and can be in many different forms. Use your imagination – take photos in rehearsal, use drawings, use colour to code ideas. Keep your log entries up to date and always try to jot down some quick notes in the studio at the end of a rehearsal. You can add to them later when you have more time.

The research that Lloyd Newson and DV8 do for a new piece can take months. The research period for *Enter Achilles* (1995) went on for almost two years, so you can see how important it would be to keep a record during the process.

Many dancers are using video to tape their rehearsals and improvisations as a way of finding new material for choreography. This medium can also be used for making archives to monitor your own growth and development. You can use it to analyse after rehearsals and select or remember movements that did or did not work well. You could keep a compilation of some ideas as part of your choreographic journal on your computer.

Now you can try Task Three to help you research your ideas.

TASK THREE – *Researching*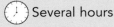

KEY SKILLS Improving own learning and performance
Problem solving
Information technology

 Several hours

Allow several hours for this work, including library, video and Internet research.

1 From the list which you prepared as a group in Task One, individually choose one of the ideas, research it and find an example which you can use as a starting point for a dance. Explore movements that would be appropriate for a dance. OR

> **2** Research the work of a choreographer who has a recognisable style. From the information which you have found choreograph a short solo in that style.
>
> This task links to Tasks Two and Six, the tables in this chapter and tasks in other chapters.

Improvisation is a crucial part of this creative process. Although you may not be intending to go into the first rehearsal with dancers with every single movement sorted, neither should you go in empty-handed. Therefore, your exploration of movement is precious time to find some key movement material. It is a time when you need to sensitively explore and assess which constituent features best interpret your chosen content. This process of *interpreting* the dance content into movement, helps you to make a start on improvising and should be a part of your preparation, or could happen in your first studio personal exploration session. Try using the log entry sheet in Table 7.2 to help start your early improvisations in the studio. Draw the table in your choreographic journal and follow the journal process that continues throughout this chapter. The tables use Task Fourteen from Chapter Six as an example for you to follow.

 Table 7.2 Log entry sheet

MY IDEAS	MOVEMENT
WEEK 1, JOURNAL: *Today I decided to use the rhyme 'Monday's child is fair of face. . .' that Ashton used for his ballet*	*I'm not sure yet whether I will use just ballet style movement, but I'll probably use other styles too – like contact and contemporary – maybe jazz and tap*
Monday's – fair of face	Dance Actions: stillness/travel/gestures of arms Space – Personal, small Time – slow Dynamics – gentle
Tuesday's – full of grace	Dance Actions: travel/gestures of arms/turns Space – Personal, large Time – triplets Dynamics – gentle, free flow Contact – helps others (helps Wednesday)
Wednesday's – full of woe	Dance Actions: stillness/travel/falls Space – Personal, low level Time – slow/sudden Dynamics – heavy, bound
Thursday's – far to go Use this as contrasting movement?	Dance Actions: travel/jumps/turns Space – direct and indirect floor patterns Time – fast Dynamics – busy
Friday's – loving and giving	Dance Actions: travel/gestures of arms/turns Space – Personal Time – slow/triplets Dynamics – gentle Contact – close

Table 7.2 (continued)

MY IDEAS	MOVEMENT
Saturday's – works hard for a living	Dance Actions: travel/jumps/turns Space – direct and indirect floor patterns Time – fast Dynamics – busy
Sunday's – bonny, blithe, good and gay *Note to research - must find out what 'blithe' means!* *May also look deeper into the history of the names of the days of the week.* *Where did they come from?*	Dance Actions: travel/jumps/turns Space – direct and indirect floor patterns Time – fast Dynamics – light *Will think about relationships later when I have some basic motifs worked out. . .*

There are several ways to approach the creative process and every choreographer has their own style of working. For example, Richard Alston described how he likes to improvise himself and so he finds motifs first, then teaches them to the dancers. Next, he guides the dancers to work in their own way with the movements and he shapes the sections of the dance. Table 7.3 shows a range of possibilities and you may feel more comfortable with one than another. None of them is better or worse from the others – but some may be harder to do! Look at Table 7.3 as part of your Weeks 1–2 *Preparation Phase* and decide on which approach you feel comfortable with with. Your choice will help guide your work in Weeks 3–4. If you're unsure which one to use, try the middle option.

Figure 7.1 May 1965: Ballet master George Balanchine (c) seated in chair directing unidentified group of male dancers as others watch during rehearsal for NYCB production of Don Quioxte at New York State Theater, scene reflected in mirror.

During preparation you will have to find some dancers. Ever wonder why certain dancers are chosen for a particular company or dance? There are a number of basic factors which we can pinpoint that influence the choreographer's choice:

■ the number of dancers required;
■ the particular role they are dancing;
■ their physique;
■ their gender.

Each of these will be considered in turn. When you are choosing dancers sometimes reliable friends are the safest choice, but also try to find dancers suited to your movement style and ideas that you will be using.

A choreographer . . . has no way of expressing himself but through movements which he must implant in the muscles of other dancers.

(David Lichine in *Ballet*, 1947)

Alvin looks for dancers who will bring some special quality and who can make a strong statement on stage. He is really quick to see if somebody's personality is the kind of personality that will give . . . Alvin has a good eye for how we'll all look together.

(Elinor Rogosin on choreographer Alvin Ailey, in *Dance Makers*, 1980)

That's why Balanchine is such a marvellous choreographer. He has a concept of his dancers . . . he knows each of them so well that he can propose something for them to try that they might not be aware they can do.

(Twyla Tharp in *Dance Makers*, 1980)

The statements above reflect various opinions about the choice of dancers. Most professional choreographers have a large number of dancers to choose from and they will choose the ones who most suit their personal style. This may mean that a certain dancer's physique will be right for a particular kind of technique; for example, Balanchine was famous for choosing very thin dancers in order to show off the lines that he required. Other choreographers may choose dancers for their inner qualities; for example, Lea Anderson prefers dancers of all shapes and sizes, but is concerned that they also be thinking people:

When you're doing lots of tiny movements that need to be linked or performed in such a way that the dancer looks as though they know why they're doing everything. Each movement has a reason behind

it . . . I'm constantly looking for things for dancers to be thinking on stage.

(Lea Anderson in interview in *Flesh and Blood*,
Cholmondeley's education pack)

When choosing dancers, you need to be clear about how they can enhance your dance.

There are those occasions when a dancer and a choreographer act as a mutual 'spark' for each other. Richard Alston and Michael Clark worked together in this way in various works including *Soda Lake* (1981) and *Dutiful Ducks* (1982). Clark's training in ballet and in the Cunningham technique equipped him with fast foot work, an ability to change direction quickly and an open torso which curved with ease and fluidity. All these technical strengths suited Alston's style perfectly.

The number of dancers

The number of dancers that is chosen should be appropriate to the choreographic idea. A large corps de ballet is clearly going to have different visual impact from that of a trio or duet. Generally speaking, the more dancers there are, the more dramatic possibilities there will be. In a duet, the possible relationship – or conflict – is 1 vs 1. With four people, there are five possibilities:

- 1:1:1:1, or
- 2:1:1, or
- 2:2, or
- 3:1, or
- 4 together.

The possibilities do not end here, however, because different dancers may, at different times, act as the odd one out and that increases the number of possible relationships again. In total, there are 15 possible combinations for a quartet.

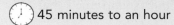

TASK FOUR – *Add it up!*

KEY SKILLS Communication
Problem solving
Working with others
Application of number

 45 minutes to an hour

In fours, use the notation placings in Figure 7.2. Decide together on the order in which to make these group shapes, and link them up with simple walking and running. Can you now find what the 15 different permutations for a quartet are? Add your findings to the original five shapes.

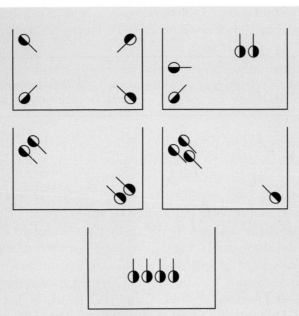

Figure 7.2 Notation showing placings for Task Four

Bearing in mind how complex the possibilities are, it is advisable to ensure that the number of dancers be appropriate for a particular choreographic idea. If your starting point is a large painting with lots of action and figures, it may be appropriate to have five, six or more dancers. And for a poem or story with a certain number of characters, the number of dancers may need to be the same.

In Robert Cohan's *Hunter of Angels* (1967), the choice of a male duet was ideal to tell the story of Jacob and Esau. It offered an opportunity to show the struggle between the twins, and it cleverly and economically involved one of the dancer's playing a dual role as both Esau and the angel which visits Jacob. The transition between these two characters was accomplished smoothly and convincingly.

The idea of a trio is, like that of a quartet, to weave the dancers together, as in Glen Tetley's *Pierrot Lunaire* (1962), where a couple is broken up by a third person (this work explores the classic story of relationships to its maximum). In ballets such as Sir Frederick Ashton's *The Dream*, (1964) and Glen Tetley's *The Tempest*, (1979) the Shakespeare stories hold many opportunities for different size groups to be used in the various dramatic situations, and for the different characters. Again, choosing the correct number of dancers is crucial to revealing the narrative.

Role

Choosing those dancers who are appropriate for a specific role is important. An individual dancer may have natural tendencies towards certain qualities and specific technical abilities which make them ideal for certain roles. In classical ballet, this may often be the case with characterisation. The same principle

applies to post-modern works, but may not be so obvious. Speaking about the choreographer Rosemary Butcher, critic Stephanie Jordan points out:

> Her works, physically simple as they might appear, demand fine, experienced dancers and can be extraordinarily diminished in their absence.
> (Stephanie Jordan in *Striding Out*, 1992)

Butcher works in dialogue with the dancers, making dances as a collaborative process, therefore to be a dancer in her company you would have to be able to contribute and develop movement material.

Other post-modern choreographers like Bill T. Jones choose total 'non-dancers' as well as those with superb technique. In *Still Here* (1994), Jones used people whom he had met through a therapy workshop for those who had lost loved ones through AIDS and other long-term terminal illnesses. Their taped testimonies, together with their role as actual performers in the piece, made the work 'undiscussible' for some critics (Arlene Croce in the New Yorker).

Similarly, Lloyd Newson's work with DV8 demands that dancers dig deep into their own life experiences to create roles and material for the works. This is an intense way of working and demands mental strength from the dancers in order to ensure in-depth exploration of the serious issues which are the main motivation of DV8 choreography.

Physique

Choreographers can tap into specific physiques sometimes. For performing lifts in pas de deux, body strength in the legs and upper body is required. Similarly, in the post-modern genre, where responsibility for lifting is often shared equally throughout the group, suitable physiques are more likely to make for safety and injury prevention, and the dance itself should also look better for the audience as a result.

The choreographic demands of the corps de ballet are such that a uniform physique is a prerequisite. This may also be observed in some mainstream modern dance companies. By contrast, in the post-modern genre we see diverse physiques, as in The Cholmondeleys and The Featherstonehaughs.

Gender

A not dissimilar situation exists in choosing dancers for their gender. Certain roles in classical ballet demand specifically male or female performers, according to conventional stereotyping, and this may also be the case in some modern dance choreography. Take, for example, Martha Graham's 1944 *Appalachian Spring*, with herself as bride and Eric Hawkins as groom (Hawkins went on to become her husband in real life). See Figure 4.9 on page 180.

Merce Cunningham's works, by contrast, tend to be rather more androgynous in that roles can be interchangeable between males and females. This is also a feature in the work of post-modern choreographer Richard Alston. *Soda Lake* (1981) was originally choreographed for Michael Clark, but in a later revival for the Rambert it was danced by Mark Baldwin and Amanda Britton. The nature of the movement is such that it has a gender neutrality. It is the fact that the dancers have a similar training in Cunningham and ballet techniques that is the main reason for choosing them.

In Britain in the late 1970s 'New Dance' sprang up as a post-modern development and the politics of gender were addressed. Ian Spink's choreography, such as *De Gas* (1981), reversed roles of men and women. Spink based the dance on the paintings of female nudes by painter Degas, but the roles were danced by men. Spink challenged his audience to unpack how they stereotype the male gender.

Much later in the development of contemporary dance in England, Matthew Bourne (Adventures in Motion Pictures) would use a similar strategy with his all-male swans in *Swan Lake* (1995). In Act Two, the corps de ballet of men combine soft curving lines with tensile strength to dance the roles of swans.

When the torsos are bare and male, the arms are powerfully muscled and the tutus replaced by ruffled feather breeches, the effect is both peculiar and mysterious.

. . . These are dangerous feral creatures. . . . After the second half I was snuffling into my handkerchief – which is more than I do at the Royal Ballet's or ENB's Swan Lake . . . Not bad for a small contemporary dance group with a daft name.

(Jan Parry in *Dance Now*, 1995)

Figure 7.3 *Swan Lake* by Tchaikovsky. **Choreographer:** Matthew Bourne. Sadlers Wells, London 12/04. The Prince with The Swans.

Put at its simplest, there are two obvious possibilities when choosing dancers. You could first choose the dancer and then build the choreography around their individual characteristics. Or you could choose a dancer whose style, physique and personality already suits your own choreographic idea. Alternatively, perhaps the dancers may choose the choreographer who they think suits them best.

Once you have decided on your content, some motifs and found some dancers you can head for the studio to prepare some movement ideas. You are ready to make a dance so where do you start?

In rehearsal

Once in the studio with the dancers, you will have to teach and guide them through your ideas. As you do this you may meet sticking points. The following list may help you to overcome problems:

- Remember your improvisations and be alert to when something feels right or when it requires further refinement.
- Accept that there is often little apparent logic in the order in which movements are discovered. You may find the end first!
- Be open to possibilities. Mistakes are often useful. You don't have to follow a fixed plan – if a better idea appears, go with the flow!
- Think how movement may look to an audience.
- Work in small, manageable sections, e.g. with one section of music.
- Allow form and structure to develop gradually.
- Sometimes work without the music to clarify certain moments and movements.
- Remember choreography takes time. The process of trial and error can be frustrating but it is usually necessary. Infuriatingly, sometimes you select the thing that you threw away first!
- Manage your time so that you work your schedule backwards from a performance deadline. Block in time slots for rehearsal and don't forget to book studio space.
- Keep a working log or diary of all your work whether alone or with dancers. A video record is great if you happen to have a camera.

Selection may involve working alone or with dancers and trying out some movements. In composing and rehearsing dances the interpretation process is ongoing as you make improvements to the dance. This is called *formative assessment* and it occurs in all the different phases of rehearsal as you select the movement that best expresses the content of the dance.

This process will further engage your intellect, feelings, imagination and intuition, in making creative and sensitive choices as to what movements will be most successful in expressing the content to the audience. The artistic decisions involved in transforming idea to final image are closely linked to a sense of personal interpretation:

Until the artist is satisfied in perception with what he is doing, he continues shaping and reshaping. The making comes to an end when its result is experienced as good.

(John Dewey in *Having an Experience*, 1934)

Table 7.3 gives you an idea of how you can begin to structure your motifs from your research and improvisation so that you are ready to teach them to your dancers for the first rehearsal.

 Table 7.3 Structuring motifs

MY IDEAS	MOVEMENT
WEEK 3 & 4, JOURNAL: *I'm still trying out different types of music as I improvise, but it's difficult to find one with enough changes of the mood. Perhaps I'll use dancers' voices – hmm. . . I'll have to choose dancers who don't mind speaking up!*	*I'm using the movement from my early journal ideas to make motifs. I don't think I'll have seven different motifs or 7 dancers either – it's too much. So perhaps 4 dancers and a mix of solos, a duet (Friday) trio (Saturday) and everyone Sunday. think that's what Frederick Ashton did – I hope that's OK. I'll ask my teacher.* *Below is how I've worked out my motifs, variations and developments*
Monday's – fair of face MOTIF 1	Travel on diagonal with gliding steps that change direction. Stillness using gentle arms gestures to frame the face. Use small hand movements to suggest holding a mirror and looking at face. Solo
Tuesday's – full of grace MOTIF 1 VARIATION	Vary Motif 1 by adding turns and add arabesques, triplets and larger gestures. Vary pathway to include curving floor pattern & freer flow of energy through body Contact – helps others – helps Wednesday up to feet as one exits and other enters. Solo
Wednesday's – full of woe MOTIF 2	Heavy, bound flow, travelling with sudden drops to floor/falls – rolling and sliding. Arms wringing through space – covering face. Solo
Thursday's – far to go MOTIF 3 – Contrasting movement	Busy travelling in direct and indirect floor patterns. Choose some recognisable everyday transport ideas like bicycles, planes, traffic for arm gesture ideas. Sudden stops. Lively! Cartwheels. Check out Task Six in Chapter Three for more help on this. Trio

Table 7.3 (continued)

MY IDEAS	MOVEMENT
Friday's – loving and giving MOTIF 1 DEVELOPMENT	Use Motif 1 + Contact work – gentle lifts and lowering to floor – close – Duet
Saturday's – works hard for a living MOTIF 3 DEVELOPMENT	Develop Motif 3 by changing order of movements and embellishing with some recognisable everyday working actions such as sweeping; add to busy cartwheels, travelling, jumps & turns. Quartet
Sunday's – bonny, blithe, good and gay MOTIFS 1, 2, 3, 4 fragmented	Add some social dance or folk dance steps – waltz fast & light. Quartet – some unison

Organisation of devices, form and structure may have been decided in the research stage, but will be part of a continual selection and refinement process as you work with the dancers and begin to evaluate what works best where, when, how and with whom. Task Five can give you a taste for the shaping expereince.

TASK FIVE – *Time lapses*

KEY SKILLS Improving own learning and performance

 45 minutes to an hour

Watch the video 'Time Lapses', Rosemary Lee and Sue Maclennan. Describe how the piece builds up a dance from improvisation through to performance. Use these questions as a guide: How is the structure of the dance gradually developed? What are the movements that are developed from improvisation as part of the final dance? How does the use of voice develop during the piece? How is the physical setting shaped from studio to final theatrical setting?

As choreographer you need to guide and work with the dancers, making clear what expression you require. You need to 'listen' to and answer their questions, both verbal and nonverbal. This means sharpening your powers of observation, description and interpretation. Questions such as 'Is that gesture appropriate to express the content or not?', 'Is it the step or the dancer's style which needs adjustment?' are vital in formative evaluation. Choreographers will need to make clear to dancers what the dance requires from them, working on details like phrasing, timing, transitions and physical setting. Sometimes you may need

to give physical support and adjustments in alignment, facings and line. Dancers too need skills of description, interpretation and evaluation. They may need to describe a problem or offer relevant suggestions to overcome physical or expressive difficulties in the polishing process.

As dancer or choreographer great perseverance and resilience of mind may be called for in the rehearsal process. In rehearsal, dancing with others demands that you maintain a pleasant, professional and responsible attitude to each other. The disciplines of warming up before rehearsal, punctuality, approaching problems such as timing and spacing efficiently and sensitively with others are all vital if the work is going to succeed.

Strategies for working in rehearsals for dancers and choreographers:

- building rapport;
- making movement clear;
- making content clear;
- developing the dancer's interpretive skills.

Building rapport

In dance companies this is done over a long period of time, and it is unlikely that you will have such a luxury. Your task is to achieve as much rapport as possible, between dancers and choreographer, in the short time you will have available. But the basic approach is the same: one of communication between dancers and choreographer – sharing information, questions and problems, and gradually building common ground and the understanding necessary for the dance to be shaped. Richard Alston advises dancers how to find the most efficient, expressive and musical way to perform a movement.

There are instances of choreographers in ballet and modern dance who have struck up special relationships with individual dancers. Ballerina Lynn Seymour had a long working relationship with Kenneth MacMillan. She describes how they rehearsed together at the start of a new dance.

He will perhaps just say . . . 'I had this sort of idea', and you will listen to a piece of music and he will show something and say 'Like this' or 'Why don't you start over there and dash over here?' And you try it. He doesn't name the steps but he gives examples. And the problem usually becomes to translate this idea into rhythmic form that the music has, and make it possible. This seems to be the thing that I have been best at and I do it for MacMillan.

(Lynn Seymour in *Making a Ballet*, 1974)

But what works on one occasion may not always work. Finding constructive and informative comments and questions to improve expression and performance is probably going to help you and your dancers produce results.

Making movement clear

A choreographer, though possessing the same emotions as other creative artists, has no way of expressing himself but through movements which he must implant in the muscles of other dancers.

(David Lichine in *Ballet*, 1947)

The need to prepare dancers and develop their skills when tackling new content, style or technique is illustrated here:

In company training . . . DV8 . . . bring in different people to develop new skills: in *My Body, Your Body* they did aerobics and long-distance running to build up stamina . . . and voice teachers are brought in at times . . . When we were looking at football, (we) . . . considered why is it acceptable for men to do footwork around a football, but not to do footwork around Irish dancing or ballet? So we brought in an Irish dancing teacher because I wanted to explore . . . what is acceptable and unacceptable male movement?

(Jo Butterworth interview with Lloyd Newson, 1998)

In the 1960s post-modern dance and British New Dance shifted away from traditional rehearsal strategies in preference for more collective dialogue between choreographer and dancer in making and choosing movement for dances. A magazine was started for New Dance itself by X6 Collective in 1977, although it is no longer in print.

From Ballet all the way to Cunningham technique, the dancer's body has been at the disposal of the choreographer to produce the desired effect. . . . The dancer was becoming more responsible; their direct contribution as themselves was more pertinent.

(Claire Hayes in *New Dance*, 1987)

Improvisation is used as an exploration into movement possibilities focusing on specific problems, which form the central point of the choreography. The dancers have the responsibility of discovering their own movement and energy level within the outer structure of the dance.

(Rosemary Butcher in *New Dance*, 1977)

Artists such as Siobhan Davies are typical of this type of approach in rehearsal, giving the dancers starting points such as poetry, geometry and architecture to make movement phrases, then shape the movement into motifs that help to structure the final dance.

Gradually you will find whether 'teaching steps', or giving dancers structures to improvise around and select from their movement discoveries, or a combination of these two approaches suits you best.

Making content clear

The choreographer gives the essence of the dance to the dancers by making content clear to them. Different choreographers do this in different ways. We may note the way that Lea Anderson emphasises the use of inner narrative for her dancers. She is concerned that the dancers are aware of the reason behind each of the tiny gestures which they perform.

The inner narrative is something that the audience doesn't know and is nothing to do with them . . . I'm very interested in the physical attitude of the performer. For example the traditional way of . . . holding your body and relating to the audience. I'm not much impressed with those ways of being . . . not how you remember the movement but thinking of the given image. The dancer must go through the same thought process every time.

(Lea Anderson in interview in *Flesh and Blood*,
Cholmondeley's education pack)

Discussion with the dancers is another method of making the content clear and this has been used by Matthew Bourne to clarify characters' motives so that they fit the story. From there the movements can be designed to express what the characters would feel and do.

Preparing a dancer for the role is crucial for a successful performance. Similarly, a dancer describes how the choreographer Alvin Ailey helped her to understand a role. She describes how she needs personal images in order to find the right dynamic in her movement.

In *Streams*, I'm a woman who, perhaps, is in the stream of water trying to move with it, or trying to move through it. Or I can take the idea that it's like life and then you try to move as smoothly as you can through everything.

(In *The Dance Makers*, 1980)

Sometimes you may find difficulty in giving the right information to dancers. The dancer may need more detail concerning content and you are giving movement information.

I am inspired by the dancers' bodies . . . I have to find the right thing for their bodies. I tell my cast little in the beginning therefore I like to get the whole shape of the music planned first; then I elaborate on the characterisation . . . I think I do this purposely because I like my artists to find themselves in their roles . . . so I allow the dancers to improvise within the limitations imposed by the steps . . .

(Kenneth MacMillan in *Making a Ballet*, 1974)

The quality of audience experience can be directly affected by the standard of performance by the dancers. A dance can be evaluated by how well the dancers have performed. A part of the art of choreography is making sure that it shows off the dancers to their best advantage. Finding movement which is not only successful in terms of compositional form but sits on the dancers like well-fitting clothes is essential. It should suit their abilities, being not too difficult for them, using their strengths but also challenging them. Dancers who achieve greatness in performance have at some point taken into their body and mind what the choreographer has intended. An idea is transformed and stylised into a coherent dance form using the skills and ideas that dancers and choreographer have available. During the rehearsals, the choreographer should be aware of how best to draw out those skills from the dancers in order to give a dance the most expressive performance possible. Once the choreographer hands over the dance to the dancers, he or she then relies on their skills to perform it for an audience.

Refining and polishing are ongoing up to the moment of performance. Ongoing evaluation of constituent features, form and structure should occur so that eventually movement is refined to express the content in the best way. As you see the dance motifs or sections over and over again you will evaluate and make fine adjustments and improvements. For the dancer, the repetition is an opportunity to increase accuracy and to pinpoint any problems or queries. It is rather like cooking a fine meal: starting with all the separate, recognisable ingredients and selecting the right amounts of everything, timing to perfection to make something which has a flavour all of its own.

The hard thing is . . . dropping the keystone in, so it completes itself in its language, without destroying what's gone before. So that you go: 'Oh, of course. The inevitable solution!'

(Mark Morris in *The Electronic Telegraph*, September 1999)

Remember: 'If you haven't anything worth throwing away then you probably haven't anything worth keeping.' Evaluation involves making decisions on what is successful and what is not. Sometimes this may come incredibly late in the rehearsal process:

I feel that within this form (of classic ballet) every day I will set something and then say 'You can't do that'. With *Rite of Spring* I worked for three weeks and produced fiendishly difficult choreography and then had to scrub the whole thing because I felt it was wrong.

(Kenneth MacMillan in *Making a Ballet*, 1974)

As you go through your rehearsal schedule you should shape and structure the dance gradually. Your ideas may change as you work and Table 7.4 may help you to understand the rehearsal process better.

 Table 7.4 The rehearsal process

MY IDEAS.	MOVEMENT
WEEK 5 JOURNAL: *I've been trying the voice accompaniment and it's tough. But I think I've found a solution. The dancers who are not dancing the main parts use their voices to keep a rhythm – like a rap in the background. They take it in turns to speak saying one word each and then sometimes in unison – like the dance! Sometimes they use their breath sounds and body percussion too.* I found some information online about the days of the week and I'm going to use a few ideas in the dance to make it more interesting	I let the dancers choose their day. It was lucky because they were all born on different days of the week – so everyone was happy. The sections of the dance were OK but it was very scrappy so I tried using a ground bass structure with all the dancers on stage. I introduced chairs for the dancers in the background and made a motif that involved sitting on them and walking around and between them so that they change chairs sometimes and actually move the chairs into different formations too. It looks good and works well with the voices and chants. As the dancers come and go they interact with each other as transitions
Monday's – fair of face MOTIF 1	Solo starts in front of the other seated dancers. Dancers in background say the words of the line slowly sometimes when the soloist looks at herself in the mirror. They sigh as if they are her looking at herself. As she ends she walks by 'Tuesday' as if she doesn't notice her
WEEK 6, JOURNAL: *Solos are all finished and the duet is nearly there. Still a lot to do though.* Must remember to ask the teacher in to see the dance	Contrasting movement – MOTIF 3 Travelling trio is fun because they're using the chairs as props and it's really funny. The soloist is seated at the back and the single voice works well because he speaks clearly and uses sounds like car alarms and boom box
WEEK 6, JOURNAL: *Solos are all finished and the duet is nearly there. Still a lot to do though.* Franky came in to watch the dance and used the evaluation sheet- very helpful suggestions that we can work on next week	The quartet is also fun because they're using the chairs too as if they're really hurrying up as they tidy and clean up. We're going to need to work hard in Week 7 to finish in time

At the end of your rehearsals you should show the dance informally to a small audience and your teacher. Task Six leads you into this and gives you an evaluation sheet that you could use before the first show to evaluate the dance yourself. You could ask a friend to do this too and then you can help them in the same way.

Once the rehearsal period is over it's show time! The appreciation of a performance will be the subject of the next chapter.

TASK SIX – *Evaluation*
(Continues from Tasks One, Two and Three)

 KEY SKILLS Communication
Improving own learning and performance

10 to 20 minutes

Prepare a brief programme note for the audience which includes information on content and style.

Share the final short solos with your group. Use the sheet on page 287 to evaluate each other's dances, noting how successful they are in:

■ putting across the original content;
■ compositional form and structure;
■ showing the style of the chosen choreographer.

Name	Title of dance		
In the style of:			
Evaluation of dances – composition and style			
✓ the columns			
	Needs improvement	Mostly effectively achieved	Consistently / imaginatively
1 Expresses the content			
2 Shows the chosen style			
3 Chooses interesting and appropriate			
■ actions			
■ use of space			
■ use of time			
■ use of dynamics			
4 Choice of accompaniment			
5 Relationship to accompaniment			
6 Uses appropriate choreographic devices			
7 Uses appropriate choreographic structure			

Comments and suggestions based on the above:

Set targets for improvement:

References and resources

Books

Blom, L.A. and Chaplin, L.T., *The Moment of Movement: Dance Improvisation*, Alton, Hampshire: Dance Books, 1988

Bremser, M., *Fifty Contemporary Choreographers*, London: Routledge, 1999

Butcher, R. and Melrose, S., *Choreography, Collisions and Collaborations*, Enfield: Middlesex University Press, 2005

Lavender, L., *Dancers Talking Dance: Critical Evaluation in the Choreography Class*, Champaign, IL: Human Kinetics, 1996

Minton, S.C., *Choreography: A Basic Approach Using Improvisation*, Champaign, IL: Human Kinetics, 2007

Scheff, H., Sprague, M., McGreevy-Nichols, S., *Experiencing Dance: From Student to Dance Artist*, Human Kinetics, 2005

Articles/Reviews

Lloyd Newson in interview with Jo Butterworth, published by The Centre for Dance and Theatre Studies, University of Bretton 1998

Other interviews with Lloyd Newson on: www.dv8.co.uk

Video/DVD

From www.theplace.org.uk

Lee, R. and Maclennan, S., *Time Lapses*, On *Spring Re-Loaded*, 2000

8 DANCE APPRECIATION

Applying the appreciation process in performance

> The art object . . . is a first presentation of a possibility truly felt and imagined.
>
> (Arturo B. Fallico in *Dance from Magic to Art*, 1976)

The dance is choreographed. In rehearsal the formative evaluations have now resulted in a finished dance. Now the dance meets an audience. The choreographer, audience and critics are looking on and evaluating the overall impact of the dance. The dancers are nervously anticipating their appearance and they have a large amount of responsibility for the dance from now on. This is what they have been training for. This section will examine aspects of this special moment when the process becomes the product – live and direct!

During and after performance, choreographer, dancer, audience and critic will engage with the process of appreciation. We perceive dances through the senses. We see the movement and perhaps feel it kinaesthetically. We hear the accompaniment. We see the costumes, light and set. The process now is one of summative evaluation. If you are a student maybe it is a course assessment or examination. At this stage each viewer will have differing opinions, ranging from a less informed/more personal taste 'I thought it was good' or 'It did nothing for me', to an informed and articulate response such as one may read from a newspaper critic, or expressed by a dance student!

> . . . art is vision or intuition. The artist produces an image. The person who enjoys art turns his eyes in the direction which the artist has pointed out to him, peers through the hole which has been opened for him.
>
> (Benedetto Croce in *Dance from Magic to Art*, 1976)

We will examine how the process of appreciation may differ depending on the point of view of dancer, choreographer, audience or critic.

The significance of dance

Appreciating the significance of a dance of your own, of other students or of professionals, is a complex process. You need to be able to recognise the constituent features and understand how they relate to each other, the content of the dance, the context. If you understand more about what makes a successful dance your own work will improve.

Initial response to a painting should be a starting point and not a finish line. It should lead not only to more prolonged scrutiny but also to the posing of questions. Just what is it in this picture that seems so pleasing? Is it the colour? the light? the conveying of the artist's emotion? . . . the forms themselves? . . . Above all how has the artist gone about achieving (the) effects?

(Helen M. Franc in *An Invitation to See 125 Paintings from the Museum of Modern Art*, New York, 1973)

Often dance students may think that analysis is a dry and rather unnecessary process. Indeed if overdone it can kill the impact and enjoyment of a dance. However, if it is done with passion and uses imagination, it can enhance the enjoyment. Try to write creatively about what you see. Finding the words that a dance is worthy of requires great powers of description, interpretation and evaluation. The three stages of the appreciation process are:

- Describe: the dancers, the movement, the set, costumes and accompaniment.
- Interpret: the content, meaning and styles.
- Evaluate: assess the success for the viewer in context.

As you watch dance, whether in rehearsal or performance, you respond to and appraise what you see. As a student of dance you are trying to make your response more of an informed one, not based only on personal taste.

The preceding chapters should have increased your understanding of the first stage of the process of dance appreciation – description. For instance, you may have described how a dance uses space or motif development in certain ways and how it relates to the accompaniment in your own journal. The next stage is to interpret what the selected constituent features may be expressing.

Interpretation

Interpretation involves understanding the content, meaning and style of a dance as expressed in the constituent features. It involves asking questions like: What is the theme? How does the movement express the meaning of the dance? A choreographer's choice of content and movement technique is part of their personal style.

Content and meaning

Content is the subject matter, theme or ideas chosen by the choreographer or the meanings expressed to a viewer. Content is expressed by the appropriate

selection and structuring of constituent features. This process of choosing and transforming content into a dance is described by American post-modern choreographer, Anna Halprin:

> . . . as an artist . . . essentially your job is to be a vehicle for other people. . . . when you take responsibility for an audience, you are then accepting the fact that you must go through some sort of distilling process in which the personal experience has become so zeroed and so heightened by a clarity that you know exactly what you're dealing with . . . Then you find the movement . . . essence of that idea inherent not only in how your body moves, but in . . . an awareness of the total thing.
>
> (In *The Vision of Modern Dance*, 1980)

If we scan various well-known choreographers we may see that they have themes of content running through their work. Indeed, some say that all choreographers spend their lifetime working on only one or two dances in essence.

The content of the work of Kenneth MacMillan often focused on sexual conflict and violence. In a similar way the works of Lloyd Newson address how people relate to each other and the problems that this may create. Content involved with movement for its own sake, 'pure dance', is a concern in the works of Merce Cunningham, Siobhan Davies and Richard Alston. Christopher Bruce seems interested in themes of social conscience such as political conflict and aging. The content itself may indicate certain styles in which it may be treated most successfully. This may bring about a certain 'look' or style in the movement. For example, a dance entitled *Gravity and Impulse* is likely to be post-modern genre, where movement for its own sake is the content and a Release style of technique is performed. However, when Mark Baldwin became director of Rambert Dance Company in 2005, he choreographed *Constant Speed*, based on two papers by scientist Albert Einstein, the 'Theory of Special Relativity' and investigations of 'Brownlan Motion'. Science meets the art of dance.

TASK ONE – *Meaning making*

KEY SKILLS Improving own learning and performance
Communication
Information technology

Several hours

Select a video of a dance work by a choreographer whom you are studying. View it, or a five-minute extract of it, repeatedly and make notes as you watch to help you answer the questions below:

- Identify the full title, choreographer, date and company/dancers.
- Name the genre and any styles that are in use.

■ Describe one main motif in terms of:
  (a) its constituent features; and
  (b) the meaning of the movement.
■ Identify any choreographic devices and the form/structure.
■ Explain what physical and interpretative skills the dancers need to perform this dance.
■ Describe the feature of the physical setting and accompaniment.
■ Give a brief evaluation of the success of the dance, considering any contextual factors which may be of influence.

Put your answers into a format that is suitable as a presentation to your group.
  Present your findings to your group using a variety of types of presentation, including, for example, short film clips, photos, PowerPoint demonstration.

In the world of fashion, clothes by the famous designers Katharine Hamnett, Christian Dior and Calvin Klein each have their own distinctive style. When worn, they give the wearer a certain look. Similarly, in the music world, hip hop sounds unmistakably different to classical music. Style is the key here. Style in dance is seen in the technique that a dancer performs. Look at the photographs below and you will see contrasts in the styles of the two genres – the classical ballet of Ashton and Anderson's post-modern dance.

Figure 8.1 *Les Patineurs* (1937) by Sir Frederick Ashton and *Birthday* (1992) by Lea Anderson

So genres appear different in style. However, there are different named styles within genres. New York City Ballet and Balanchine, or Ashton's style of ballet for the Royal Ballet, are quite different styles of ballet.

Similarly, in the genre of modern dance, you would not mistake Martha Graham technique for Merce Cunningham. Or in post-modern genre Lea Anderson's movement style is noticeably different to that of Siobhan Davies.

TASK TWO – *Compare and contrast*

KEY SKILLS Working with others
Communication
Problem solving

 Several hours

In groups of three or four, compare two works from different genres, e.g. *The Sleeping Beauty* (Petipa, 1890) and *Strange Fish* (Newson, 1992). List how they differ or are similar in content and style. Make a presentation of your findings to another group.

In music, literature and the visual arts there is a tradition of studying the 'greats'. This should be so in dance too. You may find that a style other than your own actually has similarities to yours, as well as containing elements which are very different. Therefore, it can reinforce your personal style as well as offer up new ideas to be explored. It may well reveal things which really do not fit your body and mind. It is useful to know what they are too. Matthew Bourne's parody of modern dance in his *Car Man* (2000) grew out of his dislike of Martha Graham's technique, which he believed wrecked his back during training. It did not stop him from making effective use of it in his choreography.

Your personal movement and choreographic style is something which will develop over time. As you analyse your own and others' dances, use your findings to inform your personal dance development. This process of development is seen in the work of many artists. In the work of Martha Graham we see times when America was the main focus of content and other times when Greek dramas or the Bible were important. In the early twentieth century, she totally rejected ballet and would not allow her dancers to attend ballet classes, but later she accepted the different genre as complementary to her own in training dancers. Her personal development used the torso in new ways in the stylised contraction, release and spirals. The harsh, angular appearance, with flexed feet and hands, suited the expression of the content she chose. New content reflecting the modern age of that time needed a new style of moving. Nowadays her style is part of modern dance tradition but it came from her invention. Similar developments of style can be traced in many choreographers.

Experience of a range of genres such as jazz, ballroom, tap, contact improvisation, contemporary and ballet can broaden the scope of your personal style. The key is to explore and not to be afraid of mixing genres and styles.

Working with other art forms can also enrich and enhance your work. Your personal style is not a limitation but a beginning.

So now that the first two stages of the dance appreciation process have been explained,you should understand more about how the chosen constituent features, structures and styles can be described and how they express content in the process of interpretation. The third and final stage of the process of appreciation is evaluation.

Evaluation

Evaluation is judging the success, or lack of it, of a performance taking into consideration how effectively the constituent features and style have been used to portray the content and the quality of the actual performance of the dancers.

> Evaluation is creation . . . is itself the value and jewel of all valued things. Only through evaluation is there value.
>
> (Freidrich Nietzsche, philosopher in *Thus Spoke Zarathustra*)

As Nietzsche describes above, the process of evaluation (and appreciation) gives value to the performance. Also, it is useful in the rehearsal process of making and refining dances. Although in rehearsal and performance you are looking at the same features, the evaluation of a dance may be from differing points of view.

Evaluation brings into play the concept of context of the dance because this will tell how successful a dance is for a specific viewer.

Context

In your dance studies your choreography may be in the context of some sort of assessment. Therefore it functions as a means to gain marks to pass the exam! Probably you will be working in your community with your peers. Can you see how this is the context of your work? We will now apply this to the wider field of professional dance work.

Dance is always created at a certain time and in a specific place. When we analyse and evaluate dance these contexts must be considered. In particular we may look at the contexts of:

- the development of an artist, genre or style over time;
- history and social conditions;
- the function and role of the dance.

The development of an artist, genre or style over time

As you saw earlier in the section on style, a choreographer's work, like that of other artists, develops over time. Similarly, genres such as ballet change in style over time. The 2000 Kirov reconstruction of Petipa's original 1890 *The Sleeping Beauty*, from the Stepanov notation, presented the problem of recreating the correct style. Even though the notation gave detail about the steps it did not supply descriptions of how they danced at that time. The Kirov ballet master Sergei Vikharev, who was responsible for this reconstruction, reported that the original tempo was faster than the versions of the late twentieth century.

Post-modern dance too, from its early experiments in the 1960s, has continued to develop and now has many different styles within it.

Richard Alston is a good example of the development of a choreographer. Originally trained in Graham technique at the newly formed London Contemporary Dance School, his *Nowhere Slowly* (1970) showed Graham influences of fall/recovery. He then went on to become one of the first British choreographers of note to work with a Merce Cunningham influence which suited his style. There are balletic influences too, of the Cecchetti style, but moulded into his personal language. Nowadays, his style also incorporates the Release techniques of post-modernism. He maintains strong links with visual art, from his art background. His experimental style has meant that he used a wide variety of accompaniments, from silence to complex word–sound collages. But later work seems more set to classical music such as that of Stravinsky in *Movements from Petrushka* (1994), or the romantic Brahms in *Waltzes in Disorder* (1998). He prefers to use formal structures, although as he admits on the video version of *Soda Lake*, sometimes the 'pure' movement and the figurative images become mixed together. For a while his work was very intellectual, 'pure' dance, like *Rainbow Bandit* (1974) and *Zansa* (1986), but there were also pieces that featured human emotion, such as *Pulcinella* (1987) where the dancers play roles of cartoon-like characters from commedia del'arte. Semi-narrative structures featured more in the late 1980s, although he still hankers to the Cunningham legacy in structure, such as *Sophisticated Curiosities* (1998) which presented excerpts from such early works as *Rainbow Ripples* (1980) and *Strong Language* (1987). A main concern of Alston's is his interest in form and structure of dances, plus his flowing and detailed movement style that tells stories, however abstract, about people's lives and living.

His working methods have stayed much the same throughout, preferring a collaborative style of relationship with dancers. This may reflect his beginnings in the early 1970s with *Strider*, *X6 Dance Collective* and *Second Stride* – all these companies worked in communal collaborations, breaking away from traditional ballet company hierarchies.

TASK THREE – *Research*

KEY SKILLS Communication
Problem solving
Information technology

Several hours

This task links with Tasks One and Seven.
Research a well-known choreographer of your choice. Write a summary of the key features of their development. These may

include: training, different techniques, preferred movement genres/styles, choice of content, choreographic structures, dancers, accompaniment, and relationship to other art forms.

Prepare your summary for presentation to your group. This may make use of some of your original resource material from this book, other texts, photos, video, and Internet images.

History and social conditions

If viewers of a dance have knowledge of the time and place when it was made it will help them to understand, interpret and evaluate the performance. Knowing about tradition and dances from the past can help to nurture the creative and innovative – not inhibit originality.

The historical and social context includes features of:

- dominant social values;
- changing social structures;
- philosophies and psychologies;
- technological developments.

Dominant social values

The world of Renaissance ballet was dominated by the rulers of European Royal courts. Manners and rules of everyday behaviour were reflected in the ballets where everyone knew 'their place'. So the ballets were successful if they glorified the Kings and Queens and maintained that social order. If dominant values are questioned in an artist's work it can affect the public reaction to a dance. Nijinsky provoked a riot in Paris because his audience expected to see 'ballet'. Isadora Duncan outraged people by her disregard for the rules of being a woman in society of the twentieth century.

The social conditions of the United States of America in the 1930s and 1940s were desperate for many people. The jazz-age dances, like the Charleston, had been lively and popular and represented the prosperous economy and optimistic times, but by the lowest point of the Depression in 1933 America's stock market had crashed, one-third of the population were unemployed and war was brewing again in Europe. The party times faded for ordinary people, but they found an escape in the romantic dance and song in Hollywood films. Films that told stories of overnight success in show business, such as *42nd Street* (Busby Berkeley, 1933), established a successful formula of a feel-good plot, fabulous costumes and sensational dance routines. These films featured the dancing for entertainment value and the final effect was one of watching both a narrative film *and* a separate theatrical performance.

This story telling, dancing and musical combination also influenced the world of theatre, marked by groundbreaking shows such as Rogers and Hart's

On Your Toes (1936). The plot was familiar – backstage life of a ballet company – but for the first time a Broadway show employed a choreographer, George Balanchine previously of Ballets Russes, rather than a dance director. He brought classical ballet to Broadway having emigrated in 1933 to USA. He quickly adapted his balletic technique, with assistance from tapper Herbi Harper, to include tap and jazz styles and these were to remain an influence on his choreography from that time onwards. *On Your Toes* also broke new ground by using the dances to tell the story, unlike the sudden appearance of a song and dance that added nothing to the plot in the films of the time. Balanchine hired the untrained but highly talented dancer Ray Bolger to dance with prima ballerina Tamara Geva in the show's famous dramatic number 'Slaughter on Tenth Avenue'.

Changing social structures

When we watch romantic ballet today, we must consider the time when it was first choreographed in order to understand its significance. We could never really experience romantic ballet as audiences did in the 1800s, because we live in a very different age from them. We can appreciate it for what it is and enjoy it, but not relate to it as new and fashionable in the way that the original audiences would have done. The changing social order, which resulted from the French Revolution, turned society upside down and the aristocracy and their classicism in the arts were no longer to be worshipped as perfect. Now was the turn of the peasants to be glorified and idealised. This directly affected the choice of content in the romantic ballet. The types of characters, roles, settings and stories resulted from the social context of the late nineteenth century, when fairies, spirits, exotic foreign places and peasants became ultra cool.

Today, dance may use the same stories but the treatment of the content will differ to reflect a different social order. The choreography of Matthew Bourne in *Highland Fling . . . a romantic wee ballet* (1994) shows post-modern treatment of a classical ballet story. It is based on *La Sylphide* (1832), the classic Romantic ballet, but twists the story to tell of James, an unemployed welder, who is lured from his nuptial bed by a rather grungy-looking fairy temptress. So the romantic vision of a classic style hero becomes the ramblings of a drug addict. The movement style mixes techniques of modern with social dance and some ballet.

Similarly in Matthew Bourne's *Swan Lake* (1995) we note the romantic references in the use of a comical classical ballet divertissement. Being in the post-modern genre, it is most appropriate that he should parody a dance style from the past and the romantic one is highly suited to the original subject matter of Swan Lake. But Bourne's treatment of content is not romantic because it echoes the context of people's lives today. Similarly Mats Ek's version of *The Sleeping Beauty* (1996) varies the original story by making the sleep representative of drug dependency. Aurora is a heroin addict who is attracted to Carabosse, the traditional villain. The Prince helps her but it has to be Aurora's own power of mind that causes her awakening.

Changing social structures were also influential in the beginnings of tap and jazz dance in America and *samba* in Brazil. In Brazil alone, between 3 and 4 million slaves were imported before slavery was banned in 1888. African traditions from Yoruba roots and *candomble* rituals were disguised as Catholic worship and survive to this day in Brazil. *Samba* rhythms and steps became popular for all Brazilians in 'Carnival', the Catholic celebration marking the start of Lent. Soon *samba* had spread in popularity to Europe and North America. It even made its way to Hollywood in the form of extravagant character, Carmen Miranda (1909–1955) who starred in many films, such as *Down Argentina Way* (1940) and *Copacabana* (1947). Famous for her sensational dresses and hats piled high with every fruit imaginable, her songs such as 'The lady with the Tutti Frutti Hat' and 'Chica Chica Boom Chic' were smash hits and by 1945 she was the highest paid female performer in America.

The 1960s was a time of great social change in value systems. 'Free love' and 'Flower Power' were signs of a changing society and dancers responded to this by experimenting with more collective methods of working. In 2000, an event called *PastForward: The influence of the Post-Moderns* in California presented some of the key innovations from the post-modern work of the 1960s of the Judson Church Dance Theatre. Works from David Gordon, Yvonne Rainer and Lucinda Childs, to name a few, were on show. Typical characteristics of this style were almost anti-dance and included the use of minimal everyday movement, simple walking, running and relentless repetition. For post-modern dancers in North America in the 1960s the success and significance of the work may only, indeed, be truly understood when looking back in time:

It may be true that neither critics nor audiences absorbed what happened in the sixties but I don't think I'd be doing what I'm doing now if that hadn't happened.

(Douglas Dunn in *The Vision of Modern Dance*, 1980)

Experimental work by its very nature pushes the boundaries of understanding for the audience. It is easy to dismiss what has been presented as obscure and pointless if you're missing the point! Sometimes to evaluate success new strategies may have to be adopted by the onlooker. When this fails evaluation may be achieved later only from a retrospective view. Hindsight may allow us to understand the impact which a dance made in its original context. The criteria by which we evaluate success must consider the whole artistic, social and historical conditions of the time.

Philosophies and psychologies

When modern art burst into existence at the start of the twentieth century it rejected the accepted values which had dominated art and society. In so doing it reflected a society in turmoil from war as well as the discovery of new psychologies and philosophies.

Martha Graham presented psychodramas, stark movement and hard-edged truths springing from the new psychologies of Freud and Jung. She demanded that her audiences contribute to the final performance by putting their own interpretation on her dances. Dance was no longer just entertainment, as it had been in the previous years of vaudeville and rather stale ballet: the audience had a greater role to play in the success of the final product.

Merce Cunningham took Eastern philosophies, such as Zen Buddhism, to influence his personal style, as shown in the use of chance procedures to make dances; of the mind set which keeps the constituent features of dances totally separate; and in his expectation that individuals will all view his dances from their own perspectives.

Recent developments in Release Techniques also draw on Eastern philosophies of meditation to internalise movement, acknowledging the holistic nature of dance.

Technological developments

The development of the pointe shoe and the stage light of ether, as used in L*a Sylphide* (1832), enhanced the ethereal presence of ballet in performance, which was such a vital part of the romantic palette.

The coming of sound to films brought new ideas to Hollywood film makers, allowing them to include more song and dance. *Singin' in the Rain* (1952), starring and co-directed by Gene Kelly, took the end of silent movies as the storyline and was voted the best musical film of all time by the American Film Insitute. Like many, Kelly had come up through vaudeville. In 1942, in his first film, *For Me and My Girl*, he co-starred with Judy Garland.

In more recent times, the explosion in computer technology has opened up the use of more film and mixed media work in dance performance. Dance can now be viewed on and is made specially for small screens via the Internet, or in the new form of videodance.

The function and role of dance

Most Western theatre dance has significance as art and/or entertainment. The audience is the final judge of whether a dance has been successful in enriching and energising their lives. Each one of them will have their own thoughts, preferences and interpretations from any single performance. On other occasions the role of the dance is more for participation and this can include classes in ballet, ballroom, folk dances such as morris and Irish, as well as community classes in creative dance, contemporary and contact improvisation.

In the multicultural world of today, dances of Asia and Africa, amongst many other ethnicities, are performed more and more for their artistic function rather than for any spiritual or social role. However some companies, such as *Adzido* in Britain, aim to preserve traditional African culture in what they perceive to be its clash with Western contemporary social values.

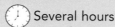

TASK FOUR – *Think of a context . . .*

KEY SKILLS Improving own learning and performance
Communication

🕐 Several hours

Test your understanding of a specific dance genre.
Choose a dance genre. Name it and complete the questions below:

- When was the genre first developed?
- What is the context of the genre?
- What is the purpose and function of the genre?
- Are there any influences on it from other dance traditions or art forms?
- What are the significant characteristics of the style of the chosen genre? This may include a choice of physical constituents, structure and form, accompaniment and relation of dance to it, physical setting, dancers, content.

Over time there may have been changes in the genre. Select a specific context, time and place, and describe:

- how any of the following changed: social conditions; function/role;
- any resulting changes in significant characteristics of the style (as listed above).

Putting appreciation into practice

Appreciation involves a set of comparisons to judge how effectively the constituent features are combined with the content, style, context and function in determining how successful a dance is. A three-stage process is useful in different ways depending on the situation:

- Choreographers will evaluate as an ongoing process of developing a dance in rehearsal and performance.
- Dancers will evaluate according to the specific demands that the choreographer's style and performance places on them.
- Audiences and critics will evaluate the significance and success of a dance in performance.

The remainder of this chapter will look at how you may find the process of appreciation useful in making and watching dances.

Appreciation of a performance as choreographer

During a performance the choreographer has a job to do. On stage a dancer may show weakness in some type of interpretative skill, or unsafe practice may have been noticed and the choreographer should note this and give constructive criticism after the show so that over time the performance improves.

Many dances are changed after initial and subsequent performances. The choreographer may detect something that could be improved upon in the choreography itself. This is a continuation of the formative evaluations and consequent refinements that took place in rehearsal. It may take into consideration comments from dancers, audience or critical reviews in the media. Generally speaking, it is unusual for a choreographer to perform in their own work because they need to be the outside eye in rehearsal and in performance.

. . . now I sit through almost every performance . . . giving notes and making changes . . . it never stops. For example, when *Bound To Please* first showed . . . it was a totally different piece to what was presented in London three months later . . . Without constant change and development, a work becomes dead for performers and audience.

(Lloyd Newson in interview with Jo Butterworth, 1998)

Equally, recognising why something is a success is just as important. Once Matthew Bourne saw the large audiences that were attracted to *Swan Lake* he realised that his work was a success. He figured out that many audiences were used to seeing films and theatre but were perhaps new to dance, and that the attraction was seeing a story without words for the first time.

There may also be technical and production problems, like sound or light cues, or a badly fitting costume that need correction. So choreographers employ the procedures of appreciation to evaluate degrees of success and respond appropriately.

Appreciation of a performance as audience

When the choreographer starts to work on the dance the target audience should have been a consideration. A dance for an audience of young children will be different to one for a 1970s' post-modern audience, or for a group of dance students.

Dances which have significance as art, and function to impact on an audience, are judged by specific criteria. Is the content of the dance presented to the audience in a form which they can understand? Or is there little to interest or stimulate an audience? Is there a flaw in structure or form which makes it difficult for the audience to interpret the content? Sometimes the audience and critic may perceive a weakness in a dance.

A dance is an intense and potentially confusing experience for an audience. So why not go and see a dance more than once, like you would listen to music or read a book or look at a painting? Unfortunately cost is the problem. Maybe there should be a discount scheme for repeated viewings of a dance! As a dance student this would be good, wouldn't it? Meanwhile, however, video observation for study purposes will have to do, fraught with problems though it is (see next chapter). So we are stuck with the 'see it once and hope' scenario. This being so, choreographers have a duty to create dances with clarity of expression and form.

Some may say that dance audiences need educating, because if they were informed they may understand and perhaps enjoy dance more. Many companies have outreach work such as post-performance talks by choreographers, lecture-demonstrations/ showing extracts from dances with explanation and opportunity for questions. One scheme being run in New York, called *New Faces/New Voices/New Visions*, was founded in 1990 by Laura Greer at the Aaron Davis Hall, home to Alvin Ailey Dance Theatre. The aim was to nurture audiences in a predominantly black neighbourhood. The scheme included chances for beginners to do a class with famous choreographer Bill T. Jones as well as attend open rehearsals and discussions, and tickets were discounted – 3 for the price of 2.

At last a discount scheme! Indeed the theory that audiences might like to think about what they see on stage is refreshing. Others disagree:

I feel exactly the opposite. Most dance people need to be educated in the ways of normal living and learn what body movements mean to other people, both consciously and unconsciously. When the average person in the street watches a dance in which women fling their legs wide open, for the dancer it's just a technical event, but for the person watching it, it can have immense emotional, sexual and psychological implications . . . we should understand what we do and what that difference in perception means.

(Lloyd Newson in *Enter Achilles* programme note, 1995)

Is it enough to entertain an audience as the work of Matthew Bourne does so well? Some would say that is insufficient, as Lloyd Newson maintains that his work should challenge audiences.

Audiences of innovatory dance or sometimes the 'pure dance' style may struggle to find ways of appreciating it. Consequently, audiences for these works may be smaller in number. Some may go once but never again feeling that they did not enjoy themselves because they did not find 'a meaning'. So how can audiences find a way to appreciate this less mainstream style of dance? Perhaps a clue lies in the process of making such works. Richard Alston in the video of *Soda Lake* comments on the wide variety of images, from animal to emotional, that he worked with during the creative process. Therefore if viewers see many different meanings, they can all be correct.

The difficulty is encouraging audiences to have the courage of their own convictions and enjoy the dances on that level. As Merce Cunningham said, the audience complete the dance by being there.

Seeing an older work such as *Les Patineurs* (1937, Sir Frederick Ashton) can help audiences to appreciate and understand later work.

Presenting dances in context of their development of a particular artist's work is something that could inform audiences. Nurturing audiences is important and involves being able to offer them contextual information both past and present, especially if, as many think, the Internet is the opportunity to share opinions on dance and take criticism out of the small élite circles of critics and

into the public arena. Forums and blogs abound now and it would be good to be able to think that the opinions shared are based on informed appreciation and not on personal taste alone.

Appreciation of a performance as critic

And so to those whom everyone loves to hate – the critics.

A critic is a bundle of biases held loosely together by a sense of taste.
(Whitney Balliett in *Dinosaurs in the Morning*, 1962)

The job of the critic is the process of appreciation and, many consider, to be publicly accountable. Their professional concerns are to be able to describe, interpret and evaluate accurately and for this they must have thorough knowledge of context. Critics contextualise in terms of history, literature, current events and whatever else is relevant to a performance in terms of content and the artists themselves. Critics themselves do not have to have been a dancer. They do need to be able to write well, be knowledgeable about arts generally and dance in particular. Perhaps what critics should be trying to do is distil:

The visceral aspect of dance (which) precedes conscious thought . . .
(Lloyd Newson in *Enter Achilles* programme note, 1995)

Just as the choreographer is distilling content into a dance for the audience's gut reaction, the critic is attempting to represent it in another physical act – writing!

Critics' styles can differ from the poetic to the documentary, advisory or informative. It is hoped that they give sufficient detailed analysis so that in its way the review can provide a document for history. Perhaps we can expect some information on principles like genre, context, content and style in dance and reasons for opinions expressed in reviews. This would increase understanding generally of the elusive art of dance. Dancers, choreographers and audiences alike may read the reviews and find useful information within.

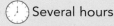

TASK FIVE – *Your theatre notebook*

KEY SKILLS Improving own learning and performance
Communication
Information technology

 Several hours

The next time you go to see a dance performance, imagine that you are the dance critic for a newspaper. Write not more than 200 words about the show, trying to inform someone who has not seen the performance. Remember that the article is not only about your personal taste but should be written from an informed viewpoint,

describing constituent features and physical setting, interpreting content and style, evaluating in context.

OR

The next time you go to a professional performance find two reviews in the newspapers or research them online (see Resources list at end of chapter). Compare the two critics' viewpoints and list differences and similarities in their writing styles and opinions.

Even with excellent contextual knowledge and a degree of objectivity, a professional dance critic's review is only one person's opinion. A good review, however, will be able to give the reader a sense of a performance that they have not seen. The reader then decides whether or not to go. Clearly if the review is bad the audience may not go, so critics bear a great responsibility and wield great power.

TASK SIX – *Review the reviews*

KEY SKILLS Improving own learning and performance
Communication
Information technology

 Several hours

Read the reviews that you found online from Task Five and match quotations from them to the stages of the process of appreciation; description, interpretation and evaluation.

Next to each quote write which of the following features are identified:

■ constituent features;
■ form and structure;
■ style;
■ content;
■ interpretative skills;
 context.

Below is an example of a list of headings under which a dance may be described, interpreted and evaluated:

Title of dance
Choreographer
Date of first performance
Genre/style
Content
Accompaniment

Dancers/company
Any specific demands placed on the dancers in performance
Movement and form/content
Set
Costume/prop
Lighting
Designer name(s)
Context and social significance
Evaluation

An example of a specific dance analysis and evaluation is now given below:

Isadora Duncan's 1920s Brahms Waltzes inspired *Five Brahms Waltzes in the Manner of Isadora Duncan* (1976).

Choreographer: Sir Frederick Ashton.

Date: 1975–76.

Genre/style: modern dance.

Content: Isadora Duncan's style.

Accompaniment: originally Brahms's Waltz Opus 35, number 15. In the 1976 version, four more waltzes were added (Nos. 2, 8, 10 and 13) and the first waltz (No. 15) was played as a prelude as in the original Isadora Duncan performance. The piano was played live on stage, again as in the original Isadora Duncan version.

Dancers/company: solo female. Originally, Lynn Seymour for The Royal Ballet, and later Lucy Burge for the Ballet Rambert (1984).

Specific demands placed on the dancers in performance: a very wide range of dynamics was required.

Movement and form/content: Ashton had strong memories of Duncan in performance – in particular, a lasting impression of the freedom of her movement – and this influenced his choice of movements, which included:

subtle, light shifts of weight;
movements relating the body to a universal space and not just to the stage space;
plastic, fluid, expressive head, body and upper-torso movements;
movements conveying a range of emotions. The choreographic form of each waltz was wide-ranging, and so were the dynamics.

Set: a bare stage except for a piano.

Costume/prop: a long piece of floaty fabric was used to enhance the spatial patterns of the movements. The costume was a tunic made of flimsy fabric

very similar to the original worn by Duncan. This emphasised the free flowing, rippling movements.

Designer name: David Dean.

Context and social significance: originally choreographed for the 1975 Hamburg Gala night to celebrate the 50th anniversary of the Ballet Rambert and entitled *Homage to Isadora*. The later version (1976) was entitled *Five Brahms Waltzes in the Manner of Isadora Duncan*, danced by Lynn Seymour and dedicated to Dame Marie Rambert who, like Ashton, had been inspired by Duncan.

In 1921, Ashton had seen Isadora dance in London. He went back many times, fascinated by her grace, intensity and use of arms. He later stated that he used these influences in his own ballet.

The original Duncan waltzes were choreographed in 1902 and performed with great success in North and South America, Europe and Russia until 1924.

Evaluation: As a piece of modern dance it has historical, retrospective value. Ashton's memories of Duncan's work go some way to record what otherwise would be lost to dance history as there is little remaining of her legacy. As a piece in its own right its revival recognises its worth. The dancers were recognised as having the high degree of technical control required for the wide range of dynamics and the authentic Duncan expressive style.

Ashton's gala piece was so successful that, unusually for a gala piece, it was placed in the Royal Ballet repertoire in a fuller version. Later still, it was revived for the Rambert repertoire.

TASK SEVEN – *Show your appreciation*

KEY SKILLS Improving own learning and performance
Communication
Information Technology

Apply the list of headings to a dance of one of the choreographers which you are studying.
Present your findings to a group on PowerPoint, in text, film images and the spoken word.

Appreciation – a summary

In appreciating the many dimensions of a dance, its value and worth are enhanced. It may be treasured as a precious jewel in the lives of all who come into contact with it. A written record, analysis and evaluation of it are vital ways

of preserving the history of dance. Whether in writing, on film or in a notation score, the description, interpretation and evaluations are lifelines for preservation and progress in the art of the dance.

References and resources

Books

Adshead-Lansdale, J. and Layson, J. (eds.), *Dance History: An introduction*, New York: Routledge, 1999

Anderson, Z., *The Royal Ballet 75 Years*, London: Faber and Faber, 2006

Bland, A., *Observer of the Dance 1958–1982*, London: Dance Books, 1985

Jordan, S. and Allen, D., *Parallel Lines*, London: Libbey & Co, 1993

Kurth, P., *Isadora: a sensational life*, New York: Little Brown, 2001

Mackrell, J., *Out of Line*, London: Dance Books, 1992

Patsch-Bergsohn, I., *Modern Dance in Germany and the United States: Cross-currents and Influences*, New Jersey: Harwood Academic Publishers, 1996

Preston-Dunlop, V., *Dance Word:, a review of words used by the dance world*, London: Routledge, 1995

Spencer, P., *Society and the Dance*, Cambridge: Cambridge University Press, 1985

Stearns, M. and Stearns, A., *Jazz Dance: the Story of American Vernacular Dance*, New York: Da Capo, 1993

Video/DVD

Mark Baldwin, *Constant Speed*, 2006. From www.rambert.org.uk

Articles/Reviews

Dance magazines
Dance Now: www.dancebooks.co.uk
Dance Theatre Journal: www.laban.org
www.ballet.co.uk
www.culturekiosque.com/dance
www.londondance.com
www.danceumbrella.co.uk
www.dance magazine.com

Lloyd Newson in interview with Jo Butterworth, published by The Centre for Dance and Theatre Studies, University of Bretton 1998.
Other interviews with Lloyd Newson on: www.dv8.co.uk
Other useful sources of newspaper reviews online:
The Electronic Telegraph: www.telegraph.co.uk
The Independent: www.enjoyment. independent.co.uk
The Guardian:www.guardianunlimited.uk/Archive
www.sunday-times.co.uk
www.artsworld.com/dance
www.artsjournal.com

> Ballets are the most transitory of things – once a step has been danced it is dead.
>
> (In *Making a Ballet*, 1974)

This chapter will identify ways to record dances so that they may be a part of the future.

As we saw in the previous chapter a review can be a way of documenting dance. The writings of dancers, choreographers and critics are a form of recording dance history. There are many examples: Petipa's scenarios, Jean-Georges Noverre's *Letters on Dancing and Ballet* (1760), Fokine's reforms in 1914, and many books, newspaper and magazine articles. As a part of your dance studies, you will appreciate and record dances. For instance, you may be improvising in your research for a solo and record the movements as you find them. A written record will make it easier to remember them, to teach them to other dancers and to build a expressive form and structure. It will also record valuable information to help to write a programme note and identify movements and devices which you chose to interpret the content of your dances. You can use words, diagrams, numbers, or a prescribed notation such as Labanotation or Benesh notation. These are all written records for your own dance diary .

Recording dance in picture form is another way of preserving it. Archaeologists have found possible evidence of dancing dating back as far as from 5,000 to 9,000 years ago. Recent finds of carved stone and painted scenes from sites in the Balkans and the Middle East depict figures holding hands in lines or circles.

Nowadays, we have much more sophisticated technology to record dances. Film is a fairly accurate way of making a record of a dance which can be used for study, or for choreographers' and dancers' personal development.

Nowadays, access to films of dance is easy. Famous choreographers such as Cunningham or companies such as Rambert and music videos are found regularly on television, DVD and online sources such as *YouTube*. Cameras are more available too, as is editing software on computers. Keeping a record of your past and for the world of dance generally, is much easier now compared with times when film and notation were not available.

A simple camera set-up may be adequate to make a journal record of your own studio work, but is it able to deal with the complexities of teaching largegroup choreography to new dancers? This may be made more difficult if the original dancers are not present at a reconstruction, or if the original dancers remember it differently. Is video adequate to record complete and accurate versions of dances? What if a video recording of a particular performance contained mistakes, and this then becomes the archive? What if the camera could not cover the whole stage area? Questions and problems arise if video is the only record. What, then, are the alternative options?

Certainly, it is worrying to think of how much of our dance heritage has been lost forever. In comparison to music, visual art and literature, we have little record of the past. These days, most large dance companies employ choreologists and their job is to notate during rehearsals when new dances are being choreographed. They give advice to the choreographer about what was done in previous rehearsals, how much music is left in a section, and so on. Choreologists also are responsible for reconstructing old repertoires. This means that a dance can be reconstructed and performed centuries after it was created, just like a Mozart symphony. Many dances, however, are revived without scores, from the living memories of dancers.

Although the legacies of dance may be passed on verbally between artists the real way ahead must be to document and record. From accurate records, classics may be reconstructed, appreciated and reworked in updated forms for new audiences.

Sometimes reworks are intended by the choreographer to explore dances that were created earlier in their career. Siobhan Davies reworked her solo *Sphinx* (1977) in 1995 in view of how her style had changed. Working from memory and video, she incorporated new material which used Release style and fluid energy, these being more typical of her later work. There is no doubt that live performances of authentic reconstructions contribute an immediacy of energy and a view of history that film and notation may not be capable of providing.

Being able to access dance from the past is vital. For young choreographers, studying originals in a systematic way brings them into line with students of other arts. The research and study of tradition is not as inhibiting as the dance world sometimes seems to think. It is a way of moving on and improving on the past, and this can only be done if we have an accurate knowledge of the past. Video, being such a relatively recent form of recording, is limited in terms of how far back into the past it can go. It also fails to give the kind of detail, depth and accuracy that a notation score can offer.

Important choreography such as that for *The Sleeping Beauty* may have been lost for ever if it had not been notated in Russia. We cannot afford to ignore our past, nor to neglect putting on record the present, as this will be the past for students of the future. Your dance journal is part of your own future too.

Filming dance

The growing interest in dance for screen is connected to the availability of new technology and the breaking-down of barriers to 'what dance can be and do'. This is not a huge step away from creating virtual realities. Certainly, with the massive range of special effects now available, dancers on film can perform superhuman feats beyond their wildest dreams. For example, in the 3-minute 1994 video *Waiting*, directed and choreographed by Lea Anderson, with The Cholmondeleys dance group, the dancers are seen to be flying and floating around in a state of suspended animation as they simply wait around. Similarly, in *Mothers and Daughters* (1994), choreographed by Victoria Marks and directed by Margaret Williams, the dancers spin at unbelievable speed in a close embrace.

Dance on film – a short history

To understand why this new art form within dance is developing so quickly, it would be worth looking at where and when it all started.

Hollywood stardom, fame, fortune

Throughout this book you will find references to the dance films from Hollywood in the 1930s and 1940s. Early Hollywood films featuring dance often made unimaginative adaptations of stage shows, but when Busby Berkeley's film and choreographic style hit the screen things changed dramatically. His first film *Whoopee* (1930) featured the groundbreaking overhead camera angle that he became famous for. This shot showed tight, symmetrical formations of chorus dancers – like looking down a kaleidoscope. Berkeley's moving camera must have literally lifted the spirits of audiences, allowing them to escape the depressing times, even if only for a short while.

If Berkeley's film gave audiences spectacle, a different approach was to be found in other films of the time. Gene Kelly (1912–1996) was a highly skilled dancer, singer and actor. He brought ordinary characters to life in films where the dances were part of the story, as had been happening in Broadway musical theatre. Kelly worked with producer Arthur Freed and his team of script writers, composers, designers and directors at MGM studios in Hollywood, on many memorable films. Kelly's style of dance crossed over several genres including jazz, modern, tap, vaudeville, social and ballet. Kelly worked with the Nicholas Brothers (*The Pirate*, 1948) and he acknowledged their influence in his characteristic energetic, athletic and down weighted style of tap. Having studied modern dance with Martha Graham, her style of expression of meaning through movement underpinned his dramatically expressive dance style used to create 'real' and likeable characters that audiences would have identified with. A typical scene that would have endeared him to audiences can be seen in *Anchors Aweigh* (MGM, Producer, Joseph Pasternak 1945). Playing a sailor on leave from the war in Hollywood, the famous scene features Kelly with cartoon character

Jerry Mouse in a gymnastic and charming duet. The opening section of the duet uses call and response relationship and then goes onto explore relationships of over, under, around, unison, canon and contact with wit and imagination. This scene was a technological breakthrough of its day combining animation with film. This was accomplished by laborious process by William Hanna and Joseph Barbera. The use of the moving camera also energised the dancing on screen of the time.

Figure 9.1
Gene Kelly in *Anchors Aweigh* with Jerry Mouse

Ballet had featured in early silent movies, stereotyping the ballerina as a fragile sylph such as in *The Dumb Girl of Portici* (1916), starring Anna Pavlova. By the 1940s, ballet became popularised through such feature films as *The Red Shoes* (Rank, choreography Leonide Massine, and Robert Helpmann, 1948) in which ballerina Moira Shearer was typecast and the story reflected that of a classical ballet plot when the leading female committed suicide. The story adapted a Hans Christian Andersen fairytale about a dancer who was possessed by an enchanted pair of shoes and could not stop dancing. The film was famous for its beautiful use of Technicolour technology. However, the substantial dancing scenes in *The Red Shoes* did bring real ballet to viewers who may not have seen it before.

During this time, after much upheaval in Ballets Russes after Diaghilev's death in 1929, Les Ballets Russes de Monte Carlo was formed by Colonel de Basil (director) and René Blum (artistic adviser). This newly energised company changed its name several more times, and was highly influential in Europe. As the 'Original Ballet Russe' tours to America and Australia were highly successful

also and artists such as Massine (1895–1979) and Balanchine influenced the look of dance in America with their Russian balletic legacy. At the time ballet was becoming 'Americanised', blended with jazz, folk and social genres, as seen in the choreography of Balanchine and American, Agnes de Mille. De Mille's ballet-based choreography featured in *Rodeo* (1942, for Ballets Russes in New York) acclaimed to be the first truly American ballet. She used images of cowboys, roping, riding and hoedown folk steps to depict America, but not the hard-edged view of Graham. From *Rodeo* she reworked the imagery for a Broadway musical, *Oklahoma* (1943) and this set new tones for musicals. As well as the inclusion of ballet vocabulary, there were darker plot lines and dance became fully integrated with the narrative. *Oklahoma* toured for ten years in the USA and overseas, until in 1955 Hollywood made it into a film. The influence of ballet and more modern expressive dance styles demanded more technical dancers and eventually won over tap dance as the style of choice. De Mille also choreographed *Carousel* (1945) and *Brigadoon* (1947) and both were made into films later.

The combined effect of these films and musicals inspired many to take up dancing. Films such as *The Turning Point* (1977), *Fame* (1983), *Flashdance* (1983), *Strictly Ballroom*, *You Got Served* (2004) and *Hairspray* (2007) continue this role into the present day.

Alternative approaches

In the USA in the late 1960s, the concern shifted towards making dance films of quite another kind. For example, Merce Cunningham, who is often regarded as the pioneer of dance on video, collaborated with composer John Cage and CBS-TV on a version of *Field Dances* (1963). Cameras panned everywhere and there were out-of-focus shots, unexpected interruptions with fragments of interviews and shots of Cage at the piano. Sometimes there was no sound or picture at all! Cunningham's usual strategy of random composition was clearly in place.

Cunningham decided to research further into how the two art forms of dance and video may work together, and this led to a later collaboration between Cunningham and Charles Atlas in the early 1970s. This produced some innovative ideas. They experimented with making a new form of dance especially for the screen, called videodance. Locating the camera amongst the dancers, moving with the action rather than relying on a zoomlens close-up, gave a greater feel for the energy involved in dance, a factor which can be washed out in film/video productions. The camera strapped to the body of the operator – called a Steadicam – brought the dance 'to life'. Cunningham and Atlas went on to make many more videodances, including *Walkaround Time* (1973) and *Torse* (1977).

Atlas went on in the early 1980s to develop a distinctive style which had the following characteristics:

- quick-moving, hand-held cameras to give a look of spontaneity;
- abrupt editing which looks almost amateur and experimental;
- documentaries that have a slight fictional, surreal feel.

313

These techniques, combined with very careful planning, created intense visual interest for the viewer. The film-biography on dancer Michael Clark, *Hail, The New Puritan* (1986), shows these characteristics very clearly. It portrays Clark's life in punk London, mixing everyday street scenes, dances, dream and surreal imagery to blurr reality and fantasy.

In Britain, more and more television coverage in artmagazine-type programmes like *The South Bank Show* and *Arena* increased the public exposure of dance. These usually involved straightforward films of stage works. In the 1970s, producers Bob Lockyer and Colin Nears led the field. Lockyer collaborated with the London Contemporary Dance Theatre, concentrating mainly on the works of choreographer Robert Cohan. From then on, dance-on-film series featured more regularly on television.

One such early series of *Dance on 4* (Channel 4, 1983) showed a range of genres and styles, including: a documentary of *Backstage at the Kirov* with excerpts from *Swan Lake*; *Plainsong* and *Carnival* by Siobhan Davies with Second Stride; Robert North's *Troy Games* for the London Contemporary Dance Theatre; and Twyla Tharp's *Dance Scrapbook*. There was a wide range of use of camera and approaches to the filming of dance across the whole series. A conventional use of film in the stage performance of *Troy Games*, used camera angles and timings that shut out some of the humour of the original. When cameras were used more freely, moving amongst the dancers, there were varying levels of success. In *Swan Lake*, there was an increase in the physical impact for the viewer, as the camera almost became one of the corps de ballet. However, in *Plainsong*, the same technique produced rather a mismatch. Here, the cameras seemed to intrude on the calm quality and clear structure of the choreography.

In 1986, television directors Terry Braun and Peter Mumford formed 'Dancelines', an independent production company . This aimed to research the different possibilities involved in making dance for television. Their first project, itself called *Dancelines*, involved a collaboration with Siobhan Davies, Ian Spink and a group of dancers/choreographers including Paul Clayden, Lucy Burge and Matthew Hawkins. The idea was to involve the whole team in the use of camera, editing and choreography. Dancers used the cameras, and camera operators joined in with the dancers' daily class. In this way, a close exchange of skills and understandings occurred. Everyone was on a very steep learning curve, and very valuable communication channels between the different art forms opened up. The final programme documented the whole process.

The *Dance on 4* series was repeated in 1988. All the featured work was made specifically for film or television. *Dancelines 2* featured in this series and it carried on, in a more sophisticated way, from where the earlier research had left off. As a part of this series, Richard Alston collaborated with Peter Mumford on an adaptation of the stage work *Strong Language*. This was no simple adaptation. It is still very recognisable as *Strong Language*, but it shows off certain features of the original dance which were less emphasised in the live performance. For example, the music and overall form of the piece were reorganised to suit a 25-minute programme and there was substantial re-choreographing: one whole section of the original was missed out. Furthermore, the use of sudden changes in images, angles and perspectives resulted in more highlights than the original dance had. In place of the original contrapuntal structure, a new concern with close-ups involved the audience more with each individual dancer, This approach was far more suited to small-screen viewing than to a live stage work.

Figure 9.2 The Featherstonehaughs in *Immaculate Conception* – to show the use of photographic effects similar to the use of video, to distort and create unusual images

From the 1980s into the 1990s there were many more series of specially commissioned works. Channel 4's *Tights Camera Action Series 1* and *2* in 1993 and 1994 showed many videodance works from Europe, the USA, Canada and the UK. The point was clearly being made that dance made for film had matured into a new genre. In 1995, a series broadcast on BBC2 called *Summer Dance* showed a wide mix of work including Cunningham's *Beachbirds for Camera*, *White Bird Featherless* (Siobhan Davies) and *Rooster, Ghost Dances* and *Moonshine* (Christopher Bruce).

The manipulation of video images in creating 'virtual' environments and performances is common these days. The use of green screen technology has brought even greater possibilities for what a dancer can achieve as seen in Cunningham's playful videodance solo, *Blue Studio: Five Segments* (co-directors Cunningham and Atlas, 1989). The sudden changes of location from street scenes to coastal landscape and the appearance of frogs, dogs and a gorilla-costumed dancer were reflected in the dance motifs such as a mime-like running, a slow goodbye wave and ape-like floppiness. The technology was also used to abruptly change colours of costume and background and to multiply

Cunningham himself so that he can dance duets, trios, quartets and quintets that fragment motifs from the five sections of the dance.

Often video footage is mixed with light, sound and human movement in computer operated interactive mixed media performance. Computer technology can serve a variety of exciting purposes. You can choreograph on it, notate on it. With virtual reality, the flesh-and-blood human dance may even be a thing of the past! No need to put ourselves through all that agonising training and injury any more. Well, this may be an extreme view, but it is certainly a consideration. Preferences for the human presence may well still be the final choice over virtual reality.

The computer can be a tool but can also be the medium itself. Software packages such as 'Life Forms' animate the human body and may make the physical presence of dancers no longer necessary. A free demonstration of Life Forms (developed by Thecla Schiphorst) can be obtained online. Merce Cunningham has been using it increasingly to choreograph with the aim to challenge the body's usual 'habits'. Here he describes his explorations with the software Sequence Editor:

> . . . one can make up movements, put them in the memory, eventually have a phrase . . . This can be examined from any angle . . . certainly a boon for working with dance on camera . . . On the computer the timing can be changed to see in slow motion how the body changes from one shape to another. Obviously it can produce shapes which are not available to humans, but as happened with the use of chance operations, followed by the use of camera on film and video, and now with the dance computer, I am aware once more of new possibilities with which to work.
>
> (Merce Cunningham, www.merce.org/technologylifeforms)

In this way he choreographed a commission for the Barbican, London (2000), *Biped*, which combined footage of virtual dancers on a front screen overlaid with digital footage of real dancers, whilst the dancers performed live behind the screen.

Problems of filming dance

The future of dance on film is a complex one, needing a close regard for the aim behind the filming of any particular dance. Depending on why a dance is being filmed, various problems arise from a certain amount of incompatibility between how the human eye works and how the eye of the camera – as controlled by the film director – operates.

Problem: long shots versus alternative options

Long shots from one or several static cameras show the broad structure of a work but do not allow the viewer a clear image of the movements involved because the figures appear so small. A conventional use of cameras, when transferring the stage work onto screen creates a problem that makes adapting stage works for film quite tricky. The basic problem is that if the usual number of cameras is employed, the field of view is insufficient to include large casts in one shot,and because the director is trying to be faithful to the choreographer, the result is a no-win situation. Long shots from static cameras are thus not an answer. Figure 9.3 shows the problem. (For a fuller explanation of this, see Bob Lockyer's article 'Dance and video: random thoughts' in *Dance Theatre Journal*.)

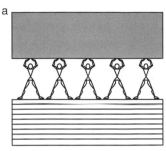

a Bob Lockyer called this the '2/3:1/3' problem to film a line of dancers, the final image shows 1/3 floor. 1/3 cyclorama, 1/3 dancers.

Figure 9.3 Showing problems of filming dance caused by camera angles/field of vision

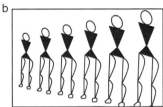

b Looking down a line of dancers affects the look of choreography, and it is still not possible to fit them all in. This was used quite effectively in the filming of Robert North *Troy Games*.

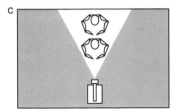

c Here the field of a camera is a cone. The closer the dancers to the camera, the tighter the shot. This can make stage placings look quite different on film. This is used to good effect by Cunningham in *Points In Space*

Possible solutions

Bob Lockyer went some way to solving this problem in attempting to stay true to the original stage work of Robert Cohan's *Forest* (filmed for television in 1980). At the start of the dance, the company enters in canon from stage right. Lockyer adapted this for the small screen by playing with the time element of the film. He superimposed one dancer doing the calling motif over the next and the next. This gave a filmed look which was close to the canon that the audience would have seen in the original stage work.

In his early research, Merce Cunningham discovered an important strategy in regard to this problem:

The triangular floor (as seen by the camera's eye) has led Merce's exploiting depth as a way of choreographing. One of his achievements is that he has

made dancing look very spacious in a very small area so that you don't necessarily feel that the camera is confining the dancers.

(Charles Atlas in *Dance Theatre Journal*, 1983)

In *Points in Space* (1987) for BBC2, Cunningham collaborated with director Elliot Caplan to create a videodance plus a documentary of the process of its making. The footage shows Cunningham watching rehearsals in New York through a camera viewfinder, in preparation for the later filming which took place in London. There is a clear concern with making exits fit into the small screen scale, and some clever uses of foreground and background. It also shows the cameras moving amongst the dancers – Caplan calls this 'cameras dancing'. Interestingly, the final dance was later reworked for the stage – a complete turn-around from the usual convention of filming a stage work.

The problem of adapting stage works and long shots was also encountered by the Mumford–Alston collaboration on *Strong Language*. The form and structure of Alston's choreography did not work on film because it relied on the eye seeing broad shots of how movements played off one against the other. The restructuring of the choreography for television opted for close-ups in order to build the interest of the viewer in the small subtleties of dancers' movement. Braun and Alston also used split screen so that a number of different images from the dance could be seen at once. This helped to fit the dance into the small screen without losing a sense of the original contrapuntal form. In order for dance to have an impact on the small screen, alternative ideas for how best to put across the original kinetic feel and energy need to be generated.

Problem: the camera's eye versus the spectator's eye

'You're the choreographer,' Glen Tetley said to me a few years ago . . . 'You select the images the viewer sees.'

(Bob Lockyer in *Dance Theatre Journal*, 1983)

The human eye, when watching dance at the theatre, will choose what to watch and when – from a broad overall scan, including exits and entrances, to a focus on a particular piece of detail or a particular soloist. As an audience watches the dance on the stage, both their eyes and the choreography itself work mainly side to side. Television, by contrast, works mainly foreground to background, so the two are not easily compatible. Also, filming diminishes the three dimensions of space – as well as the raw energy, which is scaled down enormously.

There is a key question to be asked here: should the director use the camera simply to present the dance to us, or should there be a creative freedom in the use of the camera which generates something entirely new? The first assumes that the camera is a mere substitute for the audience's eyes. The other is more about film using the dance as the subject matter to be worked on – just as a choreographer would choose certain ideas to work on. The choices of camera focus and angle and of editing styles are like choreography, but in a different

medium. The reality of being true to a stage work is not, however, quite so straightforward as it may first appear. At a basic level, each member of an audience will see and perceive a performance in their own individual way. So what hope is there of filming a 'perfect' view? The camera can never see the same as the human eye. The director's view will always be the one finally seen, and this can never reproduce the whole of the live performance with all its dynamics and visual freedoms.

Possible solutions

One solution preferred by some is to move the camera itself rather than to zoom in and out from static cameras. This solution recaptures the kinetic feel of dance and it is often seen in work by Merce Cunningham in collaboration with directors like Charles Atlas and Elliot Caplan. It may not act as the perfect human eye, but it perhaps behaves more like one than do any alternative approaches. It still reduces the choices that the eyes of an audience in a theatre may have in what to watch – or what not to watch – but when combined with appropriate choices of effects, editing and cutting, it can give an enjoyable and fresh view of dance. For example, in the videodance *Outside In* (1994) featuring Candoco (with Margaret Williams as director and Victoria Marks as choreographer), the choice of changing locations adds interest for the viewer. The locations switch from green countryside to dark warehouse space. It also uses overhead shots in order to give greater insight into the differing qualities and ways of moving of the different performers. In this way, the director becomes like an additional choreographer, directing the viewer's eye in a very specific, organised way.

In adapting stage works to film, there may be more success to be found in looking for imaginative solutions which will enhance the original qualities rather than water them down. This may require subtle or drastic changes to the choreography in order for it to be better seen in a small-scale format. This reinforces Cunningham's approach that the film and the dance are separate entities that only come together in the mind of a viewer.

The videodance *Changing Steps* (1989) is an example of such work. Co-directors Elliot Caplan and Cunningham mixed footage from rehearsals (black and white, 1974), performances of the original 1973 stage version and colour footage of an indoor-outdoor performance (1976) of the dance *Changing Steps*. Originally, the dance was designed in various groupings to be performed in any order or overlap. This complexity is added to by the videodance with the barn/studio that opens onto a garden setting. The colours of the costumes reflect that of the natural surroundings and this is emphasised further by splicing in occasional shots of plants, birds, water, rain. Editing constantly shifts the viewer in time and space between 1973 and 1989 – the video is a time travel capsule and uses crossfades, blurred images, closeups and longshots and negative space to increase the original permutation possibilities of duets, trios, quartets and quintets. Cunningham's manipulation of the viewer's sense of time and space by various editing techniques and shot selection depicts how editing

can be used to bring renewed energy to a performance, *as well as act as an archive* of a dance that was never the same in two performances and always adapted to the type of space available. On this occasion that space is a screen.

The art form of videodance is about creating new possibilities in how dance uses time, space and dynamics. It requires a different approach to the filming of dance, and could not operate in the way that a straightforward stage performance does, as found in Lea Anderson's *Cross Channel* (1991). This witty video diary of a day trip to France places the dancers in ever-changing locations – the city, travelling on trains, bicycles and the ferry, on beaches, campsites and clever editing enhances the feel of the pace and excitement of the journey. At the end, as a party inside a beach hut goes wild, outside the viewer sees the hut being swept out to sea as the sun sets – a must-see!

TASK ONE – *Action, camera*!

KEY SKILLS: Problem solving
Communication
Information technology

🕐 30 to 40 minutes

Using a dance which you have choreographed, think about how you might treat it in order to make a videodance. Remember, this is only a paper exercise, so let your imagination run away with you!

Consider the possibilities of distorting a movement to enhance its inherent qualities and structures. What special effects and use of cameras would you choose? Which parts might be better shot in close-up, or in a long panning shot? Would you consider using any of the following: blurred shots, speeding up or slowing down, reversing the action, pauses, chopping up and rearranging movements into a different order from that in which they appeared in the original piece, overhead shots, upside-down shots, harsh cuts, moving cameras, the superimposing of one image over another, changing the accompaniment completely?

Problem: working with dancers

Dancers in rehearsal have to repeat many movements over and over again in order to improve the quality of execution and so that the choreographer has a better idea of whether the dance is working or not. This repetitious and potentially injurious process is worsened by the addition of the demands of the camera operators and the film director, since there may be long gaps between shots when the dancers' muscles can cool down very quickly.

Possible solutions

There are various solutions to this problem, most of which require adequate preparation by the director in collaboration with the choreographer and the

film team. In describing his approach to filming stage works, Bob Lockyer explains how he initially tries to remember his reactions on seeing the dance for the first time, before learning the dance and then, finally, writing it down. Clearly this is a time-consuming process, but a necessary one if dancers are to be spared endless repetitions and long waiting times. After such detailed preparations, Lockyer gives copies of the action plan to the camera operators and the vision mixer. Detailed lists of shots are made and given to the crew, so that after the dancers have done their usual warm-up, it's straight into the action. In this way, hopefully, excessive repetition may be avoided.

Equally, careful preparation by the dancers is also needed and occasionally such preparation, in combination with brilliant dancers, can solve several problems. When Astaire and Rogers danced a Latin American number, 'The Carioca' in *Flying Down to Rio* (1933) the dancing was so well rehearsed that it was possible to film it almost completely in one long shot without losing the energy, technical ease and romantic mood.

Problem: expense

Detailed preparation can help to keep down costs on what is already an expensive process. Everyone seems to own some sort of camcorder these days, but producing a videodance is not always that simple. For the best results, more than one camera is needed – ideally, three at different angles and levels, and each of them with their own monitor so that shots can be seen clearly. On a low budget and with a single camera, there would have to be a great deal of imagination and skill in the treatment of the dance and its filming to make up for the lack of equipment.

The cutting and editing process is where much of the creativity and artistry of the art form lies, and access to editing suites may not be so easy to obtain, although recent technological developments in digital cameras and software are making production easier. Collaborating with students on media courses may be helpful here. A joint assignment for a team of dancers, film crew and musicians would be exciting.

Recording dance – final words

Recording dance on film is an important part of creating an archive of dance for the future. Films and videos of dance for reconstruction can be most useful if the limitations and problems of such recordings are recognised. When supplemented with a notation score and dancer's memory, as full a record as is possible will result. If the aim of using a film/video record is to rework a new version of the original then it is a vital source of reference. Similarly, texts such as reviews record dance for future reference.

Videodance is an exciting art form with many possibilities. As a record of dance, if well directed, a videodance can add to our understanding of the original stage work by emphasising features such as the structure, dynamics and dancer's interpretation. As a stand-alone work, it is a dance in its own right and

may never have come from a live stage version. It is the record of itself! In some cases the videodance can develop into a 'live' version. In turn this may have to be recorded for archive.

For the purposes of study, dance on film, scores and writings about dance are vital records of dance for the future.

References and resources

Books and articles

Atlas, C., 'Filming Cunningham dance', *Dance Theatre Journal*, vol. 1, no. 1, 1983

Burnside, F., 'Television's summer of dance', *Dance Theatre Journal*, vol. 12, no. 2, 1995

de Marigny, C. and Rubidge, S. (conceived and devised), the 'Dance and television' issue, *Dance Theatre Journal*, vol. 6, no. 1, 1988

Lockyer, B., 'Dance on video – random thoughts', *Dance Theatre Journal*, vol. 1, no. 4, 1983

Videos/DVDs

www.britishcouncil.org.il – The British Council has many videos of dance available for hire to institutions for an annual fee

The videos listed below can be ordered online at: Dance Books www.dancebooks. co.uk

Other stockists include:
National Resource Centre for Dance
www.surrey.ac.uk/NRCD
www.arts-books.com

Alvin Ailey: For Bird with Love & Witness; Black Dance America, includes work by Alvin Ailey among many

Anchors Aweigh, 1945 Warner Brothers, DVD

Anderson, L. *Cross Channel* (1991) order from MJW Productions; tel; 020 771 30400

Ballets Russes. Produced & directed, Goldfine & Geller, 2005

Merce Cunningham: *Changing Steps and Blue Studio: Five segments*. (1989)

Siobhan Davies: *Rushes; An analysis of Three Duets*, 1981

Martha Graham: *Martha Graham in Performance*, includes: *A Dancer's World; Night Journery;* and *Appalachian Spring*, 2005 Lloyd Newson, DV8: *Enter Achilles; Never Again*, 1996

Paris Dances Diaghilev – Petrushka, Spectre de la rose, Faune, Les Noces, Paris Opera Ballet, 1991

The Red Shoes. Produced & directed, Pressburg and Powell, 1948

Websites

www.art.net/~dtz – Thecla Shiphorst
www.ballet.co.uk – dance companies

www.bfi.org.uk – British Film Institute National Archive

www.dancefilmsassn.org – American dance films.

www.danceonvideo.com

www.credo-interactive.com – Life Forms

www.laban.org – some interesting links here

www.preserve-inc.org – USA archive, but useful information on storing tapes, paper and photographic records

Notation software

www.bham.ac.uk/calaban – CALABAN for p.c.s – free

www.benesh.org – The Benesh Institute

www. Labanotation.institute – Labanwriter for AppleMacs – free

Figure 10.1
Dancers –
'Assemblage'
composite
photograph of
various
dancers. This
picture is part
of a larger
image called
'Assemblage'
by Chris Nash,
2001.

Dancers are
(L–R): Gill
Clarke, Zenaida
Yanowsky,
Desiree
Kongered, Paul
Liburd, Pari
Naderi, Greig
Cooke, Cathy
Marston, Javier
De Frutos,
Lorena Randi.

This chapter will focus on the opportunities open to you to continue your dance studies or training and the possible career options which may lie ahead. In the many parts of the world today, dance activity is rapidly expanding. Whether as recreation or education, for social or health benefits, or for entertainment and artistic purposes, nowadays dance is easily accessible to all.

As a dance student, you may well be considering making dance a career, therefore it is important to be in touch with the ever-increasing possibilities that are available to you. The traditional options of stage school, West End musicals and performing are nowadays only one part of a much wider range of possibilities in dance careers. In this chapter, various options and considerations

will be presented to support your decisions concerning where you might be heading next.

Dance study and training – where to next?

There are many options available to continue to study or train in dance full-time when you have finished school. Opportunities to train as a professional dance performer, choreographer, teacher, administrator, work with the community, or as a researcher are just some of the possibilities. However, whichever option you prefer, specialist dance study will be essential to prepare you for a career. A simple way to view your options is to choose between vocational training, that emphasises skill and technique-based work, or a university degree or diploma that prepares you for wider career options. Most courses are three years long and require hard work, commitment and dedication, so it is important that you research different courses so that you know what will suit you.

There are many vocational, performing arts schools to choose from and generally they offer specialist training in ballet, contemporary, jazz and musical theatre. There are scholarships available, but competition is fierce – the Council for Dance Education and Training offers online advice about applying for funding. There are also many university courses to choose from and currently on the UCAS website there are about 30 different possibilities in higher education around England. University courses offer technique work, but usually accompanied by other areas such as choreography, critical analysis and appreciation, socio-historical study, film and technology and notation. Some niche training opportunities exist in South Asian, African and for dancers with special needs.

When deciding on a course that is right for you, consider what kind of career you may want. Possibilities include choreologist for dance companies, dance administrator, manager, producer, dance therapist, working in the community, private studio teacher, teacher in school, dancer researcher, journalist, writer, dance science/kinesiologist, dance with film and technology.

Auditons and interviews are usually held in the spring, so you should start looking for ideas in early winter and have all your application forms ready for completion by January. Each course has different requirements, including application forms, telephone interviews, auditions and video evidence of your dancing. Application requirements can vary and you need to be clear about which ones you should provide. The application form is important too, so complete it carefully and check your spelling and grammar. Better still, ask someone to double check it for you.

You should prepare carefully for the audition physically and orally. Your interviewers will be interested in you as a person as well as a dancer, so prepare your thoughts about why a specific course is right for you so that you can talk articulately about your reasons for wanting to pursue a career in dance. Try to

have something dancey to talk about – a performance or dance video you have seen recently, or a book you have read (this one for example) or something that you're working on that you are enjoying. Sometimes there's a great deal of waiting around on audition day, so take food, water, warm clothing and something to read - you could take this book! Make sure you have the dance clothing that has been stipulated and check that your apppearance is neat and tidy. Remember to switch off that phone too – interviewers will *not* be impressed if it rings.

Prepare your solo, if needed, carefully and stick to the time limit if there is one. Show it to your teacher and a friend for advice. In an audition class, work calmly and don't try to be perfect – the institution is looking for potential. Ensure a good night's rest so that you arrive bright and breezy. You will need to plan your journey carefully and allow for delays. Arrive early if anything, then you'll have time to warm up. Never be late! There is an excellent leaflet about auditions on the CDET website (address at the end of the chapter). Remember to thank the interviewers for the opportunity and say how much you enjoyed your visit – they might ask you back again. . .

The next section gives you insights into a few sectors of possible careers in the dance industry that make dance available for all and offer employment to suitably qualified individuals.

Dance for all

You may have had dance lessons at school before you started your sixth form studies, as well as lessons out of school time at a private dancing school. Dance became part of the UK National Curriculum in 1992 and the 2008 government report by Tony Hall has met with recognition for greater funding for dance in schools and for youth dance opportunities. Dance UK is the national voice for dance and its Dance Manifesto in 2006 laid down five pledges that promise further development across the dance sector. The pledges envisaged dance development to:

1 Be available and affordable for everyone to watch and participate in.
2 Be an integral part of every child's education.
3 Be supported and developed as an art form.
4 Be a sustainable career with world class training.
5 Invest in dancers' healthcare.

In the larger community the chain of National Dance Agencies in Britain generate opportunities for increased public participation and for employment in dance. Recent research internationally is finding the benefits of participation in dance for those in ill-health. Dance has also benefited from exposure in the media such as on television programmes such as *Dancing with the Stars*. The music industry has cashed in too and music videos have featured dancers more frequently over the last few years. Likewise, the fitness industry includes far

more dance content in their exercise programmes. All this activity adds up to more employment opportunities.

Similarly, the work of such companies as Green Candle, Motionhouse and CandoCo has done much to increase opportunities to dance for all, and raise awareness of issues of equity in dance. A contact-improvisation and release workshop being taught to an integrated group (that is one consisting of dancers with and without disabilities) is well documented on the video *Different Dancers, Similar Motion* (1989). It shows work done on a residency over a fortnight in Oxford with integrated groups of adults and youth and it demonstrates:

- how people can learn to overcome ignorance, anxieties, prejudices and inexperience through constructively led workshops;
- how some forms of movement, such as contact improvisation, are especially suitable for integrated workshops;
- how everyone can value everyone's role in the workshop;
- how people can learn to respect different rhythms, energies and styles of movement in one another.

(From the sleeve notes for the video *Different Dancers*, Similar Motion, 1989)

Such techniques as contact improvisation and release work have allowed far greater access to dance for those with learning difficulties, but there is a strong body of opinion that it should not end there, i.e. that dancers with disabilities should be encouraged, where appropriate, to attend other technique classes, say for ballet, in order to articulate arm and hand gestures. Technique classes could be adapted for the benefit of certain individuals, and training programmes could be made more flexible.

It is not just steps up to the studio that prevent dancers with disabilities training; it is the lack of teachers who know what they're doing when you get there.

(David Toole in *CandoCo* programme notes)

Such issues are becoming more a part of the whole dance picture. At Coventry University, a partnership has been struck up with the integrated dance company CandoCo to establish the first course which runs through further and higher education. It allows students both with and without disabilities to study together on a BA Hons Degree in Dance. The Laban Centre also reserves places on its Community Course for students with disabilities.

CandoCo's work is based on confronting the élitism of a dance world where only perfect bodies matter. In an article by Adam Benjamin, joint artistic director of CandoCo, the point is made that if disabled and non-disabled people are encouraged to study dance together, there is a chance to develop much more the possibilities of employment and research, as well as other opportunities

Figure 10.2 CandoCo piece. Can Do Dance Company. Choreographed by Rafael Bonacela.
Photographer: Hugo Glendinning.

generally, for the disabled dancer. He reflects on problems that will have to be solved, and on lessons that should be learnt from dance history:

> . . . the lessons we learn therefore will be more than academic; they will have an impact not only on dance as an art form, but on the way we perceive, treat and respect each other as human beings. Surely this, in the end, is the test of a vital, effective and truly contemporary art form.
>
> (Adam Benjamin in *Dance Theatre Journal*, 1995)

Another issue of interest to many is that of age and dance. No longer is it considered necessary to be a bright young thing to qualify as a dancer. Fergus Early's *Tales From The Citadel* (1996) for his Green Candle Dance Company was devised and performed by older dancers, including Jane Dudley who was a soloist with Martha Graham, 1936–1946. Early founded Green Candle in 1987 basing it on his belief that '. . . everyone has a birthright to communicate, express themselves and enjoy themselves through dance'.

The 2007 programme for older adults, *Falling About*, explored a theme that many older adults would relate to and the programme offered sensitive, humorous and informed thinking about the risks of falling. Early also works in hospitals and with children in his community projects.

Similarly 'From Here To Maturity Dance Company' developed from a mature dancer's event which was part of the South Bank's 1999 Blitz Festival. Their performance of *Legs To Stand On* included dancers such as Lucy Burge (danced with Ballet Rambert 1970–1985) and their director Ann Dickie who returned to the stage after a double hip replacement. All the dancers were between 40 and 54 years old. In previous times, the dance world would have regarded such dancers as retired, but now we recognise the wealth of physical intellect that they hold as interesting and important.

Figure 10.3 *Tales From The Citadel*, Green Candle, 1996, Jane Dudley seated centre

When we see and make dance we need to bear in mind such developments. Perhaps for too long dance has lived in a Ken and Barbie world. Well, not so much the Ken bit, but that too is changing. Male dancing is surrounded by controversy, most of which results from ignorance. The issue has been raised in many films. *Turning Point* (1977) starred dancer Mikhail Baryshnikov as Yuri, a Russian defector to the USA. In the film a character comments, 'Yuri is going to make it more respectable for American boys to dance'. Twenty-three years later in *Billy Elliott* (set in 1984) the battle is still going on, although perhaps there has been some progress and it is possible that more males are dancing these days, but the social pressures and prejudices still exist. While street dance, such as hip-hop, offers a niche of respect for male dance, the question is whether there is much transference of positive values between genres.

Conclusion

Perhaps after your studies you may choose to pursue a career in something completely different from dance, keeping it as a life-enhancing interest. Remembering the pleasure, challenges and value it gave you, you could still be part of the growing supporters of dance for the future. The dance world needs dancing dentists, accountants, health workers and, most of all, politicians! Peter Brinson, the famous dance educator, commented that the dance world:

> . . . doesn't pay half enough attention to the powers and the politics which have sustained it, or cast it down, throughout history.
> (In *Dance as Education: Towards a National Dance Culture*, 1991)

The story of dance is still being written and choreographed, and you as a student of dance are a part of it, walking backwards into the future. Your own contribution to making dance a part of a truly human world is important, unique and vital.

References and resources

Books and articles

Beal, R. and Berryman Miller, S. (eds.), *Dance for Older Adults*, USA: NDA/ AAHPERD, 1988

Brinson, P., *Dance as Education: Towards a National Dance Culture*, London: Falmer Press, 1991

Green Candle Dance Company, *Growing Bolder*, a start-up guide to creating dance with older people, 1997

Websites

Resources for applications to study and train in dance

From NRCD www.surrey.ac.uk/NRCD – a useful booklet *Dance Education, Training and Careers*

Council for Dance education and Training www.cdet.org.uk

Universities and Colleges Admissions Service www.ucas.org.uk

From www.artscouncil.org.uk/futurealert/ – useful booklets, *Work in Dance* and *Your Creative Future*

www.greencandledance.com

Foundation of Community Dance – www.communitydance.org.uk

National Dance Teachers Association – www.ndta.org.uk

www.dancer.com/dance-links

www.theplace.org.uk

www.balletcompanies.com

www.dancenorthwest.org.uk

www.url.co.nz/arts/dance

www.britishcouncil.org/arts/theatredance/companies

ANSWERS TO TASKS
CHAPTER ONE

Task Two:
Your torso and spine should be in a C curve – scooped out in the front with tailbone (coccyx) tucked under.

Your back muscles should feel long and extended.

transversus abdominis, rectus abdominis, pelvic floor, obliques, quadratus lumborum.

Task Four:
1 Contraction.
2 Martha Graham.
3 Two of the following: rectus abdominis, external obliques, internal obliques, transversus abdominis.
4 Extend or an eccentric contraction.

Task Seven:
1 Inferior (below).
2 Anterior (on the front).
3 A criss-cross weave to give more core stability to the ribs and lumbar spine.
4 Two from: improve leg strength, alignment, turn-out, safety and quality of jumping, travelling and lifting.
5 There are four arches. They allow ease of movement when weight is transferred during travelling and jumping. They also support the body weight and protect the bones and muscles of the foot.
6 Seven bones make up the tarsus. They are at the back of the foot – the ankle and heel.
7 The curves of the spine spread the stress in weight-bearing.
8 There are four types: long, short, flat and irregular. The size of these depends on their function: bones bearing larger body weights are bigger and denser, whereas those bearing lesser body weights are smaller and lighter.
9 Calcium maintains bone density and strength.
10 Plantar flexion or on pointe.

Task Ten:
(Possible total of 20 marks)

1 (a) Flexion and rotation. (2 marks)
  (b) The dancer on the left is extended and the dancer on the right is flexed. (2 marks)
2 (a) Quadriceps. (1 mark)
  (b) Hamstrings. (1 mark)

3 (a) Synovial or ball and socket. (1 mark)
   (b) Three. (1 mark)
   (c) Triaxial. (1 mark)
4 (a) Dorsi flexion. (1 mark)
   (b) Plantar flexion. (1 mark)
5 (a) Extension. (1 mark)
   (b) Cervical. (1 mark)
   (c) Seven. (1 mark)
   (d) Because it has to bear the weight of the head. (1 mark)
6 (a) Thoracic curve. (1 mark)
   (b) Twelve. (1 mark)
7 (a) Between the vertebrae. (1 mark)
   (b) Cartilage. (1 mark)
   (c) To absorb shock. (1 mark)

Task Fourteen:
1 Any two of the following: improves flexibility, reduces risk of injury, enhances muscle mass and the toned 'look' of the body, improves co-ordination and performance.
2 Progressive overload builds strength by increasing: (give one of following) frequency – increasing the number of repetitions or the speed of a movement; intensity – adding more and more resistance, as with weights; duration – increasing the length of time a movement takes.
3 Eccentrically (they lengthen).
4 Gravity.
5 Insertion.
6 Agonist.
7 If a dancer is well conditioned, stamina can help them to keep working longer and lessen the onset of fatigue and risk of injury.
8 Aerobic activity uses oxygen and anaerobic does not.
9 Heart and lungs.
10 Oxygen.

Task Twenty-two:
1 Two of: balance, control of energy, accuracy.
2 A small picture that is remembered in the movement memory.
3 It transmits information to the body and brain about the status of the body regarding balance and posture.
4 An image of a rainbow from the fingertips as they make a curve in the air overhead during side-to-side triplets.
5 Two of: aural, skin or visual righting reflexes.
6 Physiological centre of gravity and psychological feeling of being grounded.

CHAPTER TWO

Task Eight:

Across:
1) PROJECTION
2) & 2 DOWN – TURN OUT
3) ELBOW
4) PELVIS
5) See 4
6) & 5 DOWN – GROUP
   AWARENESS
7) EMPHASIS

Down
1) PERIPHERAL
2) See 2 ACROSS
3) FACINGS
4) & 5 ACROSS – COOL DOWN
5) AWARENESS
6) LUMBAR
7) FEMUR
8) FOCUS

CHAPTER THREE

Task Thirteen:

(Answers similar to those below are acceptable.)

You may note here that the four phrases in section one are as follows:

Phrase 1: Slow rolls, arm gesture, roll, stillness, rise to sit, stillness = 49.36 secs.

Phrase 2: Rise to stand, quick steps, turns, tilts, return to sculpture, 'wing spread' = 22.74 secs.

Phrase 3: As for phrase 1 on other side of body = 48 secs.

Phrase 4: As for phrase 2 plus balance in attitude then run to sculpture, 'wing spread' = 17 secs.

1 The phrases differ: in length (long and short) (1 mark)
   in weight (light and strong/heavy) (1 mark)
   in speed and duration (slow and fast) (1 mark).
2 Extension and contractions (of torso), travelling (rolling), gestures (arms and legs), stillness. (5 marks – 1 for each action)
3 Personal and General space – as seen in the movements close to the body and those travelling around the floor. (2 marks)
4 (a) Sometimes it ends a phrase. (1 mark)
      It marks a part of a phrase. The energy in the body is continuous throughout a pause and so gives certain phrases their unique shape. (1 mark)
   (b) It echoes the idea of landmarks such as rocks, plants and telegraph poles, which are in the desert landscape. (1 mark)
5 (a) Inward and outward. (2 marks)
   (b) The feelings of being 'in' the land held by gravity and of looking out across the landscape, marking territory, guarding. (2 marks)

6 The movement: travels away from and towards the sculpture (1 mark)
occupies the space under the 'hoop' (1 mark)
reflects the idea of the balance or quality of suspension that the
sculpture has. (1 mark)

Task Twenty:
Answers

Paragraph 1.
travels
two foot jumps
torso curves
gestures   rotation   suddenly
phrase
extend
hops   leaps
level
vibrating
stillness
pattern

Paragraph 2.
Forwards, sideways, backwards
Extend sharply and directly side-side to second position
Torso curves forward, one arm curved and one flexed, on a low level
Arms shoot out one after the other in the sagittal plane – direct,
sudden

Paragraph 3
unison
softer   space
formation   medium
over
three direct arm gestures in different directions
sideways, turned out with gesturing leg flexed at knee
quivering leg gesture and a small upper torso contraction

CHAPTER FOUR

Task Seven:
Answers:

1 Contraction and release of the torso; Flexed feet and hands;
floorwork; the sequential arm gestures of the Angel's wings were a
part of Graham technique.
2 A selection from the following: strength and stamina; flexibility;
balance; awareness of partner; co-ordination; involvement of whole
self in the characters being portrayed.

3 ■ Sustained upwards reaches – express the struggle to leave the womb first.

■ Slow bound climbing of the ladder and equally forceful pushing down on Jacob of Esau – express the struggle and effort of the conflict.

■ The Angel uses faster, more explosive movement, making appear him powerful and dominant.

■ Jacob uses percussive, quick, staccato arm gestures combined with a twisting torso, as if trapped and struggling to reach a more spiritual state.

4 ■ Symmetry of body shape in a mirror relationship establishes the characters of the twins.

■ The space inside the ladder is used fully, as the dancers continually struggle in the confined space – the womb.

■ Contact, for example when the Angel, now as the man by the well in the bible story, literally turns Jacob's world upside down. Or when the Angel drops onto Jacob's shoulders in the fight.

■ Towards the end in the fight the dancers cover more of the general space on diagonal pathways away from the ladder. This prolongs the struggle in time.

5 ■ Near the beginning of the dance Jacob covers Esau's eyes with his hand as if to confirm that he is the leader.

■ As the Angel descends the ladder, there are forceful curving gestures with alternating arms. The energy moves through the arm successively – shoulder/elbow/hand on the raise and lower of the arm – wing-like. Almost like a bird of prey.

6 As they struggle in the womb movement tempo increases and decreases.

7 The dancer Jacob holds the heel of Esau's flexed foot.

8 Esau also plays the Angel.

9 Travelling, running, leaping to circle Jacob.

CHAPTER SIX

Task Nine:

1 (a) AB.
(b) Ground bass.
(c) Fugue.
(d) Episodic narrative.
(e) Collage.
(f) Natural forms.
(g) Rondo.
(h) Chance procedures.

INDEX

Note: page numbers in *italic* indicate tables and figures.